THE PHILOSOPHY OF
THOMAS JEFFERSON

WOODBRIDGE PRIZE ESSAY
1942-43

NUMBER 14 OF THE
COLUMBIA STUDIES IN
AMERICAN CULTURE

THE PHILOSOPHY OF
THOMAS JEFFERSON

BY

ADRIENNE KOCH

GLOUCESTER, MASS.
PETER SMITH
1957

To

My Father and My Mother

The Woodbridge Prize in Philosophy

The Woodbridge Prize in Philosophy is awarded annually, from the income of the Woodbridge Memorial Fund, for the publication by Columbia University Press of the most deserving research conducted in the Department of Philosophy.

The Woodbridge Memorial Fund was established in 1940 by Professor Frederick James Eugene Woodbridge (1867–1940). During the more than thirty years of his career at Columbia he gave impetus, character, and inspiration to much of the research carried on by his students and colleagues. After his death the Fund was enlarged by a group of his friends, in order to provide also for the endowment of a Woodbridge Memorial Lectureship.

The publication of Dr. Koch's research marks the second award of the Woodbridge Prize.

Columbia Studies in American Culture

Edited at Columbia University

A series bringing together scholarly treatments of those aspects of American culture that are usually neglected in political histories and in histories of American literature and education: the arts and sciences, philosophy and religion, folkways, industry, and agriculture—in short, whatever has contributed significantly to the patterns of American life and to its heritage.

BOARD OF EDITORS

Acknowledgments

The author is happy to thank Professor Herbert W. Schneider, whose explorations in the field of American philosophy have long since made his students aware of its separate dignity. Professor Schneider was most generous in presenting the author with his own good ideas and tolerant enough to sanction her use of them.

Thanks are due also to Professor Curt J. Ducasse, for revealing the promise of philosophy; to Professor Philip Wheelwright, for his skillful communication of the bond between letters and logic; and, most deeply, to her friend Professor Sidney Hook, whose wisdom in human and technical affairs has been a constant and challenging example.

ADRIENNE KOCH

Washington, D.C.
July 6, 1943

Contents

Introduction

THE CONTROVERSIAL DISCUSSION which Thomas Jefferson ex- cited in his own time has grown, until today, two hundred years after his birth, it has become a habit of the American political imagination. In recent years the discussion has been going deeper. To be sure, scholars have still been focusing upon the purely political import of Jefferson's career. This is, in one sense, defensible; but it dwarfed our understanding of Jefferson's intellectual lineage and fostered our ignorance of the world in which he was mentally at home —his philosophic outlook. Not all statesmen can be expected to have philosophy, or to be philosophers. Jefferson, in the richness of his nature, happened to possess a speculative vein, luckily fostered by a favorable cultural tradition. He was a man so vitally interested in exploring ideas that to deny him the title of "philosopher" is to argue adherence to a prejudiced definition of the term.

Gilbert Chinard, for example, perhaps the most thorough Jefferson scholar of our age, has more than conceded that Jefferson had philo- sophic substance, but he has stubbornly withheld from him the title. Years ago Chinard set himself the job of digging into the little-known roots of Jefferson's intellectual world. The vast collection of Jefferson papers at the Library of Congress was an ample primary source to challenge the most patient or profound historian of democracy. Forti- fied by the accident of loyalty to both republican France and America, Chinard worked tirelessly upon these letters until he had disentangled several strands in Jefferson's opinions and inquiries very little adverted to in the past. However, Chinard did not cultivate his discoveries about Jefferson's ideas to the point of insuring full yield. The outlines of Jefferson's philosophy in all but its markedly political significance were left undeveloped and unrealized. Chinard's predilection for a formal tradition of philosophy made him unreasonably set against admitting Jefferson to that high estate. The climax in paradox came when Chinard, whose researches so amply furnished the data for the judg-

ment that Jefferson was a full-time thinker in the primary sense, refused to grant him even the humbler status of a "philosophe."

The point might be shaded finely; but the question at issue is: What
would it mean to call Jefferson a philosopher? Think of the "great tradition" in philosophy—Plato, Aristotle, system-builders like Aquinas,
Spinoza, Kant, Hegel—and there is no dispute; Jefferson is not to be included. Think instead of the men who tried to find out the worth of
new hypotheses, who offered their own formulations on data they had
diligently collected, who stood ready to accept and interpret the tests
of public verification, and who had a natural bent for every intellectual
inquiry which could advance knowledge or improve science. Jefferson
not only belongs to this company, but also he extends its value by the
cosmic coverage of his intellectual habit.

Remember that Jefferson was a disciple of scientific method when
it took courage and ingenuity to be one. He was a devotee of *res publica*,
to the extent of serious and sustained analysis of the principles and
practice of desirable social living in its many facets—the state, local
government, education, the law, the army, and the protection of citizens. He was, moreover, a vivid interpreter of the classics, literary,
historical, moral, and a level-headed innovator in the art of public
order.

Suppose the device of defining philosophy keeps one confined within
a technical world; then Jefferson was, in part, inside it. Even if he had
not been, there would still be an obligation to see whether his political
philosophy is related to any other set of ideas that he held. To learn
where his ideas came from (so far as is now possible), to learn first just
what those ideas were, to begin to see the connections among them is
to find his philosophy.

The interesting fact we are so prone to overlook is that Jefferson
wanted people to pay attention to the philosophical side of his nature;
and he gave more than one clew to what he meant by philosophy.

When a learned man once wrote to Jefferson to ask approval of a
"methodical encyclopedia of all human sciences," which he had "classified" into categories of "matter, mind, and the union of both," Jefferson
replied that every system of classification ever devised was only the
repository of its owner's purpose. Start simply, by classifying your
library, for example, and you will be contented with the divisions and

subdivisions which "throw convenient masses of books under each separate head." But a lawyer will group books (and ideas) differently from a physician; and both will be right.

At other times, however, Jefferson carried further the matter of classifications, of systems, and of outlining the "fields" of knowledge. Two of these practical impositions of order are instructive. One is the formal classification of the fields of knowledge which is the basis of the elaborate library catalogue prepared by Jefferson for his extensive library—a library which was, at the time, "without doubt the best chosen collection of its size in this country." Since his library was the product of extraordinary devotion and, as he said, "hand-picked," it is a valuable index to his intellectual attachments. When the bill providing for its purchase by the nation was on the floor of Congress, it is amusing that the only objections the House could muster were: "too philosophical," "too many books in foreign languages," "too large for the wants of Congress," and that it was, in fact, "irreligious—especially Voltaire."

The second significant grouping which makes apparent Jefferson's unusual respect for the claims of philosophy occurs in one of those long letters on education which nephew Peter Carr occasionally received. This letter is plain proof that Jefferson recognized the primary importance of philosophy for educated people. It helps, also, to identify the precise connotation of the word for Jefferson.

Philosophy is made one-third of a "General School" curriculum which was designed to contain "all the branches . . . of useful science." And the very first division under "Philosophy" is one which is logically prior to the others in Jefferson's estimate—viz., "Ideology." The components of Philosophy are given in the following order: (1) Ideology, (2) Ethics, (3) The Law of Nature and Nations, (4) Government, (5) Political Economy. These are the things Jefferson meant when he thought of "philosophy." These topics are therefore used as the plan of this study of Jefferson's philosophy.

One immediate conclusion to draw from the above is that in Jefferson's mature thought there is not the slightest suspicion of an antiphilosophical bias, although we shall see that there is considerable and founded resentment against "metaphysics."

To present Jefferson, as many have tried to do, without taking account of ideology, ethics, law of nature and nations, government, and political economy is to fail to recognize what he himself considered necessary understanding for every successful graduate of his "General School."

History has been generous in singing Jefferson's praises, but we know how often praise obscures the man. The easy shibboleths "democracy," "equality," and "the rights of man" have been used to enthrone him as a kind of vapid eighteenth-century saint (an unorthodox one, to be sure). Those who enjoy such a vision fail to see Jefferson in the true refinement and vigor of his thought. A more careful appraisal brings its reward to the student of ideas; for Jefferson always had much to say that the pressure of events could not then dissuade him from writing and should not now prevent us from pursuing.

PART ONE: ETHICS

Chapter I

EDUCATION AND PHILOSOPHICAL
SOURCES

IT IS exceedingly difficult to reconstruct the sources of Jefferson's early ethical outlook, because the usually copious supply of letters, nicely reflecting the thoughts uppermost in his mind from day to day, is disappointingly meager for the years up to 1785, which was Jefferson's forty-second year. It is clear, however, from his "commonplace books," [1] as well as from what we can infer on the basis of the letters of later years, that the Greek and Roman classics had a profound influence upon Jefferson during his school and college years.[2] Evidence of Greek and Latin sources are numerous and intimate in the Jefferson letters, and his commonplace books depend heavily upon the ancients. *The Commonplace Book of Philosophers and Poets* has extracts from Homer, Euripides, Herodotus, and Anacreon; from Virgil, Ovid, Horace, Cicero, and Seneca. Nor does it seem that Jefferson's interest in the ancients was primarily to cull personal comfort or guidance for his immediate problems. It was broader than that—an effort to formulate a moral pattern, for both public and private affairs, joining the

[1] *The Literary Bible of Thomas Jefferson; His Commonplace Book of Philosophers and Poets* and *The Commonplace Book of Thomas Jefferson; a Repertory of His Ideas on Government.* Gilbert Chinard is the editor of both commonplace books.

[2] James Parton, in his *Life of Thomas Jefferson*, p. 18, points out that for the two years that Jefferson attended the Reverend James Maury's school, he supplemented his elementary school training in Greek and Latin by intensive study in these languages only. See also the famous letter of advice on studies to Peter Carr, Paris, August 19, 1785, in Jefferson, *Writings* [Memorial ed.], V. 84. [Further references to the Memorial Edition of Jefferson's *Writings* will be designated "M.E."] In addition to valuing Greek and Latin as "models of pure taste in writing," incomparable for "matter" as well as for style, Jefferson urged the usefulness of such knowledge. See letter to John Brazier, Poplar Forest, August 24, 1819, M.E., XV, 207. "To sum the whole, it may truly be said that the classical languages are a solid basis for most, and an honest ornament to all the sciences."

basic art of living well and living wisely to the special art of good government.

Jefferson's apprenticeship in the classics was more intense than that of his contemporaries; but it is significant that most educated young men drew upon similar sources.[3] Since a close intellectual affinity has been shown to connect the period of the Enlightenment in France and the revival of interest in classical antiquity, perhaps we are justified in assuming that the American enlightenment drew its nourishment from the same rich sources.[4] Certainly if Jefferson, Adams, Hamilton, and Madison (to mention only a few) are typical products the assumption is more than warranted. Chinard is probably correct in saying that "Homer, Euripides, Cicero were the masters who provided him [Jefferson] with strong moral standards. . . . It is only later in his life that he found in Christianity a set of moral teachings transcending the standards of antiquity." [5]

No systematic moral philosophy emerged from Jefferson's apprenticeship to the Greek and Roman moralists. However, he seems to have been greatly impressed with the respective attractions of the two moral philosophies which he judged the best that pre-Christian Western society had offered, namely, Stoicism and Epicureanism. Despite the familiar opposition between the two doctrines, an opposition more insuperable in theory than in practice, Jefferson was deeply sensible of the moral advantages inherent in each program. Passages in *The Literary Bible* [6] are almost equally divided between striking Epicurean aphorisms and majestic Stoic invocations to control of will.[7] If we try

[3] Chinard, Introduction, *The Literary Bible of Thomas Jefferson*, p. 18. Hereafter referred to as *The Literary Bible*.

[4] See Harold Talbot Parker, *The Cult of Antiquity and the French Revolutionaries*, especially pp. 1–26. In fact, there is good reason to believe that classical learning was more important in the American republic than in France. Jefferson, for example, buying as many classics as he could for friends at home and for his own library when he was in France, commented sharply: "Greek and Roman authors are dearer here [France] than I believe anywhere in the world. Nobody here reads them, wherefore they are not printed." (To James Madison, Paris, September 1, 1785, M.E., V, 107.) Granting the exaggeration of this statement, it seems that the argument for classical influence applies *a fortiori* to America.

[5] Chinard, Introduction to *The Literary Bible*, p. 34.

[6] See pp. 78, 80, 88, 102, 132.

[7] The man who copied passages as divergent as the following illustrations may well have found them suited to different aspects of experience. From Horace, for instance,

to determine the degree of acceptance of the respective doctrines, we must look beyond the testimony of this commonplace book [8] to one of Jefferson's earliest letters [9] on record. Speaking with evident philosophic enthusiasm and youthful gravity, Jefferson advised his young friend in the following manner:

Perfect happiness . . . was never intended by the Deity to be the lot of one of his creatures in this world; but that he has very much put in our power the nearness of our approaches to it, is what I have steadfastly believed.

The most fortunate of us, in our journey through life, frequently meet with calamities and misfortunes which may greatly afflict us and to fortify our minds against the attacks of these calamities and misfortunes, should be one of the principal studies and endeavors of our lives. The only method of doing this is to assume a perfect resignation to the Divine will, to consider that whatever does happen, must happen; and that by our uneasiness, we cannot prevent the blow before it does fall, but we may add to its force after it has fallen. These considerations and others such as these, may enable us in some measure to surmount the difficulties thrown in our way; to bear up with a tolerable degree of patience under this burden of life; and to proceed with a pious and unshaken resignation, till we arrive at our journey's end, when we may deliver up our trust into the hands of him who gave it, and receive such reward as to him shall seem proportioned to our merit.

Jefferson extracts "Enjoy today and put as little trust as possible in the morrow," and immediately following an excerpt from Euripides, "More easily shalt thou bear thy sickness with quietness and a noble courage; to suffer is man's fate." The Stoic strain becomes even more apparent in a quotation from Cicero: "We follow our fate here and there wherever it takes us. Whatever will happen, destiny must be overcome, by bearing it." But it is even more to the point to notice that Jefferson is taken with the typical Epicurean argument against an immaterial soul, and immortality. Using Cicero's version, he wrote: "For if either the heart, or the blood, or the brain is the soul, then certainly the soul, being corporeal, must perish with the rest of the body; if it is air, it will perhaps be dissolved; if it is fire, it will be extinguished." If Chinard is right in maintaining in his Introduction to *The Literary Bible* (p. 27) that all these selections were made early in life, then Jefferson was already forming an attachment to the materialistic moral theory which he only elaborated in his later years.

[8] The inadequacy of the testimony of the Commonplace Books is apparent to the writer, since there is no reason to believe that Jefferson approved everything he selected or that he approved everything equally. But information for the years prior to 1785 is so scarce that every hint of what Jefferson was thinking must be used to the full.

[9] To John Page, Shadwell, July 15, 1763, M.E., IV, 8. Jefferson was just 20 years of age at that time.

Such, dear Page, will be the language of the man who considers his situation in this life, and such should be the language of every man who would wish to render that situation as easy as the nature of it will admit. Few things will disturb him at all: nothing will disturb him much.[10]

Here I think we can find the clew to Jefferson's youthful moral opinions. In fact, on the basis of this letter alone Chinard fails to justify his contention that Jefferson was first a Stoic and then "transferred his moral allegiance to Epicurus, at a time which remains to be determined —quite possibly under the influence of the French 'philosophes' of the Helvetius group. During his later years . . . it is Epicurus he calls 'our master,' deploring the fact that he has been misrepresented by Cicero." [11] Clearly, Jefferson was not a literal disciple of either sect. The Stoic discipline of the will seemed morally praiseworthy to Jefferson, while the Epicurean belief in necessity and intelligence (yielding an *understanding* of destiny) was in line with his confidence in "natural" science, and his wish to extend its achievements to every field of human enterprise.

What this letter does suggest, then, is that Stoicism and Epicureanism were not sharply distinguished for Jefferson; that he used them as complementary techniques in the realization of the good life. This use was to develop later into a new synthesis, when Christian morality was to supply the basic frame of benevolence and neighborly love. Indeed, if one speculates on the historic function of Epicureanism and Stoicism and also upon their reintroduction into Europe in the sixteenth and seventeenth centuries, Jefferson's attitude may be better understood. In brief, they both functioned as systems of independent morality, needing no sanction from Church or State.[12] This alone would have been sufficient to evoke some interest on Jefferson's part, since authoritarian religious morality was clearly repugnant to him at this period, as always.

[10] To John Page, Shadwell, July 15, 1763, M.E., IV, 10.
[11] Chinard, Introduction to *The Literary Bible*, p. 16.
[12] A recent essay, "Epicurisme et stoïcisme," points this out: "Epicuriens et Stoïciens ont eu ainsi dès l'origine et sous la pression des mêmes besoins, ce mérite commun de se proposer l'organisation philosophique de la morale indépendante, rendue nécessaire par le déclin des croyances religieuses et du patriotisme." For this point, see a recent essay "Epicurisme et stoïcisme," by Theodore Ruyssen in *La Tradition philosophique et la pensée française*, p. 9.

With respect to Epicureanism, additional factors probably explain Jefferson's acceptance. In England, Hobbes and the revival of Epicurus's philosophy embodied the materialistic adversary to orthodox Christianity [13] from the latter half of the seventeenth century to the first quarter of the eighteenth. Then "materialistic hedonism . . . resigned its role of chief heresy to the less alarming figure of Deism, an intellectual offspring, ironically enough, of that useful champion of 17th century orthodoxy, the 'New Science' of the Royal Society." [14] For Jefferson's purpose either phase of the anticlerical tradition was serviceable.

The emphasis on the Epicurean tradition, however, was probably due to its contribution of a scientific materialistic cosmology harmonized with an autonomous ethics of prudence. Gassendi's formulation of Epicurean doctrine seems to have been the source of Jefferson's knowledge and the model which he found so persuasive,[15] and presumably the reason was that Gassendi had already made room for Stoic and Christian elements in his interpretation. For example, Gassendi's formula is that happiness is the end of life; happiness is defined as tranquillity of soul, which can be attained only through self-discipline. The subsequent analysis of happiness reveals that happiness must be considered an active state, not a dead repose.[16] A critic appropriately comments that the Epicurean pursuit of pleasure, in Gassendi's modified version, was "an exacting, almost an austere thing, attained and maintained only by the most vigilant intelligence and the most rigorous self-control." [17]

It is interesting to notice that Gassendi's version of Epicureanism had been popularized in England. What was fashioned by the "holy priest of Digne" was borrowed by an ingenious Anglican clergyman. In 1724 Wollaston's *Religion of Nature Delineated* was written; it offered a remarkable section on "Happiness." Wollaston makes clear

[13] See Mayo, *Epicurus in England* (*1650–1725*). E.g., "Epicurus and Hobbism shared the position of central heresy, about which rallied most of the radical forces in the thought and life of the age" (p. 112).
[14] *Ibid.*
[15] Jefferson's library lists show that his first library included a six-volume Gassendi *Opera*, and the second one, the *Syntagma; Epicuri philosophiae.*
[16] Mayo, *Epicurus in England*, p. 3.
[17] *Ibid.*

several *postulata*, the first of which is: "Pain considered in itself is a real evil, pleasure a real good." [18] And the true quantity of pleasure or pain is given by the excess of either feeling, because "when pleasures and pains are equal, they mutually destroy each other." [19] Happiness is nothing other than "the true quantity of pleasure, unhappiness of pain. Or, any being may be said to be so far happy, as his pleasures are true," [20] but, fearing that the implication was not sufficiently plain, Wollaston added: "That being may be said to be ultimately happy, in some degree or other, the sum total of whose pleasures exceeds the sum of all his pains; or, ultimate happiness is the sum of happiness, or true pleasure, at the foot of the account." [21] So far, the tone is precisely the utilitarian one of calculation of pleasures and pains, a tone which is thoroughly foreign to Jefferson's thinking. But Wollaston's argument is now ready for a novel climax. "To make itself happy is a duty, which every being, in proportion to its capacity, owes to itself; and that, which every intelligent being may be supposed to aim at, in general." [22] Nothing remains to obstruct the good religious conscience except the identification of "the way of happiness" with the "practice of truth," so that the happy life is, without possibility of error, to be seen as coincident with the reasoning life. Wollaston concludes his section on happiness with the explanation that now his choice of the term "natural" to qualify "religion" has shown its double justification; it is natural because "grounded upon truth and the nature of things," and it is natural again because its other support is "true pleasure and pain, which are physical [or natural] good and evil." [23]

Jefferson rejects this account of the role of truth, referring to the "most whimsical" theory of Wollaston, "who considers truth as the foundation of morality." [24] But he is engaged by the peculiar conjunction of duty with happiness. It is exactly this combination which Jefferson appeared to have in mind in the letter to Page quoted above.

[18] Wollaston, *Religion of Nature Delineated*, p. 58.   [19] *Ibid.*, p. 59.
[20] *Ibid.*, p. 62.   [21] *Ibid.*, pp. 63–64.   [22] *Ibid.*, p. 64.
[23] *Ibid.*, p. 69. It is hard to refrain from quoting the triumphant last sentence. "And since both these unite so amicably, and are at last the same, here is *one* religion which may be called natural upon *two* accounts."
[24] To Thomas Law, Esq., Poplar Forest, June 13, 1814, M.E., XIV, 139. Jefferson maintains that the Creator implants "in our breasts a love of others, a sense of duty to them, a moral instinct, in short . . ." (*ibid.*, p. 142).

This is more than a suggestion of the blended Stoic-Epicureanism which Christian philosophers, of one sect or another, had been interested to develop.

It happens that the period starting with this letter and including the years of Jefferson's twenties and thirties is the time of his severest criticism of institutionalized religion. In this period Jefferson formed an implacable anticlerical attitude and fought in the legal and political campaign for separating Church and State and freeing educational curricula from outside domination. He further fortified his policy by liberal provisions in the Bill for the Diffusion of Knowledge. It may therefore have been more agreeable to him to stress the concrete moral advantages of the ancient moralists as a demonstration that an adequate moral theory and practice could really exist shorn of supernatural sanction or the dogmatic services of a priesthood. A good deal later the ancient "pagan" moralists were declared to be "highly and justly esteemed," but Jefferson was moved to continue: "although in my own opinion the moderns are far advanced beyond them in this line of science." [25]

If at this early period Epicureanism seemed to provide the goal for the good life, Stoic discipline was the method for attaining it. It is true that Jefferson derived more personal inspiration from the Greek and Roman Stoics than from the Epicureans. An elaborate letter of advice to Jefferson's young ward, designed to guide the latter's reading, recommended: "In morality read Epictetus, Xenophantis Memorabilia, Plato's Socratic dialogues, Cicero's philosophies, Antoninus, and Seneca." [26] The preponderance of Stoic influence is obvious here, and tends to represent Jefferson's conception of the highest practical moral counsel, at that time.

But surely there is no ground for saying, as Chinard does, that

Jefferson, who at first was attracted by the doctrine of the Stoics, transferred his moral allegiance to Epicurus, at a time which remains to be determined,— quite possibly under the influence of the French "philosophes" of the Helvetius group. During his later years . . . it is Epicurus he calls "our master," deploring the fact that he has been misrepresented by Cicero. [27]

[25] Thomas Jefferson to John Brazier, Poplar Forest, August 24, 1819, M.E., XV, 207.
[26] To Peter Carr, Paris, August 19, 1785, M.E., V, 84.
[27] Chinard, Introduction to *The Literary Bible*, p. 16.

This statement is misleading on two counts. First, it assumes that Jefferson was at one time or another a disciple of the Epicureans or of the Stoics. In fact he never gave his unqualified "moral allegiance" to either philosophy. Secondly, a false time interval is postulated to allow for "transferring" his discipleship from the Stoic camp to the Epicurean. Apparently the presupposition is that support of the ideas of Epicureanism are necessarily incompatible with a selective appreciation of Stoicism. The rigidity of this conventional presupposition deprives us of the close give and take, in practice, between Stoic and Epicurean moral goals and disciplines. Jefferson, even in his early period, is properly to be regarded as loyal to both Stoic and Epicurean principles. Both were rich for him in the integrative devices of individual morality.

A certain warmth in Jefferson, however, remained unsatisfied with the egoistic strain of these doctrines. Some years later, when he was ready to formulate his intellectual estimate of morality, he formulated explicit criticism along this line. And ultimately it was to the "morals of Jesus" and the current moral sense theory, with its stress upon native feelings of sympathy and benevolence, that Jefferson turned for the social reënforcement of his ethical position.

Chapter II

JEFFERSON AND BOLINGBROKE

THE INFLUENCE of the classical Greek and Roman moralists upon Jefferson was not confined to that of the Stoics and the Epicureans; it included the great literary figures of Homer, Horace, Euripides, for example, from whom moods and attitudes could be culled, and flashes of insight or wisdom treasured. *The Literary Bible* is therefore graced with quotations revolving about the broader human themes, namely, the unhappiness of man's fate,[1] the burden of mortality, the evanescence of time, the roguery of men, especially the rulers of cities, the inconstancy of women, and so forth. The mood of the book is not always far from that of an adolescent disillusioned with man and man's fate. A purely personal tone is not sustained for long, however. Anyone at all familiar with Jefferson will expect his reflections about morality to drift inevitably to questions of political principle. Not only are Cicero, Homer, Euripides, Herodotus, and Vergil plundered for counsels of good government, but the moderns, too, come in for attention on this score. Thus Jefferson chooses exactly those quotations from Shakespeare which are freighted with

[1] See quotations from Homer (both *Iliad* and *Odyssey*), and Cicero, e.g., " 'What is there agreeable in life, when we must night and day reflect that, at some time or other, we must die?" And Euripides, to effect "Alas, alas, races of mortals, wholly inspiring tears, much lamenting and much toiling! Behold how contrary to expectation fate goes her way! Now to one now to another, and to each in turn she metes troubles after a long season, and all the life of men is unstable.' " *The Literary Bible*, p. 94. Also:

> "I cannot tell, what you and other Men
> Think of this Life; but for my single self,
> I had as lief not be, as live to be
> In awe of such a Thing as I myself.
> I was born free as Caesar, so were you;
> We both have fed as well; and we can both
> Endure the Winter's cold as well as he."
>
> *Julius Caesar*, Act I, scene 3.

political feeling; for this reason Shakespeare is represented by *Julius Caesar*, *Henry IV*, *Coriolanus*, and *Troilus and Cressida* rather than by the more private and universal insights of the other psychological tragedies and dramas.[2]

The general orientation of political principles in ethical terms grows clearer, however, in the section where Jefferson devotes himself to the modern writers on ethics and politics. A particularly long section on Bolingbroke reveals Jefferson's close dependence for ideas upon fundamental methodological principles, which in turn generate specific attitudes on moral questions—such as the relation between morality and authority, between belief and knowledge, and so forth. Jefferson's deism, as well as his enlightened acceptance of the concept of ethical relativity, was thoroughly steeped in Bolingbroke's presentation. As a first principle of method, for example, the following statement, which Bolingbroke had intended to direct against those theological arguments advanced without fit obeisance to fact, Jefferson copied down and used as a sweeping indictment of political, as well as religious, forms. "No hypothesis ought to be maintained if a single phenomenon stands in direct opposition to it." [3] To Bolingbroke no single phenomenon seemed to stand in opposition to his Tory preferences about government: to Jefferson the same "law of nature" to which Bolingbroke appealed appeared incontestably ranged on the side of Republican government. Indeed, with the help of this principle Jefferson was able to justify militant defiance of British vested interests in colonial America when the right moment presented itself. Submit authority of any kind to rational question even once, and it becomes the only legitimate method for judging every type of social institution.

The literary commonplace book also shows that the idea of "ethical relativity" impressed Jefferson in his reading of Bolingbroke. The latter's statement of the issue made much of the quarrel with institutionalized Christianity. The following passage is typical:

Who are to be reputed good Christians? Go to Rome, they are papists. Go to Geneva, they are Calvinists. Go to the north of Germany, they are Lu-

---

[2] How typical that Jefferson should have chosen to quote "This man / Is now become a God, and Cassius is / A wretched Creature, and must bend his Body, / If Caesar carelessly but nod on him." *Ibid.*; quoted twice, pp. 94, 148.
[3] Quoted in *The Literary Bible*, p. 41.

therans. Come to London, they are none of these. Orthodoxy is a mode. It is one thing at one time and in one place. It is something else at another time, and in another place, or even in the same place: for in this religious country of ours, without seeking proofs in any other, men have been burned under one reign, for the very same doctrines they were obliged to profess in another.[4]

Jefferson, living in a later age, confronting newer and broader problems, gave the dictum "Orthodoxy is a mode" full rein. Political constitutions, as we shall see in another context, were to be applied to suit the country and the people, because political absolutes, like moral or religious absolutes, were non-existent, and therefore there could be no pretensions to orthodoxy.

From a philosophical point of view it is interesting that Jefferson was by no means unaware of the basic methodological orientation of Bolingbroke's criticism of beliefs which passed for knowledge. Locke's treatment of degrees of evidence for different kinds of propositions is unquestionably the theoretical background for Bolingbroke's analysis of the unreliability of religious legends and myths.[5] The specific problem to which Bolingbroke addresses his reasoned sarcasm is the inquiry into the grounds warranting assent in so-called "true" propositions.[6] He attacks the blind approval which devout or conventional people have too readily accorded to Biblical stories. Then a scrupulous analysis follows of the difficulty of ascertaining definitely the truth or falsity of even the minutest historical "fact." Yet Bolingbroke is confident that the voice of reason can utter "natural laws," these laws being self-evident, indubitable, and consequently capable of universal acceptance. The rational knowledge of natural laws contrasts pointedly with authoritarian immersion in dogma and faith.

[4] *Ibid.*, p. 57.

[5] The atmosphere of the inquiry about degrees of evidence, done in pungent and spirited fashion by Bolingbroke, is reminiscent of Voltairean and Encyclopaedist exposés of religious superstitions, save that the French attacks are more brilliant.

[6] It may be helpful to recall that Locke made his famous analysis of propositions in terms of those which are certain (i.e., necessarily true) and those which are probable. Several sections in Book IV of *An Essay concerning Human Understanding* are devoted to just such appraisals of the evidential worth of historical judgments, the revelations of religion, tradition, legend, hearsay, rumor, mistake, and lie. The larger theoretical structure of Locke's work is not the center of attention for Bolingbroke, since he emphasizes the *social uses* of the method for verifying propositions, while the epistemological aspect of the problem is peripheral.

The missionary of supernatural religion appeals to the testimony of men he never knew, and of whom the infidel he labors to convert never heard, for the truth of those extraordinary events which prove the revelation he preaches. . . . But the missionary of natural religion can appeal at all times, and everywhere, to present and immediate evidence, to the testimony of sense and intellect, for the truth of those miracles which he brings in proof; the constitution of the mundane system being in a very proper sense an aggregate of miracles.[7]

So far, at least, Jefferson was ready to endorse Bolingbroke's position. But there is some question whether he went further, to agree with Bolingbroke's more specialized pronouncements about the ethics of Christ. Bolingbroke's repudiation of a system of ethics based on the gospel was probably acceptable to Jefferson at this time, especially since Bolingbroke's dissatisfaction with Christian ethics was based upon the relative superiority of the "antient heathen moralists," like Tully, Seneca, Epictetus, and others. Jefferson's taste coincided admirably with this judgment.[8] It was not until he had ripened in experience and many years later that Jefferson began to work on his outline, "The Morals of Jesus," with the intention of providing a core for a complete and workable system of ethics.[9] Bolingbroke's sharp criticism of Christian ethics appeared impressive enough when Jefferson compiled his literary commonplace book for him to enter it there. The tenor of the entire argument can be gauged in this selection.

It is not true that Christ revealed an entire body of ethics, proved to be the law of nature from principles of reason, and reaching all the duties of life. If mankind wanted such a code, to which recourse might be had on every occasion, as to an unerring rule in every part of the moral duties, such a code is still wanting; for the gospel is not such a code. Moral obligations are occasionally recommended and commended in it, but nowhere proved from principles of reason, and by clear deductions, unless allusions, parables, and comparisons, and promises and threats, are to pass for such. Where [sic] all the precepts of this kind, that are scattered about in the whole new-

---

[7] Quoted in *The Literary Bible*, p. 49.

[8] This is apparent throughout *The Literary Bible* and is often reiterated in early letters. E.g., letter to Peter Carr, Paris, August 19, 1785, M.E., V, 85. See passage instructing Peter on what to read for moral education, viz., "Epictetus, Xenophantis Memorabilia, Plato's Socratic dialogues, Cicero's philosophies, Antoninus, and Seneca."

[9] See Part I, Chap. IV, "Morals and Religion."

testament, collected, like the short sentences of antient sages in the memorials we have of them, and put together in the very words of the sacred writers, they would compose a very short, as well as unconnected system of ethics. A system thus collected from the writings of antient heathen moralists of Tully, of Seneca, of Epictetus, and others, would be more full, more entire, more coherent, and more clearly deduced from unquestionable principles of knowledge.[10]

From this account it would seem that the root of the difficulty is the source of authority implied in any "system" of Christian ethics. Bolingbroke objects that isolated rules alone do not constitute a system of ethics. Any genuine system of ethics must provide for deducing its rules from some first (moral) principles. In any formulation of a Christian "system" all rules would depend upon either revelation or authority; but both are unsuitable, since the first is essentially private, and the second, being motivated by private interest, is not capable of impartiality. In place of an unsystematic Christian ethics Bolingbroke recommends the "unquestionable principles of knowledge" as the only firm basis for a system of ethics. These unquestionable principles were probably none other than the statement of the law of nature, together with whatever corollaries one could "deduce." The principles were understood to be formulated by reason, offered as certain, necessary, and even "self-evident" truths.[11]

Jefferson's intellectual history is not understood until one observes how he floundered with the empty formalism of "first principles" derived from reason. Jefferson was aware that simply sloughing off supernatural sanctions and proclaiming that the realm of moral values is autonomous was no substitute for additional analysis of the concrete dictates of morality and of the source from which they spring. But his eagerness to deal with practical problems made him impatient with long intellectual stocktaking of this nature. So there are various "fun-

[10] Quoted in *The Literary Bible*, p. 50.
[11] One reason why Jefferson may have been sympathetic with Bolingbroke's assault on disparate rules of conduct was that systematic ethics, grounded on the unquestionable formulae of natural rights, was a good formal framework for the "truths" in the Declaration of Independence. The Declaration is, in one way, the political culmination of this strain of rational universalism in ethical thought, but since it is a political document, it is reënforced by attention to concrete cases, which does much to reveal the nature of particular "rights," as well as to define violations of them.

damental" explanations of ethical principles, but no energetic attempt to resolve the inconsistencies mutually entailed by them. If this doctrinal fluidity is bewildering to the student of Jefferson, it should be read as part of Jefferson's own trial-and-error procedure in handling the baffling philosophic problems of moral theory. One should not, then, be surprised to find that Jefferson supplied the lacks in Stoicism and Epicureanism by injecting the modern language and ideas of rationalistic deism; while the latter, needing further content, was padded by reassurances concerning an "innate moral sense."

Chapter III

MORAL SENSE

THE INTUITIONALIST ethics of the late eighteenth and early nineteenth centuries was a convenient stopgap for disturbing questions about the source, authority, and generality of moral judgments. Jefferson, in this respect at least, was conventional.[1] Without anything approaching exhaustive analysis, he could not resist the verbal reassurances of a "special moral faculty" or "moral sense." His early letters mention such a belief, while some of his late ones investigate the philosophic implications of this position. The form of the doctrine which seems to have drawn his attention, was closer to so-called "perceptional intuitionalism," the variety accepted by Shaftesbury, Hutcheson, and to a large extent Hume, than to the rational variety of Clarke, Price, and Reid. Jefferson was acquainted with the works of Shaftesbury and Hutcheson particularly, if his library catalogue is any guide to his reading.[2] Apart, however, from the circumstantial evidence of quoting Shaftesbury in *The Commonplace Book* on government [3] and of reordering Shaftesbury's *The Characteristics*

---

[1] See Shearer's *Hume's Place in Ethics*, p. 6. Intuitionalism, developed chiefly in the eighteenth century, "was then known as the 'moral sense theory.' The bond among all forms of intuitionalism is the assumption that there is a special moral faculty. As a faculty it cannot of course be derived from any other element of consciousness." Shearer further comments that despite the usual classification of Hume as a "Utilitarian," Hume classified himself as a moral sense theorist, along with Shaftesbury and Hutcheson. (pp. 7 ff.)

[2] The works of the two influential deists, Lord Shaftesbury and his Scottish pupil, Francis Hutcheson, are listed in the catalogues of both of Jefferson's libraries. See *Catalogue of the Library of the United States,* and the manuscript "Catalogue of the Second Library," Jefferson Collection, Library of Congress. The significance of items which appear in both catalogues is due to the fact that Jefferson sold his first library, because of financial distress, to the United States Government and proceeded to collect a second library in the last years of his life. The second library, then, represents those books which he valued enough to duplicate, in addition, of course, to books which he had not possessed before.

[3] *The Commonplace Book of Thomas Jefferson,* pp. 388–89.

and Hutcheson's *Introduction to Moral Philosophy* and *Beauty and Virtue,* there is the important similarity in doctrine which makes Jefferson combine the ethics of deism and moral sense with utilitarianism, exactly in Hutcheson's formula, namely, "the greatest happiness of the greatest number."

This is not to suggest, however, that Jefferson was consistently loyal to the notion of moral sense. Rather, there is an occasional appeal to the unequivocal deliverances of instinctive moral "faculties," which furnished the authority in ethical matters that a belief in "Nature" demanded. From this point of view Jefferson's declarations in favor of perceptional intuitionalism never function more deeply than to criticize immoralism and hypocrisy [4] and to substitute a Rousseauistic idealization of the simple, untainted life of farmers and savages. Perhaps one typical quotation from Jefferson's earlier letters will reveal his usage of the idea of moral sense. Writing to his nephew Peter Carr, in 1787, Jefferson expressed himself with unusual severity:

I think it is lost time to attend lectures on moral philosophy. He who made us would have been a pitiful bungler, if He had made the rules of our moral conduct a matter of science. For one man of science, there are thousands who are not. What would have become of them? Man was destined for society. His morality, therefore, was to be formed to this object. He was endowed with a sense of right and wrong, merely relative to this. This sense is as much a part of his nature, as the sense of hearing, seeing, feeling; it is the true foundation of morality, and not the *to kalon*, truth, etc., as fanciful writers have imagined. The moral sense, or conscience, is as much a part of man as his leg or arm. It is given to all human beings in a stronger or weaker degree, as force of members is given them in a greater or less degree. It may be strengthened by exercise, as may any particular limb of the body. This sense is submitted, indeed, in some degree, to the guidance of reason; but it is a small stock which is required for this; even a less one than what we call common sense. State a moral case to a plowman and a professor. The former will decide it as well and often better than the latter because he has not been led astray by artificial rules.[5]

[4] For example, when Jefferson wrote about moral sense to Peter Carr, he was in Paris, his nephew in America. The idle, corrupt society of European court life had not contrasted favorably with the memory of hard-working farmers and pioneers, or even the unbroken harmony and dignity of Indian tribal life with which Jefferson was so impressed.

[5] To Peter Carr, Paris, August 10, 1787, M.E., VI, 256.

The strikingly anti-intellectualist tone of this letter, more marked here than in the temperate letters of later years, places more faith in virtue than in reason. Beyond this there is distinctly visible the influence of Henry Home (Lord Kames), whose works Jefferson knew in detail.[6]

Kames, in the *Essays on the Principles of Morality and Natural Religion*, launches a criticism of Shaftesbury, Hutcheson, and Hume for their treatment of the concepts of "obligation" and "duty." According to Kames, moral sense, the "guide and director of our principles of action," is direct feeling without reflection. Its authority lies in the fact that we feel and perceive an action to be our duty, that is, something which we "are indispensably bound to perform." Education and experience can never have the power of creating any one sense or feeling.

They may well have the effect of cherishing and improving the plants of nature's formation, but they cannot introduce any new or original plant whatever.[7]

We have no reason than to conclude . . . that even the greatest savages are destitute of the moral sense. Their defect rather lies in the weakness of their general principles of action, which terminate in objects too complex for savages readily to comprehend.[8]

Home adds to this the interesting modification that the moral sense develops—"improves gradually like our other powers and faculties, 'til it comes to be productive of the strongest as well as most delicate feelings." [9] This last statement is one which Jefferson practically reproduces in his letter to Carr.[10] A much more striking illustration of Jefferson's agreement, however, occurs in a lengthy note written by hand into his copy of Kames's *Essays on the Principles of Morality and Natural Religion*. The existence of this note seems to have escaped notice completely in the past, and yet it is of utmost importance in showing that Jefferson conceived the moral sense, as Kames did, in a developmental way, rather than as fully formed and instinctively operating

[6] Jefferson had an extravagantly high opinion of Kames; he owned nearly all his books. There is a marked copy (initialed with the characteristic "T" and "J") of Kames, *Essays on the Principles of Morality and Religion*, in the Rare Book Collection at the Library of Congress; marginal notes, in ink, are in Jefferson's hand.
[7] *Ibid.*, p. 140.   [8] *Ibid.*, p. 141.   [9] *Ibid.*, p. 143.
[10] Letter to Carr, cited Aug. 10, 1787.

faculties. The character of this development is also relevant, for it places moral sense in a social, historical context.

Jefferson's comments appear as a footnote to Kames's statement that the law of nature, concerned with the moral feelings of men and society, "cannot be stationary. It must vary with the nature of man, and consequently refine gradually as human nature refines." At this point Jefferson offers the following supplementary comment.

This is a remarkable instance of improvement in the moral sense. The putting to death captives in war was a general practice among savage nations. When men became more humanized the captive was indulged with life on condition of holding it in perpetual slavery; a condition exacted on this supposition, that the victor had right to take his life, and consequently to commute it for his services. At this stage of refinement were the Greeks about the time of the Trojan war. At this day it is perceived we have no right to take the life of an enemy unless where our own preservation renders it necessary. But the ceding his life in commutation for service admits there was no necessity to take it, because you have not done it. And if there was neither necessity nor right to take his life then is there no right to his service in commutation for it. This doctrine is acknowledged by later writers, Montesquieu, Burlamaqui, etc., who yet suppose it just to require a ransom from the captive. One advance further in refinement will relinquish this also. If we have no right to the life of a captive, we have no right to his labor; if none to his labor we have none to his absent property which is but the fruit of that labor. In fact, ransom is but commutation in another form.[11]

Although this passage shows that Jefferson held the theory of moral sense in an unorthodox form, giving ground to historical change and social "refinement" of our moral judgments, he is still bound to other traditional features of it. On the issue of the universality of moral sense, for example, he is fairly conventional; and in the midst of a glowing description of American Indians, Jefferson is moved to underscore Kames's arguments about the universality of the moral sense.[12] "Their only controls are their manners, and that moral sense of right and wrong, which, like the sense of tasting and feeling in every man, makes a part of his nature."[13]

From a broader point of view the implications of this moral theory

[11] Written into Kames, *Essays on the Principles of Morality and Religion*, pp. 147–49. Jefferson Collection, Rare Book Division, Library of Congress.
[12] *Notes on Virginia*, M.E., III, 228.   [13] *Ibid.*

are twofold. First, it provided a convenient explanation for optimistic expectations of honesty and genuine goodness on the part of average men. Second, the political corollary was highly useful—namely, that the possession of an innate faculty of moral perception was nothing other than the concrete expression of the source of every man's civil rights. At a time when it was necessary to justify one's belief in equal opportunities for education, no better proof of the prior right of "the people" in all governmental matters could be given than their possession (from some mysterious but powerful hand) of the gift of direct, infallible judgments about the best conduct. How much more sensible it would have been to expect a developed benevolence in ordinary men if one could have trusted them to have unerring perceptions of right and wrong.

The doctrine crops up again in Jefferson's later writings, but then with emphasis upon its social implications. At this period the influence of Helvetius [14] and the other French philosophers had worked itself deep into Jefferson's thought. In 1814 Jefferson explicitly stated his appreciation for the "social advantages" of moral-sense theory.

These good acts give us pleasure, but how happens it that they give us pleasure? Because nature hath implanted in our breasts a love of others, a sense of duty to them, a moral instinct, in short, which prompts us irresistibly to feel and to succor their distresses. . . . The creator would indeed have been a bungling artist, had he intended man for a social animal, without planting in him social dispositions. It is true they are not planted in every man, because there is no rule without exceptions; but it is false reasoning which converts exceptions into the general rule. . . . When it is wanting, we endeavor to supply the defect by education, by appeals to reason and calculation, by presenting to the being so unhappily conformed, other motives to do good and to eschew evil, such as the love, or the hatred, or rejection of those among whom he lives; and whose society is necessary to his happiness and even existence; demonstrations by sound calculation that honesty promotes interest in the long run; the rewards and penalties established by the laws; and ultimately the prospects of a future state of retribution for the evil as well as the good done while here . . .[15]

[14] Jefferson quoted extensively from *De l'homme* in *The Commonplace Book . . . on Government*, pp. 328–34. Chinard seems to think there is some evidence that these inserts were made before Jefferson went to France. (Introduction, p. 47.)

[15] Thomas Jefferson to Thomas Law, Esq., Poplar Forest, June 13, 1814, M.E., XIV, 141.

Jefferson repeatedly defends this judgment that the social nature of man is in every respect as natural as his physical equipment or mental make-up. Innate moral faculties emerge as the means of maintaining the harmony necessary for living in society. Altruism and benevolence are essential ingredients of every sound person. Only moral defectives will need to be educated to understand that self-realization demands social coöperation and mutual, neighborly helpfulness. The others will know this natively; and since they are the rule, and the others the exception, the prospect for social accord is bright.

The union of innate moral sense with the principle of "utility" is an interesting climax to the belief in innate moral sense. As Jefferson phrased it:

The moral sense is as much a part of our constitution as that of feeling, seeing, or hearing; as a wise creator must have seen to be necessary in an animal destined to live in society; that every human mind feels pleasure in doing good to another . . .[16]

Virtue, therefore, "does not consist in the act we do, but in the end it is to effect." [17] And the end, which permits such a wide range of particular actions, is only the well-being of the person to whom the act is directed, which well-being (happiness of others) ensures the fullest and deepest "pleasure" to a normally moral human being.

This utilitarian strain in Jefferson's intuitionism had already presented itself in eighteenth-century English and French thought. Wollaston expressed one version of it,[18] Hume another,[19] Bentham gave it "scientific" statement, and the French sensationalist philosophers, Helvetius, D'Holbach, and Cabanis,[20] for example, made an attempt at a logical system founded upon these very ideas. Jefferson's utilitarianism was less pretentious and closer to sources of personal practicality

[16] To John Adams, Monticello, October 14, 1815, M.E., XV, 76. The context of this statement is a criticism of Destutt de Tracy, who was his master in almost everything except the belief in the Hobbesian principle, viz., "that justice is founded in contract only" (*ibid.*).
[17] *Ibid.*
[18] See Wollaston, *Religion of Nature Delineated*, especially Section II, "Of Happiness."
[19] See Shearer, *Hume's Place in Ethics*, for connection between hedonistic theory of values and intuitionalism. Hume, e.g., "takes it for granted that the good and the pleasant are identical" (p. 23).
[20] Cf. Part II, "Ideology," below.

and sentiment. Besides, other ethical formulations proved to be equally, if not more, attractive to Jefferson as he thought further about moral questions. However, Jefferson's habits, socially and politically speaking, reënforce his theoretical humanitarian ideals. Whether moral sense or utilitarianism furnished reasons, Jefferson saw to it that standards of justice and honor were manifested in all dealings with minority groups, such as the Indians and the negroes. In principle this was extended to any group which might find itself powerless and at the disposition of other ruling groups.[21] To gauge the quality of feeling which animated Jefferson's thinking about the problems of the hard-working but down-trodden poor, one might consult his own statements [22] or the record of his public efforts.

On the assumption that overt behavior is a more reliable index of a person's real beliefs than verbal protestations, we may list some of Jefferson's activities in this connection.[23]

1. The fight against the remnants of feudal aristocracy in Virginia— a fight which was not relinquished until the old legal and religious mandates had been stripped of compulsive power. Concretely, this meant the abolition of the laws of primogeniture and entail, the writing of the Bill for the diffusion of education, and the famous Statute of Virginia for Religious Freedom.

2. Politically, on a wider scale, Jefferson tried to ensure the maintenance of a genuine republican ideal.[24]

3. The emotional significance of this campaign to safeguard republicanism was centered in Jefferson's belief in common people. A sincere

[21] Jefferson's well-known policy of having the United States Government declare itself in favor of and actively practice the right of asylum is in keeping with this.
[22] For example, in a letter to Lafayette, urging the latter to acquire a true knowledge of his own country, Jefferson wrote: "And to do it most effectually, you must be absolutely *incognito;* you must ferret the people out of their hovels as I have done; look into their kettles, eat their bread, loll on their beds under pretense of resting yourself, but in fact to find if they are soft. You will feel a sublime pleasure in the course of this investigation, and a sublimer one hereafter, when you shall be able to apply your knowledge to the softening of their beds, or the throwing of a morsel of meat into their kettle of vegetables." To Marquis de Lafayette, April 11, 1787, Nice, M.E., VI, 106.
[23] Not further discussed because (1) many are already familiar to everybody, and (2) they lead us afield from a study of ideas to specific details of political maneuvering and strategy. This information is to be found in any full-length political biography of Thomas Jefferson.
[24] See Chapter XVI on "Republicanism," below.

love for the humble, everyday working people directed Jefferson's political and ethical thought to provide those minimal external devices which guarantee equalization of opportunity to the greatest possible degree. Specifically, we might think here of the Bill of Rights, free religion, free thought, free press, free speech, the right of asylum for refugees. More generally, the unswerving effort to make American farmers and laborers ("the people") the happiest, most free human beings in civilized history was further token of Jefferson's good faith.

4. Jefferson's personal tastes were an additional corroboration of his ethical beliefs. Jefferson himself found greatest peace and satisfaction in a life devoted to agricultural pursuits; he imagined that virtuous life was synonymous with agrarian existence. Moreover, he was convinced that the means to achieve the good, independent life were at hand for everyone in the vast, unused territory of the North American continent, where new land could be gotten for the toil of taking possession or for small sums of money. He was personally distressed by the stupidity of allowing crowded cities to emerge, with their incorporated vices of impoverishment, lack of independence, their wage slaves and debtors.[25] Jefferson wanted the toil-and-tax-ridden laborers of the old monarchies (especially France, to which he was most attached) to come to the new country, where the fruits of toil were not wrested from men where there were no "plundered ploughmen and beggared yeomanry."

Thus it appears that the moral caliber of Jefferson's beliefs was expressed concretely in social, political, and personal democracy and philanthropy. These values, ornamented with more or less rhetoric, as the occasion deserved, have succeeded in fixing themselves in American popular consciousness for the duration of the republic. To recapitulate, they are: a deep suspicion of entrenched classes with fixed privileges; a steady faith in the educability of ordinary people, without which a reliance upon "the will of the people" becomes impossible; a profound belief in tolerance as the social attitude necessary for the settlement of public differences and conflicts; sympathy and affection for those made to suffer under the heel of tyranny (whether political, economic, or personal), fortified by ever-renewed vigilance to guarantee each successive "right" that previous battles have wrested for the people.

[25] *Notes on Virginia*, Query XIX, M.E., III.

Chapter IV

MORALS AND RELIGION

THE MORE INTIMATE side of Jefferson's moral theory, and a true reflection of the gentle character advancing it, was his humanistic interpretation of Christian morality. From the hectic years of his presidency Jefferson had one moral project close to his heart—an extensive but unorthodox version of the life and "morals" of Jesus. Due to the pressure of events the plan was never realized in full. But there are several lengthy letters, mainly to Rush and Priestley, which state Jefferson's thesis about Jesus, the man. There is also the now famous *Jefferson Bible*.

The *Jefferson Bible* [1] first appeared as a brief syllabus and extracts from the evangelists—amounting in all to forty-six pages. It was later issued as a book almost twice as large entitled *The Life and Morals of Jesus of Nazareth*, bearing the explanatory subtitle *Extracted Textually from the Gospels in Greek, Latin, French and English*. This editing of the Gospels by selecting only the "genuine" statements of Jesus and rejecting the "spurious" ones written by his misguided or dishonest disciples, Jefferson trusted to disclose a new picture of Christianity. Jefferson asserted that the sayings could never confuse him, since those of Jesus were as easy to separate from the others as "the gold from the dross." [2] He was confident of his ability to "winnow this grain from the chaff." [3] When he tired of these metaphors, but not of the sentiment, he tried another, proclaiming that the bona fide maxims were "as easily distinguishable as diamonds in a dunghill." [4] Jefferson

---

[1] This is not to be confused with Jefferson's literary commonplace book, which Gilbert Chinard edited and titled *The Literary Bible of Thomas Jefferson*. The latter title is not, on grounds of clarity and specificity, the best one possible.

[2] To William Short, Monticello, April 13, 1820, M.E., XV, 245.

[3] *Ibid.*, August 4, 1820, M.E., XV, 259.

[4] To John Adams, Monticello, October 13, 1813, M.E., XII, 390.

was afraid that his "Bible" would bring a hue and cry, but in this one instance the expected attack never materialized.[5]

The letters to Rush and Priestley discussed the needs of a theory which would blend the purity of religious idealism with the practical demands of social intercourse. Jefferson was reminded of conversations which he had had with Rush on this subject in the years 1798 to 1799, when Priestley sent him his own recently-published little book comparing the views of Socrates and Jesus.[6] In the earlier conversations Jefferson had promised Rush to develop his ideas by writing them out in book form, and Priestley's book was a quickening reminder. By 1803 Jefferson had still not completed his project, and he wrote to Priestley, "I have reflected often on it since, and even sketched the outlines in my own mind." [7]

These outlines show that Jefferson intended to extend the examination of Christian morality further than Priestley had done, making a subsection out of the comparison between the morals of Socrates and Jesus. Later it became clear, however, that Jefferson's project would require more research and time than he could afford to devote to it, so he urged Priestley to make use of his outline and suggestions and give them the careful development they merited. "You are the person of all others would do it best, and most promptly. You have all the materials at hand, and you put together with ease. I wish you could be induced to extend your late work to the whole subject." [8] But, not happy to relinquish the subject, Jefferson finally composed a "Syllabus of an Estimate of the Merit of the Doctrines of Jesus, Compared with Those of Others," which he sent to Rush in a letter written from Washington, April 21, 1803.[9]

The drive of Jefferson's entire approach is manifested in the descriptive phrase he employed about the subject: "the morals of Jesus." The

[5] Instead, in time it actually achieved a little official success—in a surprising quarter. In 1890 a Congressional amendment was adopted, providing that "there be printed and bound . . . for the use of Congress, 9,000 copies of Thomas Jefferson's *Morals of Jesus of Nazareth* . . . 3,000 copies for the use of the Senate, and 6,000 copies for the use of the House." Since that time other editions have appeared. See Introduction to the Jefferson Bible, M.E., XX, 19.

[6] To Dr. Joseph Priestley, Washington, April 9, 1803, X, 374.

[7] *Ibid.*   [8] *Ibid.*

[9] To Dr. Benjamin Rush, Washington, April 21, 1803, M.E., X, 381–85.

plainness of this phrase is intentional and needs no expatiation. The spirit Jefferson looked for and found in the recorded sayings of Christ was one of the utmost purity and simplicity, so that the figure which emerges is at one and the same time more noble and more homely than any traditional religious interpretation allows. Jefferson was aiming to humanize the deified conception of Christ. He says again and again that Jesus must be understood only as a man, whose way of life was one unexcelled for integrity. Christ was first and foremost a man, but one of magnificent inspiration. His inspiration must not, however, be shrouded with mystical properties or with talk of supernatural origin and destiny. Like the early deists, Jefferson stressed the fact that primitive Christianity was free from mystery and asserted that the Judaic and Greek sources were responsible for the intrusion of the idea that mystery is that which transcends reason.[10]

For positive suggestion, Jefferson selected two aspects of the teachings of Jesus as distinctive of Christian morality. The first was the elementary emphasis upon the inward motive and intention. The second was the spirit which animates Christian conduct, the spirit of benevolence, charity, and love of one's fellowmen, extending from the nearest neighbor to the vast brotherhood of mankind.[11]

Since Jefferson felt that this was the heart of Christian morality, the bitterness of his attack upon the corps of priests, theological apologists, and orthodox fanatics everywhere is understandable. He could not forgive them their obscurantist accretions to the true Christian doctrine, which misled honest believers and fortified some who were altogether alien to the spirit of Jesus. On this subject it was difficult for him to conceal his resentment. He wrote to John Adams, for example:

In extracting the pure principles which he taught, we should have to strip off the artificial vestments in which they have been muffled by priests, who have travestied them into various forms, as instruments of riches and power to themselves. We must dismiss the Platonists and Plotinists, the Stagyrites and

[10] See, e.g., Section on Toland's *Christianity Not Mysterious* in article "Deism," in *The New Schaff-Herzog Religious Encyclopedia*, p. 393.

[11] Jefferson may have found this tendency to interpret Christian morality as the practice of benevolence in Shaftesbury. Mossner, in *Bishop Butler and the Age of Reason*, says concerning Shaftesbury: "In man, naturally benevolent, may be developed a 'taste' in morals leading to an unalterable perfect virtue, benefiting alike both society and individual," p. 60.

Gamalielites, the Eclectics, the Gnostics and Scholastics, their essences and emanations, their Logos and Demiurgos, Aeons and Daemons, male and female, with a long train of etc., etc., etc., or, shall I say at once, of nonsense.[12]

Jefferson's contempt was by no means confined to the fantasia produced by the feverish minds of theological philosophers; for its anticlerical vein became especially harsh when turned against philosophical theologians. As a believer in natural religion, Jefferson aired his deep-seated objection to the role played by the self-chosen "followers" of Jesus, a role which obscured and perverted the reality of that pure ethical code which Jesus had originally fashioned for mankind. But the fate of Jesus was that

. . . his principles were departed from by those who professed to be his special servants, and perverted into an engine for enslaving their oppressors in Church and State: that the purest system of morals ever before preached to man has been adulterated and sophisticated by artificial constructions, into a mere contrivance to filch wealth and power to themselves; that rational men, not being able to swallow their impious heresies, in order to force them down their throats, they raise the hue and cry of infidelity, while themselves are the greatest obstacles to the advancement of the real doctrines of Jesus, and do, in fact, constitute the real anti-Christ.[13]

With so marked an antichurch bias, the disputed question of Jefferson's church membership seems wholly beside the point.[14] If one must take sides in the sectarian contest, it really seems fair to admit that Jefferson, at least toward the end of his life, was content to call himself a Unitarian. There is one very important letter, curiously omitted from the "definitive " edition of Jefferson's writings, which Jefferson wrote

[12] To John Adams, Monticello, October 13, 1813, XIII, 389.
[13] To S. Kercheval, Monticello, January 19, 1810, M.E., XII, 345–46.
[14] Claims have been made by Episcopalians and Unitarians, on the one hand, while during Jefferson's own lifetime and thereafter, the hue and cry of atheism, irreligion, and deism never abated. Jefferson has at times been called atheist, deist, freethinker, Unitarian, Episcopalian, Socinian. For some of these claims see: (1) Lewis, *Jefferson the Freethinker*; (2) Gould, "The Religious Opinions of Thomas Jefferson," *Mississippi Valley Historical Review*, XX (1933), 191–209; (3) Hall, "The Religious Opinions of Thomas Jefferson," *The Sewanee Review*, XXI (1913), 164–76. The truth of the matter is that Jefferson wrote specifically against the Congregationalists, Episcopalians, Presbyterians, and Calvinists. He did approve very much of Unitarianism, and in his early days he was attracted by the Quakers, until he felt that their political and social role had become unpatriotic.

one year before his death. Here he explicitly refers to himself as a Unitarian.

I am anxious to see the doctrine of one god commenced in our state. But the population of my neighborhood is too slender, and is too much divided into other sects to maintain any one preacher well. I must therefore be contented to be an Unitarian by myself, although I know there are many around me who would become so, if once they could hear the questions fairly stated.[15]

Intellectually, we have Jefferson's word [16] that his religious opinions were based on Priestley's writings, especially on the latter's *Corruptions of Christianity* and *Early Opinions of Jesus*. Therefore, it appears that Jefferson's brand of deism was definitely English in orientation, rather than French: which is to say that no matter what critical judgments might be passed upon organized religion, there would be no open, radical abandonment of the church for the furtherance of a thorough materialistic philosophy. One critic delineates the difference between French and English deism in this way:

Newton and Boyle succeeded in reconciling the creed of the church with their mechanical metaphysics; and this union remained characteristic of England, so that even men like Priestley and Hartley did not shrink from supporting their materialistic theories by theological arguments.

But when deism entered France from England (although early deists like Fontenelle and Bayle had been native French, their doctrines had created no immediate deistic movement there), "only its materialistic and revolutionary phases were seized upon, to the exclusion of that religiosity which had never been lost in England. French Deism stood outside of theology." [17]

Interestingly enough, Jefferson was aware of this broad division in

---

[15] To Benjamin Waterhouse, January 8, 1825; manuscript letter in the Jefferson Collection, Library of Congress. Also reproduced in Honeywell, *The Educational Work of Thomas Jefferson*, p. 92. This letter is also omitted from the Ford Edition of Jefferson's *Writings*.

[16] Letter to John Adams, Monticello, August 22, 1813, M.E., XIII, 352. In this letter Jefferson also said that "Middleton's letters from Rome and to Waterhand" [*sic*] had been important in molding his religious opinions.

[17] See Ernst Troeltsch's article "Deism," in *The New Schaff-Herzog Religious Encyclopedia*, especially pp. 392–95.

deistic ranks and accepted it with the tolerance required by his own principle of historical relativism. There is a moving passage in a very earnest letter discussing the foundations of morality, in which Jefferson, decidedly not an atheist, defends the morality of the French atheists.

If we did a good act merely from the love of God . . . whence arises the morality of the Atheist? . . . idle to say . . . that no such being exists. . . . I have observed indeed, generally, that while in Protestant countries the defections from the Platonic Christianity of the priests is to Deism, in Catholic countries they are to Atheism. Diderot, D'Alembert, D'Holbach, Condorcet are known to have been among the most virtuous of men. Their virtue then must have had some other foundation than the love of God.[18]

We can infer several things about Jefferson's religious and moral position from the above quotation. First, that his own "defection from Platonic Christianity" occurring in a Protestant country, would be likely to be deistic, rather than atheistic. And this is substantiated by other passages.[19] Secondly, the field of morality was not to be regarded as essentially bound up with the practice of any religion. And the third point is really an extension of the second; namely, that atheism or any outright renunciation of religion was not only to be tolerated socially but also might be just as constructive a base for morality as the orthodox one of religion.

The general drift of Jefferson's thinking is unquestionably toward

[18] To Thomas Law, Esq., Poplar Forest, June 13, 1814, M.E., XIV, 139–40.

[19] *Ibid.* See also the letter to John Adams, Monticello, April 8, 1816, M.E., XIV, 468–69. Here Jefferson refers to the "system of Atheism" of Diderot, D'Alembert, D'Holbach, and adds: "It was a numerous school in the Catholic countries, while the infidelity of the Protestant took generally the form of theism. The former always insisted that it was a mere question of definition between them, the hypostasis of which, on both sides, was '*Nature*,' or '*the Universe*'; that both agreed in the order of the existing system, but the one supposed it from eternity, the other as having begun in time. And when the atheist descanted on the unceasing motion and circulation of matter through the animal, vegetable and mineral kingdoms, never resting, never annihilated, always changing form, and under all forms gifted with the 'power of reproduction'; the theist pointing 'to the heavens above, and to the earth beneath, and to the waters under the earth,' asked, if these did not proclaim a first cause, possessing intelligence and power in the production, and intelligence in the design and constant preservation of the system; urged the palpable existence of final courses; that the eye was made to see, and the ear to hear, and not that we see because we have eyes, and hear because we have ears; *an answer obvious to the senses, as that of walking across the room, was to the philosopher demonstrating the non-existence of motion.*" Last italics mine.

the autonomy of moral values; and there is enough in his writings to make it safe to hazard a guess that should he ever have been freed from his own conviction concerning instinctive moral sense, which the "Creator" had made "so much a part of our constitution as that no errors of reasoning or of speculation might lead us astray from its observance in practice," [20] he would have emerged a full-fledged altruistic utilitarian. The concrete social reforms and even the humanitarian spirit which characterized Jefferson would have remained pretty much the same in the changed theoretical framework.

What Jefferson was seeking in his religious morality was an appreciation of *motive* and *intention*. His own moral theories had always been centered on the conception of the good man, whose acts are "right" or "good" as much because of their intention as because they were directed by a prudent concern for the welfare of those affected by the contemplated action. Even duties had to be intimately connected with impulsive feeling in order to be properly moral. Jefferson quoted Kames (fifty years after reading him) to the effect that "a man owes no duty to which he is not urged by some impulsive feeling." [21] Jefferson feels that this is altogether correct "if referred to the general standard of feeling in the given case, and not to the feeling of a single individual." [22]

In an interesting early letter to his nephew Peter Carr advising an open-minded and critical reading of the New Testament, Jefferson urged the boy to draw his own conclusions about whether Jesus was a "living divinity" who "suspended and reversed the laws of nature at will, and entered bodily into heaven" or a natural and noble man, "of a benevolent heart, enthusiastic mind." [23] He pointed out that there was no need to be frightened, no matter how the inquiry terminated. "If it ends in a belief that there is no God, you will find incitements to virtue in the comfort and pleasantness you will feel in its exercise, and the host of others which it will procure you. [24] Whereas if it ended in a belief in God, that should provide "a vast additional incitement" [25]

[20] To Thomas Law, Poplar Forest, June 13, 1814, M.E., XIV, 139.
[21] *Ibid.*, p. 144.
[22] *Ibid.* Jefferson is anxious to preserve a *social*, majoritarian check for a man's "impulsive feeling."
[23] To Peter Carr, Paris, August 10, 1787, VI, 260.
[24] *Ibid.*   [25] *Ibid.*

to moral behavior. And then Jefferson adds: "Your own reason is the only oracle given you by Heaven; and you are answerable, not for the rightness, but uprightness, of the decision.[26] Jefferson later came to believe that this was exactly the spirit of the morals of Jesus, this spiritual concern primarily for the uprightness, not the rightness, of moral decisions. And uprightness was wedded forever to impulsive feeling.

After he had studied the teachings of Jesus with even more care, he decided that this advantage in moral theory pertained exclusively to them. Neither the ancient Greeks or Romans, nor the Hebrews had ever approached such a conception of the inward spirit, without which morality could be nothing but formal.

The precepts of philosophy, and of the Hebrew code, laid hold of actions only. He [Jesus] pushed his scrutinies into the heart of man; erected his tribunal in the region of his thoughts, and purified the waters at the fountain head.[27]

"How" something is done and "why" is made equal in importance with "what" was done. Thus responsibility penetrates even into the fringe of feeling accompanying actions, because the attitude, the inward disposition and will in which an act is launched, is now conceived as partially determinative of its moral worth.

However, to know more about the character of the feeling which should be termed "good" and the converse character termed "bad," we must remember the second distinctive feature of Christian ethics—benevolence. Jefferson considered this element of benevolence, or active affection for others, as the true expression of our natural, instinctive moral equipment.[28] Any moral system which should attempt to ground morality on self-interest was foredoomed to failure, in Jefferson's eyes. Self-love is no part of morality for Jefferson; it is "exactly its counterpart." [29] "Take from man his selfish propensities, and he can have nothing to seduce him from the practice of virtue. . . . Or subdue these

[26] To Peter Carr, Paris, August 10, 1787, VI, 261.
[27] To Dr. Benjamin Rush, Washington, April 21, 1803, M.E., X, 385.
[28] Hutcheson, in *An Inquiry into the Original of Our Ideas of Beauty and Virtue*, said: "The universal foundation of this moral sense is benevolence." Treatise II, "Con. Moral Good and Evil," p. 203. This may have influenced Jefferson's ". . . nature hath implanted in our breasts a love of others" (letter to Thomas Law, P.F., June 13, 1814, XIV, 14).
[29] *Ibid.*, p. 141.

propensities by education, instruction or restraint, and virtue remains without a competitor." [30]

Self-love may be natural (although not in all forms), but there are no duties to the self and no morality stemming from the ego. "I consider our relations with others as constituting the boundaries of morality. . . . To ourselves . . . we can owe no duties, obligation requiring also two parties. Self-love, therefore, is no part of morality." [31] As a climax, Jefferson disposes of the subtler form of the egoistic doctrine (egoism "in a broader sense"), which he associated with the name of Helvetius. Jefferson quotes the following passage from Helvetius, *De l'esprit:* "The humane man is he to whom the sight of misfortune is insupportable, and who to rescue himself from this spectacle, is forced to succor the unfortunate object." [32]

Jefferson sensed that the "language" of Jesus was in perfect harmony with the moral need to regard others and to make their welfare count. Jefferson therefore draws attention to the strength of Christian morality, which allows for sympathetic impulses toward others as the source of morality. He shows that other ethical codes are weak in this respect.

His [Jesus's] moral doctrines, relating to kindred and friends, were more pure and perfect than those of the most correct of the philosophers, and greatly more so than those of the Jews; and they went far beyond both in inculcating universal philanthropy, not only to kindred and friends, to neighbors and countrymen, but to all mankind, gathering all into one family, under the bonds of love, charity, peace, common wants and common aids. [33]

Even the great Epicurean and Stoic philosophers failed to formulate a constructive and principled "social" morality. But Jefferson felt moved to grant that when philosophers like Pythagoras, Socrates, Epicurus, Cicero, Epictetus, Seneca, Antoninus addressed themselves to individual duties they were truly successful. "Their precepts related chiefly to ourselves, and the government of those passions which, unrestrained, would disturb our tranquillity of mind. In this branch of philosophy they were really great." [34]

In an instructive footnote which Jefferson appended to the preceding

[30] *Ibid.*   [31] *Ibid.*
[32] To Thomas Law, Poplar Forest, June 13, 1814, M.E., XIV, 142.
[33] To Dr. Benjamin Rush, Washington, April 21, 1803, X, 384–85.
[34] *Ibid.*, p. 381–82.

statement the chapter headings of Seneca's and Cicero's philosophical writings were analyzed, clearly proving that the preponderance of subject matter was concerned with the individual. If the individual's contact with others entered into discussion at all, Jefferson perceived that the perspective would be the network of conventional duties and services which defined the individual's status in his community. Jefferson was disinclined to acccept the assumption that individual duties and claims were the heart of moral philosophy; he found the new vision which Jesus brought more valuable to a world of common life than the vision of the ancient moralists had been.

In developing our duties to others, they were short and defective. They embraced, indeed, the circles of kindred and friends, and inculcated patriotism, or the love of our country in the aggregate, as a primary obligation; towards our neighbors and countrymen they taught justice, but scarcely viewed them as within the circle of benevolence. Still less have they inculcated peace, charity and love to our fellow men, or embraced with benevolence the whole family of mankind.[35]

In remaking this point some years later, he was more succinct.

Epictetus and Epicurus give laws for governing ourselves; Jesus a supplement of the duties and charities we owe to others.[36]

The essence of Christian morality for Jefferson is revealed in the above statement, namely, its recognition of (1) the duties owed to others and (2) the charities to others. In the performance of the latter an individual would manifest the degree of his goodness or virtue, while compliance with the former would merely result in conformity to the minimal requirement of morality. Division 1 insures an operative principle of social compromise, very much in the manner of the utilitarians; while 2 supplies the moral ideal of benevolence and love as the spiritualizing force for moral conduct. Although Jefferson on occasions referred to himself as an Epicurean,[37] one can see now in what way the doctrines of Epicurus fell short of the humanitarian practice of Jesus,

[35] To Dr. Benjamin Rush, Washington, April 21, 1803, M.E., X, 382.
[36] To William Short, Monticello, October 31, 1819, M.E., XV, 220.
[37] Ibid., p. 219: "As you say of yourself, I too am an Epicurean. I consider the genuine (not the imputed) doctrines of Epicurus as containing everything rational in moral philosophy which Greece and Rome have left us."

on the one hand, and the resplendent social idealism [38] which Jefferson associated with the teachings of Jesus.

Because Jefferson did find in the ethics of Jesus the clearest expression of inspired humanitarianism, the character of his intense loyalty was somewhat akin to personal religion. But it is important to realize that this "religiousness" of Jefferson's was not based upon a point-by-point agreement with everything Jesus had taught. For example, Jefferson had a realistic appreciation of moral utilitarianism, so that the issue of repentance for him, was always one of repentance plus "good works." Referring to Jesus, Jefferson said: "he preaches the efficacy of repentance towards forgiveness of sin; I require a counterpoise of good works to redeem it." [39] There were differences as well in the way Jefferson regarded questions like immortality, eternal reward and punishment, freedom of the will, "necessary" evil and suffering. Perhaps the question of immortality is of enough moment to examine further.

Jefferson once wrote [40] that Jesus's moral code possessed the advantage of the belief in an after life. "He taught, emphatically, the doctrines of a future state, which was either doubted, or disbelieved by the Jews; and wielded it with efficacy as an important incentive, supplementary to the other motives to moral conduct." [41] But it is difficult to determine whether Jefferson approved the argument of immortality only as an extra incentive to moral behavior, a kind of Benthamite "religious sanction," but without literal or ascertainable truth value, or whether he actually believed in its promise. Unfortunately, Jefferson was reluctant to air his views on this subject. A letter of condolence to John Adams on the death of his wife, Abigail, mentions the time when Jefferson and Adams would "deposit in the same cerement, our sorrows and suffering bodies, and . . . ascend in essence to an ecstatic

[38] The "sublime idea of the Supreme Being, aphorisms and precepts of the purest morality and benevolence . . ." was Jefferson's way of referring to the doctrine of Jesus; while the actual conduct of the latter was "sanctioned by a life of humility, innocence and simplicity of manners, neglect of riches, absence of worldly ambition and honors, with an eloquence and persuasiveness which have not been surpassed." *Ibid.* See also letter to Wm. Short, Monticello, August 4, 1820, M.E., XV, 259.

[39] *Ibid.*, Monticello, April 13, 1820, M.E., 244.

[40] This is placed at the end of the syllabus comparing the morals of Jesus with those of other moral philosophers. To Dr. Benjamin Rush, Washington, April 21, 1803, M.E., X, 385.

[41] *Ibid.*

meeting with the friends we have loved and lost, and whom we shall still love and never lose again." [42] Still the context suggests a conventional formula of sympathy, more than a considered intellectual position.

The clue to Jefferson's position lies in the meaning that "materialism" had for him, so far as his ethical and religious convictions were concerned. Jefferson himself declared that his position was similar to Priestley's; and the tone of the latter's materialism can perhaps best be gauged by the key quotation prefaced to his *Disquisitions relating to Matter and Spirit*. "Si quelqu'un demontreroit jamais, qu *l'âme est materielle* loin de s 'en alarmer, il faudroit admirer la puissance, qui auroit donné a la matiere la capacité de penser. (Bonnett)." Priestley was a materialist "necessarian" [43] who had taken over Hartley's argument that spirit could not exist apart from matter.[44] Priestley was midway between radical French mechanism and New England unitarianism, which considered Priestley too materialistic. Jefferson was thus a conservative materialist. He once argued, in reference to Locke's speculations about matter being endowed by the creator with the power of thinking, that he was "partial to Locke's one incomprehensibility rather than two." [45]

But about Priestley's more specialized beliefs Jefferson was inclined to be critical. For example, Priestley made one exception to the natural law denying preëxistence and post-existence, namely, miracle. Christ's body was supposedly rendered immaterial by miracle, and believers in him were also supposed to become immortal.[46] Priestley also retained his belief in prophecy and the millennium to the end of his life.[47] Jeffer-

---

[42] To John Adams, Monticello, November 13, 1818, M.E., XV, 174.

[43] Priestley defined necessity as: "A chain of causes and effects, established by infinite wisdom, and terminating in the greatest good of the whole universe . . . No necessarian, however, supposes that any of the human race will suffer eternally; but that future punishments will answer the same purpose as temporal ones . . . God, the author of all, is as much to be adored and loved for what we *suffer*, as for what we *enjoy*; his *intention* being equally kind in both, since both are equally parts and equally necessary parts, of the same plan." *The Doctrine of Philosophical Necessity*, pp. 184–85; published as part of Vols. I–II of *Disquisitions Relating to Matter and Spirit*, and called an "Appendix" to the latter.

[44] See Holt, *The Unitarian Contribution to Social Progress in England*, p. 310.

[45] To John Adams, Monticello, March 14, 1820, M.E., XV, 241.

[46] Holt, *op. cit.*, p. 311.   [47] *Ibid.*

son, on the other hand, rejected miracles, inspiration, and revelation without compromise; he was acridly critical of the ignorance and fallibility of the apostles, particularly denouncing St. Paul as the principal corruptor of the doctrines of Christ.[48] On the basis of this, one is entitled to conclude that Jefferson's "religion" was more radical "rational Christianity" (to use his own phrase) than Priestley's.

However, the greater consistency of Jefferson's materialistic beliefs never approached the positive and sturdy materialism of the French philosophers, for instance, Holbach, Diderot, D'Alembert, Helvetius,[49] and others. Since Jefferson stopped short of the logical development of complete materialism, it is puzzling to ascertain what exactly he had had in mind by his self-claimed materialism. His repeated accusations against those he called "Spiritualists" may possibly furnish the clue. Jefferson meant by the term (which he nowhere carefully defined) the Platonic philosophers and theologians ("mystifiers" generally), Cartesian dualists,[50] and perhaps also Berkeleyan idealists.[51] The ground for classifying these together philosophically seems to have been their anti-scientific transcendental metaphysics. From the viewpoint of morals and politics these figures represented the conservatism which supported the union of morality and the church, a practical tendency, in short, which led to a point-by-point defense of the *status quo*. Feeling that the belief in an immaterial, immortal soul would open all avenues to mysteries, miracles, and incomprehensible "logomachies," Jefferson set out to show that there was a tradition of materialism with as good a lineage as that of spiritualism.

Mr. Locke . . . openly maintained the materialism of the soul; and charged with blasphemy those who denied that it was in the power of an almighty

[48] See Hall, "The Religious Opinions of Thomas Jefferson," *The Sewanee Review*, XXI, 169.

[49] See *Ideology*, Part II, following.

[50] Priestley, for example, was primarily opposed to the tradition of Cartesian dualism; the division into soul and body presented insoluble problems, for either "one seemed extraneous" or the "union mysterious." See *Disquisitions* . . . p. 111. Jefferson seems to be in agreement on this point. Also, Holbach's *System of Nature* (a copy of which is penciled in Jefferson's writing, in the Jefferson Collection, Rare Book Department, Library of Congress) argues against the system of *Spirituality*, which "owes all its pretended proofs to Descartes," pp. 98–99.

[51] John Witherspoon meant by "immaterial system" the philosophy of Berkeley. Possibly Jefferson uses the term to include this also.

creator to endow with the faculty of thought any composition of matter he might think fit. The fathers of the church of the first three centuries, generally, if not universally, were materialists, extending it even to the creator himself, nor indeed do I know exactly in what age of the Christian Church [52] the heresy of spiritualism was introduced.[53]

Three years later Jefferson allowed Cooper to convince him that the doctrine of materialism was that of Jesus,[54] although his earlier judgment had been that Jesus was a spiritualist.[55] It was evidently agreeable to Jefferson to rank Jesus with the materialists (although he had lacked the scholarly proofs to back such a hypothesis on his own initiative), for this was metaphysical support in favor of the humanistic values of the morals of Jesus.

In fact, it may almost be said that Jefferson had conceived a moral preference for the position of materialism. He apparently used it as a heuristic principle—assuming materialism to be true, man's self-reliance is increased, his moral responsibility developed, his social obligations inescapably defined: therefore it is true. Nevertheless, he did make an effort to inform himself on the scientific status of the issue; but partly because of the real paucity of information and experimentation at that time and partly because of the limited time he could allot to such research, his understanding of materialism was not profound.[56]

The pattern which finally suggests itself, on the basis of the fore-

[52] A marginal note is appended at this point, in Jefferson's writing: "around the council of Nicea."
[53] To Thomas Cooper, August 14, 1820, M.E., XV, 266.
[54] See the letter to Thomas Cooper, Dec. 11, 1823, which Cooper reprinted in his *The Scripture Doctrine of Materialism*, p. 329. There Cooper notes: "Mr. Jefferson was not aware that Materialism is the real doctrine of Jesus Christ, until I sent him the preceding extract. See his letter to W. Short, April 13, 1820."
[55] To William Short, Monticello, April 13, 1820, M.E., XV, 244.
[56] The specifically *scientific* problem was brought to Jefferson's attention by the work of "Flourend" (same as *Flourens*), whose experiments on the functions of the nervous system he read in 1825. He wrote: "Cabanis had proved by the anatomical structure of certain portions of the human frame, that they might be capable of receiving from the hand of the Creator the faculty of thinking; Flourend proves that they have received it; that the cerebrum is the thinking organ; and that life and health may continue, and the animal be entirely without thought, if deprived of that organ. I wish to see what the spiritualists will say to this . . ." To John Adams, Monticello, January 8, 1825, M.E., XVI, 91. The philosophical treatment of the issue of materialism interested Jefferson more deeply. See Part II, "Ideology."

going considerations, is that of an extremely liberated deist, with a primarily utilitarian emphasis for his social morality. Regretting the role of the "religion-builders" who "so distorted and deformed the doctrines of Jesus . . . as to shock reasonable thinkers, to revolt them against the whole, and drive them rashly to pronounce its Founder an imposter," [57] Jefferson tried to find his way back to "the simple structure of Jesus." [58] Specific creeds were only irritants to Jefferson; he impatiently declared that there were probably no two creeds alike, but if there were, he neither considered himself a member of any sect nor expected the world to be concerned with what must remain, in all seriousness, a man's private account, "to be settled only with Him who made us." [59] "I never told my own religion," he wrote, reprovingly on one occasion, "nor scrutinized that of another. I never attempted to make a convert, nor wished to change another's creed." [60]

Rationally, he seemed to accept the argument from design, believing it pointed to "a Fabricator of all things . . . a Superintending power, to maintain the universe in its course and order." [61] Jefferson further maintained that the creator who was sufficiently intelligent to design the harmonious "working of systems" (solar, organic, human) could not be further defined as spiritual or material. "Of the nature of this Being we know nothing." [62] Whatever its real nature, it must be akin to Mind. He insists that the cosmogony found in the first chapter of John should be "truly translated" [63] as: "In the beginning God existed, and reason (or mind) was with God, and that mind was God." [64] In short, Jefferson found the translation of *logos* as "word" to be a distortion of the meaning appropriate to that context. Reason was not merely imminent, it was creative wisdom, fashioning a world.

Over and above the belief in an intelligent and benevolent Creator ("the God whom you and I acknowledge and adore, the Creator and benevolent Governor of the world") [65] who "formed us moral agents,"

[57] To Timothy Pickering, Esq., Monticello, February 27, 1821, M.E., XV, 324.
[58] *Ibid.*, p. 323.   [59] *Ibid.*, p. 324.
[60] To Mrs. M. Harrison Smith, Monticello, August 6, 1816, M.E., XV, 60.
[61] To John Adams, Monticello, April 11, 1823, M.E., XV, 427. The discussion, pp. 425–30, is interesting from the point of view of religious beliefs—Calvinism, Atheism, revelation, etc.
[62] *Ibid.*, p. 428.   [63] *Ibid.*, p. 429.   [64] *Ibid.*
[65] To John Adams, Monticello, April 11, 1823, M.E., XV, 425.

there is practically no discussion of specific tenets. The desire for privacy, mentioned before, coupled with a frank admission that there is no knowledge of the specific attributes of God or of the manner in which his superintendence over the world was being exercised, were sufficient reasons for Jefferson's avoidance of everything resembling theological discussion. He felt impelled to recall Jesus's attitude in justifying his own.

. . . the benevolent and sublime reformer of that religion has told us only that God is good and perfect, but has not defined him. I am, therefore of his theology, believing that we have neither words nor ideas adequate to that definition. And if we could all, after this example, leave the subject as undefinable, we should all be of one sect, doers of good, and eschewers of evil.[66]

One looks in vain, therefore, for answers to the genuinely puzzling question about Jefferson's "particular principles" of religion: for example, his beliefs on the state of future rewards and punishments, the literal immortality of the soul, or the resolution of the problem of evil (in a world presumably "superintended" by God, with no specification of how much superintendence, or how far). The moral test alone was trustworthy in Jefferson's opinion; and by itself sufficient.

I must ever believe that religion substantially good which produces an honest life, and we have been authorized by one whom you and I equally respect, to judge of the tree by its fruit.[67]

Indeed, he was ready to sum up the essential features of his position by confessing to John Adams.

If by *religion* we are to understand *sectarian dogmas*, in which no two of them agree, then your exclamation on them is just, "that this would be the best of all possible worlds, if there were no religion in it." But if the moral precepts, innate in man, and made a part of his physical constitution, as necessary for a social being, if the sublime doctrines of philanthropism and deism taught us by Jesus of Nazareth, in which all agree, constitute true religion, then without it, this would be, as you again say, "something not fit to be named even, indeed, a hell." [68]

[66] To Ezra Styles, Monticello, June 25, 1819, M.E., XV, 203.
[67] To Mr. Miles King, Monticello, September 26, 1814, M.E., XIV, 198.
[68] To John Adams, Monticello, May 5, 1817, M.E., XV, 109.

In the face of this mounting evidence, it seems singularly misdirected to attach any significance to the equal inaccuracies of claiming Jefferson for some special sect and for relegating him to the ranks of "atheistical unbelievers." He was a pious man, if the religion of a humane morality is recognized as a kind of natural piety.

Chapter V

UTILITARIANISM

SOMETHING remains to be said about Jefferson's tendency to strengthen the "pure and sublime" principles of Jesus with a dash of the most hard-headed moral theory current in the Enlightenment—utilitarianism. Epicureanism, Christian benevolence, moral sense intuitionism had all been woven into the pattern which Jefferson needed to account for morality. But only utilitarianism could be relied on to cut the suggestion of absolutism out of these more single-valued philosophies, making room for that variability of moral judgment which Jefferson's historic sense made him acknowledge as one segment in the development of man in society. Social utility was apparently capable of supplying some answers which Christian idealism failed to provide.

In discussing the advantages of the doctrines of Epicurus, Jefferson had accepted "happiness as the aim of life" and "utility as the test of virtue." [1] But we have already seen that happiness cannot be assimilated to the pleasure of the self (that is, to egoistic hedonism) in Jefferson's usage. And it is not surprising, therefore, to find that happiness is qualified by Jefferson so that it depends upon virtue.[2] Virtue, in turn, is specifically described as made up of the classic cardinal virtues: (1) Prudence; (2) Temperance; (3) Fortitude; (4) Justice. To which are opposed: (1) Folly; (2) Desire; (3) Fear; (4) Deceit.[3] All four components of virtue are postulated on the assumption that the welfare of others is a real pleasure to the self. The only proof one can offer that human nature supports an unselfish morality, is that "the Creator would indeed have been a bungling artist, had he intended man for a social animal, without planting in him social dispositions." [4] He admits excep-

[1] To William Short, Monticello, October 31, 1819, M.E., XV, 223–34.
[2] *Ibid.*   [3] *Ibid.*
[4] To Thomas Law, Esq., Poplar Forest, July 13, 1814, M.E., XIV, 142.

tions to this, as to every rule, but warns that the exceptions should not be themselves "converted" into a general rule. For those individuals who lack the gift of "social dispositions," secondary safeguards must be artificially built up.

. . . by education, by appeals to reason and calculation, by presenting to the being so unhappily conformed, other motives to do good and to eschew evil, such as the love, or the hatred, or rejection of those among whom he lives and whose society is necessary to his happiness and even existence; demonstrations by sound calculation that honesty promotes interest in the long run; the rewards and penalties established by the laws; and ultimately the prospects of a future state of retribution for the evil as well as the good done while here . . .[5]

In short, where the genuine inborn morality of pure intention does not exist and function, one relies upon the descending scale of moral forces, namely, training, discipline, appeal to self-interest—both in this world and the "next."

How is it possible that within the framework of a designed universe, in which moral principles are made native to the constitution of man, there are such varieties and conflicts in the meanings of "virtuous" and "vicious" behavior? Jefferson was cognizant of the problem, and his later letters introduce the concept of "utility" for this purpose. Different actions are termed "good" and "bad," because concrete differences in adjustment are necessary to meet the requirements of dissimilar circumstances.

. . . nature has constituted utility to man, the standard and test of virtue. Men living in different countries under different circumstances, different habits and regimens, may have different utilities; the same act, therefore, may be useful, and consequently virtuous in one country which is injurious and vicious in another differently circumstanced . . .[6]

Utility was to serve as the "standard and test of virtue," but how did Jefferson understand the concept of utility? What kind of action, relative to a given set of conditions, should one designate as virtuous? At this point Jefferson connects utility and virtue with happiness—the happiness of *others*. Any specific action can be identified as virtuous if it is aimed at the well-being or happiness of others.

[5] *Ibid.*   [6] *Ibid.*, p. 143.

If it is to effect the happiness of him to whom it is directed, it is virtuous, while in a society under different circumstances and opinions, the same act might produce pain, and would be vicious. The essence of virtue is in doing good to others, while what is good may be one thing in one society, and its contrary in another.[7]

This passage is evidence that Jefferson had moved away, in his mature ethical thought, from a simple belief in moral rules, divinely inspired and innately ingrained in man. The subtler notion, of a moral principle like social utility, conceived to be sufficiently flexible to accommodate the inevitable changes of environment, completed the moral picture. Nor is it accidental that this device made workable that humanity and tolerance and unlimited good will which Jefferson had so eagerly studied in the conduct of Jesus, his one undisputed leader. On the other hand, the happiness of others, which he singled out as the essence of a virtuously motivated action, was a part of the secular, practical, and modern morality which Jefferson admired. He valued it as a realistic reënforcement of the loftier Christian morality, the latter remaining indisputably the most perfect pattern of conduct, while the former represented the desirable average compromise which a wise legislator would be glad to have realized by the citizens of a state. That is why Aristotle's "eudaemonism" is a closer approximation to Jefferson's use of the happiness concept than the more contemporary "hedonism" was.[8]

One cannot help observing the want of articulation between the varied fragments of Jefferson's ethical theorizing. Actually, these loopholes in theory might be expected to lead to an impasse in practical decisions had not Jefferson's belief in man's essential goodness remained firm. The interpretation of primitive Christian morality was the concrete form in which he put the inspiration contained in his "moral sense"

---

[7] To John Adams, Monticello, October 14, 1816, M.E., XV, 77.

[8] Sometimes Jefferson interpreted happiness in the Epicurean sense; see, e.g., letter to William Short, Monticello, October 31, 1819, M.E., XV, 222–24. But Jefferson always approached Epicureanism via Gassendi, in its Christianized and Stoicized version, so that nothing really conflicting with the eudaemonistic has a place in Jefferson's system. Jefferson says: "I have sometimes thought of translating Epictetus (for he has never been tolerably translated into English) by adding the genuine doctrines of Epicurus from the Syntagma of Gassendi, and an abstract from the Evangelists of whatever has the stamp of the eloquence and fine imagination of Jesus." *Ibid.*, p. 221.

theory. The concept of "happiness" was the logical culmination of the tendency to emphasize social health through restrained self-interest, coöperation, and compromise; technically, it destroyed the absolutist character of Jefferson's earlier moral theory, which inconsistency was a small price to pay for having done justice to the real variety of moral experiences. But without a doubt the balance was maintained by Jefferson's own behavior, by his habit of faithfully filling in the concrete values of a liberated and humane person, wherever the theoretical lacunae might have resulted in indecision or misdirection.

PART TWO: PHILOSOPHY
AND IDEOLOGY

Chapter VI

PHILOSOPHICAL DEBUT

JEFFERSON was a true *"philosophe."* The *philosophe* as a thinking type has been noticed in the German phrase *"Denker für die Welt,"* men who are interested in ideas, in the latest findings of the sciences, in the increase of knowledge, but less from the point of view of technical exactness and wire-fine detail than from the angle of amateur systematic clarity and enthusiasm. The persistence of Jefferson's intellectual curiosity and its vast range of interest and inquiry are at once the keys to his personality and the sign of the *philosophe.* No other political figure, with the possible exception of Franklin, in America, had as genuine an enthusiasm for the progress of knowledge or as tireless a devotion to the liberalizing agencies inherent in "disinterested" knowledge as Jefferson did. If any one figure can be taken as symbol of the Enlightenment in America, Jefferson must be that one. While his adventures in politics are better known, in point of vitality and significance his intellectual career requires equal attention.

Two traditions are blended in Jefferson's philosophic thinking—one spontaneous and home-grown, the other formal. The former is a type of thought which may be called scientific, empirical, or practical; Jefferson naturally inclined to it, and used it for problem solving. The latter is the school of French ideology, which managed, in a remarkable way, to round out with method and technical finish a set of similar ideas.

French ideology was as self-conscious a philosophic sect as the history of philosophy has ever produced. It was institutionalized, and centered its headquarters, *l'Institut National,* in Paris. One of its official members was Napoleon, before he became irritated with the intellectual independence of the second class, which he ordered "dissolved" in

1803. The official publication of the ideologists was the *Décade philosophique;* their official charges, the system of *écoles centrales,* spread throughout France, with curriculum, faculties, and textbooks all ideologic in orientation.[1]

Jefferson made a personal discovery of ideology through friendship with its founders and clearly considered himself the representative of the movement for America. The French ideologists were overjoyed with their statesman disciple, a joy due to the belief that their theoretical philosophy had demonstrated its usefulness by furnishing a disciplined intellectual system to the pioneering republic, in which they centered their hopes for a better world. But it is highly significant that Jefferson's choice of a philosophy, made late in his life, should reënforce a lifetime's preference for the tradition of scientific positivism (in its then-current historical form). There is no break in intellectual consistency, none in basic orientation either, when Jefferson promotes the fortunes of ideology or bestows upon it his official blessing.

These are easily the two dominant traditions in Jefferson's career of philosophic reflection, and may without artifice be viewed as two phases of one persistent philosophical tendency. There is additional evidence of allegiance in Jefferson's flirtation with Scottish intuitionist philosophy. While this may seem a quite unrelated tradition, as Jefferson viewed it, it was part of the same tendency. Scottish realism, for Jefferson, was a minor intellectual enthusiasm, rooted, however, in his past, when as a youthful thinker speculating on law and morality, the moral sense theory advocated by Lord Kames [2] caught his attention. The later Scottish systematizers were careful to avoid the word "innate," but in fact were the continuators of the same tradition.[3]

---

[1] Control of the *écoles centrales* was the result of a careful program of national instruction legislated by the politically minded educators in 1795. See Introduction to Van Duzer, *Contribution of the Ideologues to French Revolutionary Thought;* also Boas, *French Philosophies of the Romantic Period,* pp. 4–22.

[2] See letter to Thomas Law, P.F., June 13, 1814, M.E., XIV, 144, in which he calls attention to his high estimate of Kames as a thinker, but admits it is 50 years since he was referred to that author. Also, the preponderance of selections from Kames in Jefferson's *Commonplace Book* on government is further testimony.

[3] E.g., Reid's defense of "moral sense"; see Segerstedt, *The Problem of Knowledge in Scottish Philosophy,* pp. 32–33, and Stewart's further modification of the doctrine, *ibid.,* p. 38. Rogers *English and American Philosophy since 1800,* pp. 2–3, maintains that Scottish realism is identified with the tradition which explained

This, in brief, is the setting for Thomas Jefferson's realm of ideas.

Before Jefferson was sent as American ambassador to Paris, to replace Benjamin Franklin, he had led a very active political life. From his college years to the long awaited time [4] of his European pilgrimage, his philosophical thinking had been concentrated on questions more related to the law, to government, to religion, and to personal morality than to pure philosophy. His commonplace books and the *Notes on Virginia* are the outstanding evidences of his intellectual interests before his sojourn in France. In Paris, Jefferson was set down in the midst of the most aggressive intellectual group on the continent. More than that, he was received by them with the friendliest of welcomes, inspired in part by the current sentiment for Franklin, in part by the political excitement then current about the great American republican experiment, and in good part by Jefferson himself, with his modesty, his learning, and his intellectual courage. Many of the Encyclopaedists, the Materialists, and the more conservative (but still "liberal") aristocratic savants and diplomats were his friends and acquaintances.

He corresponded with them on official matters, but usually in more than the routine diplomatic spirit; and with some he discussed unofficial questions, ranging from supplements to his *Notes on Virginia* (which was enjoying a phenomenal success with the French intellectuals at the time), to broader questions of civil rights, the proper "aim" of good government, and the meaning of freedom for men in different societies. He frequented Mme d'Holbach's salon and was a favorite of Mmes d'Houdetot, Corny, De Bréhan and De Tessé.[5] There is available correspondence with Condorcet, the Abbé Morellet, Mirabeau, Lafayette, the Marquis d'Argenson, Mably, Dupont de Nemours, and others, and one can surmise there was much that is lost.

Contact with the society where encyclopaedism, materialism, and

mental processes not only by "the laws of association at work upon the material of sense" but also by "certain ultimate and unexplainable truths of intuition." For Stewart's own exposition see *The works of Dugald Stewart*, I, 7–8.

[4] Jefferson was twice prepared to represent the American Government in France, but his missions were canceled at the last minute.

[5] See correspondence, in Chinard, *Trois amitiés françaises de Jefferson*, and *Les Amitiés américaines de Madame d'Houdetot*. Also see Chinard, Introduction to *Jefferson et les idéologues*, p. 5.

even Scottish realism was represented, stimulated Jefferson's thought to activity in new directions. Jefferson had already demonstrated, in his *Notes on Virginia*, that he understood and could use scientific method. His criticisms of Buffon's natural classifications, his skillful disclosure of the inaccuracies of current theories about naturally "inferior" races (in this case, the American Indians and Negroes), his exploration of the concept of republican government, including his brilliant defense of religious freedom, could only have been made by somebody committed consciously to the ideal of impartial scientific investigation. Furthermore, the very real proofs of devotion to the cause of intellectual freedom and to its political roots are the essence of the book.

But what Jefferson knew and thus used in an independent fashion was made explicit and systematic by the French radical intellectuals who became his friends. Driving home the implications of an acceptance of reason and science, they marshaled a vast array of erudition and corroborative testimony to give solid support to their moral, political, and philosophical beliefs. In this way they managed to achieve a certain group systematization, typified earlier in the *Encyclopaedia*.[6] The unity of the *Encyclopaedia* is its most basic postulate, which almost alone constitutes its "philosophy." This unity is brought to life by juxtaposing one concrete investigation to another, in any field at all, but investigations animated by the identical spirit of scientific "objectivity" and evidence—the net effect of which was defense of progress and reason against social and religious prejudices.

Jefferson owed something to the encyclodaedic movement in thought.[7] He was well acquainted with the important introductory

[6] *Encyclopédie, ou, Dictionnaire raisonné des sciences, des arts et des metiers.*

[7] Jefferson's practical role in the popular French occupation of encyclopaedism was shown by his connection with the *Encyclopédie méthodique*, which in Jefferson's description "relates to economy politique and diplomatique." See "Notes on the Fifth Volume of Marshall's *Life of Washington*," M.E., XVII, 402. His act for Freedom of Religion, passed by the Virginia Legislature in 1786, was reprinted in this encyclopedia. He contributed articles and furnished information for them. See the letter to M. Van Hogendorp, Paris, August 25, 1786, M.E., V, 418. "The authors of the part of the new 'Encyclopédie,' which relates to political economy, having asked of me materials for the article 'Etat Unis' [*sic*], stating a number of questions relative to them. I answered them as minutely and exactly as was in my power. He has from these compiled the greater part of that article." He also pur-

essay by D'Alembert, which, with its philosophic borrowings from Bacon, Locke, and Condillac, proved to be sympathetic to the ideologues as well as to Jefferson. The famous classification of the human mind, and its correlations with specific subject matters, adopted by the encyclopaedists and made introductory to the entire work, D'Alembert attributed to Bacon. Jefferson used this same classification for his literary catalogues and seemed to accept its presuppositions about knowledge and the human mind.[8] Furthermore, this classification was the basis of elaborate plans for school and university curricula drawn up many years later by Jefferson,[9] so that one can infer that he had taken seriously the implicit epistemology and psychology of the *Encyclopaedia*.

Although the *Encyclopaedia* was the monument of the cultural and scientific achievement of eighteenth-century France and exercised immeasurable influence over subsequent ideas and attitudes, no one pretends to find in it outstanding technical philosophical value. It is better, therefore, to appreciate its influence upon Jefferson as stimulating him to familiarize himself with a popular statement of Locke's empiricism in Condillac's interpretation. In this sense, the *Encyclopaedia* was Jefferson's preparation for ideology, since the ideologists looked upon Condillac and through him Locke and ultimately Bacon as the intellectual pioneers who broke the ground for their own work.

At approximately the same time that Jefferson matured in the atmosphere of the *Encyclopaedia*, he met Dugald Stewart, who later sent him his books,[10] as they appeared, with their defense of Reid and

chased a set for himself, and other sets for friends, such as Wythe, Madison, Edmund Randolph, Dr. Styles, and others. See Parton, *Life of Thomas Jefferson*, pp. 304, 311.

[8] See Preface. See also Jefferson's second library catalogue. The entire table of contents is listed under the Baconian classification, viz., "The Faculties of the Human Mind," which are divided into "Memory," "Reason," and "Imagination." With these are correlated the subjects "History," "Philosophy," and "Fine Arts," respectively. These are further subdivided until all subjects are exhausted.

[9] For further discussion of this point, see the concluding section of this chapter.

[10] See Vol. I of Jefferson's copy of *The Elements of the Philosophy of the Human Mind* in the Library of Congress. Stewart's letter to Jefferson is pasted on the inside cover: "The book which accompanies this letter is the only performance which I have yet ventured to publish. I hope you will do me the honor to give it a place in your Library and that you will accept it as a mark of my grateful recollection of the attentions which I received from you at Paris."—signed, Dugald Stewart, College of Edinburgh, October 1, 1792.

Scottish common-sense doctrines.[11] There is little information about the relationship between Stewart and Jefferson in Paris. We know only of Jefferson's subsequent excitement about his friend's philosophic eminence. In 1820 Jefferson wrote to Adams:

Stewart is a great man, and among the most honest living. After you left Europe he . . . came to Paris. He brought me a letter from Lord Wycombe . . . I became immediately intimate with him, calling mutually on each other and almost daily during his stay at Paris, which was of some months. I consider him and Tracy as the ablest metaphysicians living; by which I mean investigators of the thinking faculty of man . . .[12]

Another confirmation of Jefferson's high opinion of Stewart is his letter written in 1824, when he wished to enlist Stewart's aid in selecting foreign professors for the University of Virginia; in the course of that letter Jefferson referred to "the publication of your invaluable book on the *Philosophy of the Human Mind,* a copy of which you sent me, and I have been happy to see it become the text book of most our colleges and academies, and pass through several reimpressions in the United States." [13] There are no further overt references to Stewart's work, so that Jefferson's admiration for Stewart is not supported by any specific analysis of his writings. However, Stewart's rejection of metaphysics and the practical tone in which he avoided excessive rational scepticism probably appealed to Jefferson.

In fact, Stewart's *Elements of the Philosophy of the Human Mind* has something in common with both the philosophy of the *Encyclopaedia* and Ideology. All three philosophies are primarily "antimetaphysical" (a favorite term of the *Idéologues*)—which seems to mean primarily anti-Descartes, medieval rationalism, "spiritualism." In Stewart's case it meant in addition anti-Hume [14] and anti-Kant. Furthermore they both regarded themselves as empirical "investigators of the thinking faculty," [15] and they considered the theory of knowledge to

---

[11] The hopes for the "future progress" of the philosophy of mind are based on "the excellent models of this species of investigation, which the writings of Dr. Reid exhibit . . ." *Works of Dugald Stewart,* I, 7.

[12] To John Adams, Monticello, March 14, 1820, M.E., XV, 239-40.

[13] To Dugald Stewart, Monticello, April 26, M.E., 1824, XVIII, 331.

[14] Stewart was anti-Hume because he regarded Hume's scepticism as a kind of paralyzed metaphysics. See Stewart, *Works . . . ,* II, 51.

[15] See excerpt, already quoted, from Jefferson's letter to Adams, March 14, 1820.

be so closely connected with society and practical problems that any philosophy which could not offer an immediately adequate approach to the real world was by that fact disqualified. In keeping with this fundamental agreement, we find all three philosophies openly claiming the same historical progenitor, Bacon.

Stewart phrases his acceptance of Bacon's positivistic theory of nature in this fashion:

To ascertain those established conjunctions of successive events which constitute the order of the universe;—to record the phenomena which it exhibits to our observation, and to refer them to their general laws, is the great business of philosophy. Lord Bacon was the first person who was fully aware of the importance of this fundamental truth. The ancients considered philosophy as the science of *causes;* and hence were led to many speculations, to which the human faculties are altogether incompetent.[16]

Jefferson himself apparently valued such an attitude because it offered a more workable pragmatic approach to scientific problems than the current "metaphysical" philosophies did. In his own investigations of scientific hypotheses (which he undertook in a highly independent spirit),[17] he had sufficiently prepared himself to receive only the philosophical positions which acknowledged and encouraged independent and critical activity in the sciences. In this connection Stewart's virtual identification of philosophy with psychology or the science of mental faculties and operations [18] was a step in the direction of concrete localization of the kind necessitated by the scientific ideal. That this was uppermost in Stewart's intentions is revealed at once in the first pages of his book.[19]

By confining their attention to the sensible qualities of body, and to the sensible phenomena it exhibits, we know what discoveries natural philosophers have made: and if the labor of metaphysicians shall ever be rewarded with similar success, it can only be by attentive and patient reflection, on the subjects of their own consciousness.

Stewart expected that the acceptance of scientific methodology, which he seems to have understood in a peculiarly limited way, would ulti-

[16] Stewart, *Works* . . . , II, 6. (Cambridge, 1829.)
[17] See, e.g., his *Notes on Virginia*, M.E., Vol. II.
[18] Stewart, *Works* . . . , II, 49.　　[19] *Ibid.*, p. 6; II, 50.

mately introduce the same "law" and order into the philosophy of the human mind that it had already facilitated in the science of physics. The aim of the new philosophy of mind was clearly and unblushingly presented.

. . . [the discovery of] a comparatively small number of simple and uncompounded faculties, or of simple and uncompounded principles of action. These faculties and principles are the general laws of our constitution, and hold the same place in the philosophy of mind, that the general laws we investigate in physics, hold in that branch of science. In both cases, the laws which nature has established, are to be investigated only by an examination of facts; and in both cases, a knowledge of these laws leads to an explanation of an infinite number of phenomena.[20]

Enough has been said in this passage to conclude that Stewart's optimistic pan-scientism had turned upon the more recondite philosophies with considerable determination. The ideal of precise scientific statement proportioned exactly to evidence receives further consideration from Stewart.

When we have once ascertained a general fact; such as, the various laws which regulate the association of ideas, or the dependence of memory on that effort of the mind which we call *attention;* it is all we ought to aim at, in this branch of science. If we proceed no further than facts for which we have the evidence of our own consciousness, our conclusions will be no less certain, than those in physics: but if our curiosity leads us to attempt an explanation of the association of ideas by certain supposed vibrations, or other changes, in the state of the brain; or to explain memory, by means of supposed impressions and traces in the sensorium; we evidently blend a collection of important and well ascertained truths, with principles which rest wholly on conjecture.[21]

These two passages, taken together, illustrate at once the attractiveness and also the inherent superficiality of the "new" philosophy. The attraction was clearly the appeal to immediate experience, to "fact," and to observation patient enough to ground "laws" and generalizations, but not so patient and so carefully analyzed as to dissolve into sceptical irresolution or suspension of conclusions and actions.[22] However, the

[20] Stewart, *Works* . . . , II, 51–52.   [21] *Ibid.*, p. 52.

[22] "It is indeed only by an examination of the principles of our nature, that they can be brought to a satisfactory conclusion; but supposing them to remain unde-

superficiality is just as plainly the limited conception of scientific investigation, verification, and evidence generally, which so easily assumes that "facts" are ready-made structures in the "real" world open to mere viewing or looking; while scientific operations are grossly oversimplified, to the point where sceptical difficulties are solved in advance by the resolution that there are general laws descriptive of our "constitution," which are based upon "the evidence of our own consciousness"; and these facts of consciousness presumably will be declared the terminus of inquiry, for fear that further inquiry would lead to remoter mental and physiological operations too elusive for sensation and introspection.[23] To this presentation of philosophy as science, Jefferson gave, as we have already noticed, verbal assent; although his own practical investigations in many instances [24] were more penetrating and subtle than this theory allowed.

However, Jefferson's interest in Scottish philosophy was probably not limited to the technical epistemological aspect. As we have seen, Jefferson was deeply preoccupied with explanations of moral judgments, and he discovered in Stewart's approach a continuation of Kames's solution. The Scottish contribution of moral faculties was akin to a reaffirmation of conventional maxims, attributed as essential furniture to the mind. Thus it was not a genuinely new interpretation. Jefferson's acceptanace of this explanation contributed very little to his own advance in ethical theory.[25]

In Stewart's work, although experience is invoked as methodological and genetic sanction, it does not prevent a solid reliance upon a priori

---

cided, our sceptical doubts concerning the certainty of human knowledge, would no more affect the philosophy of mind, than they would affect any of the branches of physics. . ." *ibid.*, p. 56.

[23] Locke's influence is still paramount in this respect; simple ideas of sensation and reflection are not forsaken as the actual desiderata of philosophical analysis. Only now more craft is required in appealing to them.

[24] See, e.g., his *Notes on Virginia*, Query VI, on Buffon's hypothesis, the question of "racial inequality," etc. M.E., II, 61–96.

[25] In fact, the disappointingly meager results of the Scottish "scientific" philosophy are only too apparent in their accounts of moral judgments. The careful method of going no further than the facts and patiently observing the succession of phenomena, etc., could not have been applied here with too much seriousness; for, had it been, one might have expected more from Stewart's ethical position than a slightly pruned repetition of Cudworth and Price. See Segerstedt, *The Problem of Knowledge in Scottish Philosophy*, pp. 38–39.

certainties. These certainties are the "faculties," "simple and uncompounded principles of action" which serve to launch subsequent empirical investigation. The authority of basic truths in morality and common sense is kept intact, so that neither dissolvent scepticism nor unknown radical innovation can act upon them. This fear of persistent analysis which might end with no end in sight, as Stewart believed it had for Hume, was part, at least, of the "realism" of the Scottish philosophers.

Stewart drew attention to this feature of his position by stating early in his *Elements of the Philosophy of the Human Mind* that his aim was "to maintain a steady course of inquiry, between implicit credulity and unlimited scepticism." [26]

From this point of view Stewart's philosophy appears to be the result of a decision to compromise, to avoid the wholesale assertions of theological or mystical philosophies which give rise to rigid dogmas and unqualified revelations. But the decision to compromise, anteceding the inquiry itself, is responsible for the introduction of an arbitrary limit to analysis. It is this which allows for the presence of "faculties" and "uncompounded principles of action" embarrassing nonempirical first principles in a revolutionary conception of philosophy as empirical science of mind. [27]

The fuller significance of Stewart's assumptions about "scientific" philosophy, including the desideratum of "laws"—as useful and extensive as those of physics are—can most easily be discovered in the explicit statements of ideology. The analogous development of the science of bodies with the (future) science of mind is thrust forward to compel philosophic attention; this cardinal thesis shapes the elaborate systematization which characterizes the ideologic venture.

[26] Stewart, *Works* . . . , II, 71.

[27] Theodore Jouffroy, who offered Stewart's works in translation to the French public, prefaced them with lengthy critical introductions, which are (with Cousin's) almost alone as serious appraisals of Scottish common-sense philosophy. Cf., the following excerpt with the criticism suggested above. "Le mot *organe*, employé pour désigner la cause de certains phénomènes, ne laisse donc pas dans l'esprit une idée plus nette de cette cause que le mot *ame;* ce sont deux mots employés pour désigner une cause inconnue, qu'ils n'expliquent pas plus l'un que l'autre." *Esquisses de philosophie morale*, by Stewart, Jouffroy's *Preface*, p. cxxvi.

Chapter VII

JEFFERSON AND IDEOLOGY

JOHN ADAMS, in one of his typical outbursts of energy and irritation, demanded of Jefferson the meaning of the curious new word, "Ideology." "'Three vols. of Ideology!' Pray explain to me this Neological title! What does it mean? When Bonaparte used it, I was delighted with it, upon the common principle of delight in everything we cannot understand. Does it mean Idiotism? The science of *non compos mentuism?* The science of Lunacy? The theory of delirium? Or does it mean the science of self-love? Of *amour propre?* or the elements of *vanity?*" [1] But after a few lines Adams grudgingly conceded to Jefferson that Tracy's work (and thus ideology) bore no signs of *non compos mentis.* "That analysis, however does not show a man of excessive mediocrity . . . Of all things; I wish to see his Ideology upon Montesquieu." [2]

Jefferson's enthusiasm for Ideology was apparently beginning to crack the irascible crust of Adams's habitual resistance. As Adams himself implied, if a man like Jefferson (then in his seventy-third year) bothered to translate, write commentaries about, and plead for the publication of the works of Destutt de Tracy [3] and other Ideologists, perhaps even an outlandish name should not impede serious study of the new doctrine. Jefferson, undaunted by Adams's manner, wrote his serene answer some weeks later. It is worth reproducing, because it is at once simpler and more revealing than other brief descriptions of ideology.

Tracy comprehends, under the word "Ideology," all the subjects which the French term *Morale*, as the correlative to *Physique*. His works on Logic, Government, Politics, Economics and Morality, he considers as making up the circle of ideological subjects, or of those which are within the scope of

[1] John Adams to Thomas Jefferson, Quincy, December 16, 1816, M.E., XV, 88.
[2] *Ibid.*   [3] *Ibid.*

the understanding, and not of the senses. His Logic occupies exactly the ground of Locke's work on the Understanding.[4]

The suggestion Jefferson makes here is supported by one connotation of the French adjective *morale* as "mental" or "intellectual." Apparently the French ideologists believed in approaching philosophy through epistemology, just as Locke and Stewart had done. Jefferson shows that Stewart and Tracy are, in his opinion, engaged in related pursuits, while he had already associated Locke with Tracy. Referring to Stewart, Jefferson said:

I consider him and Tracy as the ablest metaphysicians living; by which I mean investigators of the thinking faculty of man. Stewart seems to have given its natural history from facts and observations; Tracy its modes of action and deduction, which he calls Logic and Ideology; and Cabanis has investigated anatomically, and most ingeniously, the particular organs in the human structure which may most probably exercise that faculty.[5]

On the basis of these passages the mysterious philosophy called "Ideology" is revealed to be, from one perspective, philosophical inquiry into the operations of the mind (psychology) and into the knowledge and kinds of proof obtainable thereby (logic and epistemology). Jefferson's way of putting the case is interesting, namely, in terms of a distinction between *morale* and *physique*, but somewhat oversimplified. Jefferson tended to overstate the matter in his zeal for simple, unambiguous instruction about ideology, which, as a movement, still had to fight the epithets Napoleon had flung at its leaders: "these miserable metaphysicians," "inexhaustible nonsensemongers." [6] In fact, it had been maintained that the word *"idéologue"* should serve as a synonym for all that is vain and trivial in thought.[7] The distinction between the understanding and the senses almost suggests that the senses are to be left out of ideological analysis, yet they are implicated in the origin and the character of knowledge.[8]

Jefferson's loyalty to ideology was in no way a substitute for analysis

[4] To John Adams, Monticello, January 11, 1817, M.E., XV, 97.
[5] *Ibid.*, March 14, 1820, M.E., XV, 240.
[6] George Boas, *French Philosophies of the Romantic Period*, p. 14.
[7] *Ibid.*
[8] See letter to John Adams, Monticello, August 15, 1820, M.E., XV, 273–74 for statement of Jefferson's sensationalism.

founded upon actual reading of its painstaking and systematic text. Jefferson's role in the history of ideology was varied. He was prose-lytizer, translator, editor, sponsor for publication, and general repre-sentative in behalf of Tracy's author's rights. Some of the evidence is listed here: as early as 1803 a letter to Cabanis, warmly in favor of *Rapports du physique et du moral de l'homme;* [9] in 1812 a letter of unreserved recommendation of Tracy as metaphysician and of Cabanis as anatomist (referring to the *Rapports* as "the most profound of all human compositions"),[10] sent to Dr. Thomas Cooper to incorporate in a reading list for students in a book Cooper was preparing for publica-tion; in 1813 a letter to Colonel Duane, in which Jefferson mentions that upon his recommendation Tracy's *Review of Montesquieu* had been adopted by Bishop Madison as a fundamental textbook at William and Mary College [11] and that he is in receipt of a "MS" from the same author on *Political Economy* which is "not of greater, but of equal merit." Eager to secure Duane as printer for the manuscript, Jefferson comments further about Tracy:

He has written a work entitled Ideology which has given him a high reputa-tion in France. He considers that as having laid a solid foundation for the present volume on Political Economy, and will follow it by one on Moral Duties. The present volume is a work of great ability. It may be considered as a review of the principles of the Economists, of Smith and of Say, or rather an elementary book on the same subject. As Smith had corrected some principles of the Economists, and Say some of Smith's, so Tracy has done as to the whole. He has, in my opinion, corrected fundamental errors in all of them, and by simplifying principles, has brought the subject within a narrow compass.[12]

In a letter to Destutt de Tracy himself, Jefferson inquires whether the author's health has improved sufficiently to allow "you to pursue your

[9] To Monsieur Cabanis, Washington, July 12, 1803, M.E., X, 404.
[10] To Thomas Cooper, Monticello, July 10, 1812, M.E., XIII, 177.
[11] To Col. Wm. Duane, Monticello, January 22, 1813, M.E., XIII, 213. See also letter to Destutt de Tracy, November 28, 1813, where in reference to the *Review* Jefferson says: "I sent a copy of it to the late President of William and Mary Col-lege of this State who adopted it at once as the Elementary Book of that institu-tion. From these beginnings it will spread and become a political gospel for a na-tion open to reason, and in a situation to adopt and profit by its results, without a fear of their leading to wrong." M.E., XIV, 13.
[12] To Col. Wm. Duane, Monticello, January 22, 1813, M.E., XIII, 214.

plan through the two remaining branches of morals and legislation, which executed in the same lucid, logical and condensed style, will present such a whole as the age we live in will not before have received." [13] Despite the great difficulties encountered in arranging for the translation and publication of Tracy's *Commentary and Review of Montesquieu*, Jefferson adds that if Tracy wishes to have these new books appear in America first,[14] he hopes to be able to arrange for their appearance more promptly than he was able to do for the former book.

And certainly no effort should be spared on my part to ensure to the world such an acquisition. The MS. of the first work has been carefully recalled and deposited with me. That of the second, when done with, shall be equally taken care of.[15]

Other references to Tracy cite him as "the most conspicuous writer of the present day in the metaphysical line"; [16] "the ablest writer in France in the moral line"; "the ablest writer living on intellectual subjects, or the operations of the understanding." [17]

Jefferson's active work in behalf of translating and providing for publication of ideological works was extraordinarily energetic and patient. In America ideology was introduced solely through Jefferson's efforts in its behalf and was confined almost exclusively to the writings of Tracy, with some attention to Cabanis and J. B. Say.[18]

Since Tracy was the outstanding formal ideologist in France and indeed had even been responsible for substituting the name *Idéologie* for philosophy (understood as science of ideas),[19] Jefferson's concentration of attention upon him is in no way arbitrary. It will be convenient to give Jefferson's own account of Tracy's writings before stating his share in bringing some of them before the American public. In a letter to John Adams in 1816 he offered this information about the great ideologist:

[13] To Destutt de Tracy, November 28, 1813, M.E., XIV, 11.
[14] Tracy was afraid to publish his books in France while Napoleon was in power. See letter to John Adams, Monticello, October 14, 1816, M.E., XV, 75.
[15] To Destutt de Tracy, *op. cit.*, p. 11.   [16] To Duane, *op. cit.*, p. 214.
[17] To John Adams, Monticello, October 14, 1816, M.E., XV, 75.
[18] Jefferson repeatedly recommended Say's *Political Economy*. See letter to Duane, April 4, 1813, M.E., XIII, 231. Also, to John Norvell, Washington, June 11, 1807, M.E., XI, 222.
[19] "Idéologie," by François Picavet, in *La Grande Encyclopédie*, p. 538.

He writes me that he is become blind and so infirm that he is no longer able to compose anything. So that we are to consider his works as now closed. They are three volumes of *Ideology*, one on *Political Economy*, one of *Ethics*, and one containing his *Commentary on Montesquieu*, and a little tract on Education. Although his commentary explains his principles of government, he had intended to have substituted for it an elementary and regular treatise on the subject but he is prevented by his infirmities. His *Analyse de Dupuys* he does not avow.[20]

The "three volumes of Ideology" referred to above are not to be confused with the three works of applied ideology enumerated following them.[21] But the catalogue of Jefferson's second library corrects the preceding account of Tracy's works in two respects: the *Idéologie* is listed as five volumes; and there appears a new item, *Principes de logique*, MS, Paris, 1817.

Of these books, Jefferson recommended and circulated copies of the *Analyse de Dupuys*; [22] persistently and publicly encouraged interest in the *Idéologie*, suggesting once that Ideology be included in a "recomposed" division of the sciences, while zoology was to be divided into two parts, physical and moral.

The latter including ideology, ethics, and mental science generally, in my catalogue, considering ethics, as well as religion, as supplements to law in the government of man, I had placed them in that sequence . . .[23]

In 1814, in one of his first detailed letters on educational plans for the state, Jefferson mapped the curriculum for general schools in three broad groups: (1) languages, (2) mathematics, and (3) philosophy. His further specifications about "philosophy" are eloquent testimony to the high regard in which he held ideology. Here is Jefferson's statement on philosophy. "In the Philosophical department, I should distinguish: (1) Ideology; (2) Ethics; (3) the Law of Nature and Nations; (4) Government; (5) Political Economy." [24]

---

[20] To John Adams, Poplar Forest, November 25, 1816, M.E., XV, 81.

[21] Tracy in a letter to Jefferson from Paris, October 21, 1811, refers to his three volumes of *Ideology* already published as: (1) Ideology proper, (2) Grammar, (3) Logic. Gilbert Chinard, *Jefferson et les Idéologies*, p. 88.

[22] The reference is to Tracy's *Analyse raisonnée de origine de tous les cultes; ou, Religion universelle.*

[23] To Judge Augustus B. Woodword, Monticello, March 24, 1824, M.E., XVI, 19.

[24] To Peter Carr, Monticello, September 7, 1814, M.E., XIX, 211–21. This entire letter is interesting for a study of Jefferson's educational views. One can estimate

It was in connection with the works of applied ideology that Jefferson revealed the depth of his attachment to Tracy's ideological analyses. Single-handed, he arranged the entire presentation and reception of *The Commentary and Review of Montesquieu* and the *Political Economy*. He translated the *Commentary* in full and was so conspicuously engaged in recommending it to the public with letters which were subsequently utilized by the publisher for their commercial value that his old friend Dupont de Nemours wrote to congratulate him as the anonymous author and informed Jefferson that the book (which Jefferson had labored heroically to translate from the French) was already translated into French. Dupont hinted slyly: "Vous y avez mis une petite dédicace comme s'il était offert par un Français aux Etats-Unis. Vous aurez cru que ce qui paraîtrait pendant quelque tems venir d'une autre Nation, frapperait davantage . . ." [25] Jefferson wrote to disclaim authorship, but for at least another year [26] Dupont remained under the impression that Jefferson had written the book on Montesquieu.[27]

In fact, Jefferson not only translated a part of the *Commentary* and scrupulously corrected the section of the translation which Duane had arranged for, but he also urged Duane on with the publication when it seemed to lag and practically managed the entire publicity campaign to sell the book, once it was printed. And it is interesting to notice, as Chinard does, that Jefferson's enthusiasm for the *Commentary* did not abate at all after its publication, although he had seemed to lose all interest in Volney's *Ruines* after the translation was finished.[28]

Tracy was himself well aware of the important role which Jefferson played in making his works available and favorably regarded. He

---

the importance assigned to philosophy, incidentally, by consulting p. 220, where Jefferson suggests at least four basic professorships for the projected State University: viz., "(1) Languages and History . . . Belles-Lettres, Rhetoric and Oratory. (2) Mathematics pure, Physico-Math., Physics, Anatomy, Medicine, Theory. (3) Chemistry, Zoology, Botany, Mineralogy. . . . (4) Philosophy."

[25] Dupont de Nemours to Thomas Jefferson, January 25, 1812; in Chinard, *The Correspondence of Jefferson and Du Pont de Nemours*, p. 179.

[26] His letter to Thomas Jefferson on April 14, 1812, refers again to "votre livre"; *ibid.*, p. 194.

[27] The reason appears to be, as Chinard suggests, that Ticknor who was to deliver Jefferson's letter to Dupont arrived in France after the former had departed for America. *Jefferson et les idéologues*, p. 124.

[28] See *ibid.*, p. 95.

acknowledged this plainly in a letter written in 1811; the reference must, therefore, have been to Jefferson's work in behalf of the *Commentary*.

Je sens tout ce que je dois à votre indulgence et à votre aimable désir d'encourager quelqu'un à qui vous voyez de bonnes intentions. Mais enfin même en retranchant beaucoup des éloges que vous voulez bien me donner, il me reste la douce certitude que vous approuvez mes vues, et que par conséquent elles sont saines. Vous les avez préservées de l'oubli auquel elles sembloient condamnées. Vous les avez publiées et répandues dans un vaste pays qui est l'espérance et l'exemple de l'Univers. Je suis plus que content.[29]

The *Political Economy*, the manuscript of which followed the *Commentary* to the hands of its sympathetic American patron, was regarded as another fundamental text in political thought. Jefferson wrote to Duane in 1813, immediately after receiving the manuscript, that he had something, not of "greater, but of equal merit" with the *Commentary*.

I have received from France a Ms. work on Political Economy, written by Destutt Tracy, the most conspicuous writer of the present day in the metaphysical line. He has written a work entitled *Ideology*, which has given him a high reputation in France. He considers that as having laid a solid foundation for the present volume on Political Economy, and will follow it by one on Moral Duties. The present volume is a work of great ability. It may be considered as a review of the principles of the Economists, of Smith and of Say, or rather an elementary book on the same subject. As Smith had corrected some principles of the Economists, and Say some of Smith's, so Tracy has done as to the whole. He has, in my opinion, corrected fundamental errors in all of them, and by simplifying principles, has brought the subject within a narrow compass. I think the volume would be of about the size of the Review of Montesquieu . . .[30]

In a communication to the author,[31] which differed only in being even more enthusiastic, Jefferson tells of his arrangements for the translation and printing of the manuscript. Since Tracy had sent on his manuscript to Jefferson in November of 1811,[32] he had been forced to

---

[29] Destutt de Tracy to Thomas Jefferson, Paris, October 21, 1811; *ibid.*, p. 87.
[30] To Col. Wm. Duane, Monticello, January 22, 1813, M.E., XIII, 214.
[31] To Destutt de Tracy, November 28, 1813, M.E., XIV, 11.
[32] Destutt de Tracy to Jefferson, Paris, August 29, 1813. Chinard, *Jefferson et les idéologues*, p. 115.

inquire about the delay in publication. Jefferson replied at once, explaining the causes of the delay and showing his undiminished esteem for Tracy's work by offering better publication arrangements for his next two books, should Tracy still prefer to have them appear first in America.[33]

By 1818 Jefferson wrote to Milligan, saying that he was returning the translation of the *Political Economy,* which although now faithful to the sense of the author, still did no justice to his style, "in which no word is unnecessary, no word can be changed for the better, and severity of logic results in that brevity to which we wish all science reduced." And he again voiced his confidence in its value for America:

The merit of this work will, I hope, place it in the hands of every reader in our country. By diffusing sound principles of Political Economy, it will protect the public industry from the parasite institutions now consuming it, and lead us to that just and regular distribution of the public burdens from which we have sometimes strayed. It goes forth, therefore, with my hearty prayers that while the Review of Montesquieu, by the same author, is made with us the elementary book of instruction in the principles of civil government, so the present work may be in the particular branch of Political Economy.[34]

About a month later Jefferson hastened to write good news to Lafayette, who in addition to being Jefferson's close friend was Tracy's son-in-law.

I am rendered very happy by being able at length to send M. Tracy a copy

[33] At this time Jefferson believed that the *Political Economy* would appear almost any day (November, 1813). In fact, Duane kept him waiting until August, 1814, when he wrote to say that he was financially unable to undertake the printing of Tracy's book! Jefferson then transferred to Milligan. Arrangements for printing dragged on until 1816, when Jefferson remarked that he had worked on the translation "four or five hours a day for three months comparing word by word with the original, although I have made it a strictly faithful translation, yet it is without style, *le premier jet* was such as to render that impossible." To Albert Gallatin, Monticello, April 11, 1816, M.E., XIX, 233. But in Jefferson's opinion, the book was "all ready to be printed." However, the book still did not see the light of day, and in October, 1816, Jefferson, enthusiastic about the *Political Economy* as ever, wrote to John Adams that Tracy had published the French version in Paris, "which he thought unsafe while Bonaparte was in power." As yet no printed copy had reached America. Milligan finally brought out the first American edition in November, 1818. The book, for some reason, bears the imprint "1817."

[34] To Joseph Milligan, Monticello, October 25, 1818, M.E., XIX, 263.

of the translation of his book on political economy, the publication of which is at length accomplished. The delay has been scandalous and to me most vexatious. But I am fully repaid by the good the publication will render to our country.[35]

Miraculously Jefferson's interest in the *Political Economy* appeared not to have been worn thin by the battle for its appearance. Adams wrote to Jefferson in praise of the book, and Jefferson at once wished to use Adams's letter in behalf of the book's circulation.

I am delighted with your high approbation of Mr. Tracy's book. . . . If I had your permission to put your letter into the hands of the editor [Milligan], with or without any verbal alterations you might choose, it would ensure the general circulation, which my prospectus and prefatory letter will less effectually recommend. There is nothing in the book of mine, but these two articles, and the note on taxation in page 202.[36]

Had Tracy been apprized of the endless devotion Jefferson showed in the cause of his ideas, his reference to Jefferson as "mon ange tutélaire" [37] would have been even more appropriate. The next news conveyed to Tracy, again via Lafayette, was jubilant about the success of the *Political Economy*.

Present me with friendship and respect to M. Tracy. Tell him his *Political Economy* has got into rapid and general circulation here, that it is already quoted in Congress and out of Congress as our standard code; and that the naming him in that as the author of the *Commentary on Montesquieu* has excited a new demand for that work. . . . These two works will render more service to our country than all the writings of all the saints and holy fathers of the church have rendered.[38]

It was only in 1820, however, that Jefferson experienced the full vindication of his struggle in behalf of both the *Commentary* and the *Political Economy*. Then he was enabled to write Tracy that the *Commentary*, its first edition having been exhausted, was being reprinted with

[35] To the Marquis de Lafayette, Monticello, November 23, 1818, M.E., XIX, 270.
[36] To John Adams, Monticello, March 21, 1819, XV, 185–86.
[37] Destutt de Tracy to Jefferson, July 14, 1814; Chinard, *Jefferson et les idéologies*, p. 126.
[38] Thomas Jefferson to Lafayette, Monticello, March 8, 1819. Chinard, *The Letters of Lafayette and Jefferson*, p. 397.

a corrected translation; while "a second edition of your *Economie politique* will soon also be called for here." [39] "These two works will become the Statesman's Manual with us, and they certainly shall be the elementary books of the political department in our new University." [40] Therefore, when Tracy finally published an edition of the *Commentary* in Paris, he saw fit to do homage to Jefferson by including his name in the *avertissement* in the following manner: "Cet ouvrage existe depuis plus de douze ans. Je l'avais écrit pour M. Jefferson, l'homme des deux mondes, que je respecte le plus, et, s'il le jugeait à propos, pour les États-Unis de l'Amérique du Nord." [41]

Jefferson's extraordinary faith in Tracy's Ideology, was still not exhausted by the history of the *Political Economy*. He also made an attempt to publish the short *Principes logiques*,[42] the manuscript of which Tracy had also confided to Jefferson. Estimating that its brevity made it more suitable for an article than a book, Jefferson offered it to Robert Walsh, Jr., the editor of the *American Register*. Jefferson described the *Logic* to Walsh as follows:

It is an examination into the certainty of our knowledge, and the most complete demolition of the Skeptical doctrines which I have ever met with. You know his character and peculiar strength in Ideological enquiries. I place him and Dugald Stewart so much in a line, that I can decide no more than that they are the two greatest men in that line at present known to the world. It will require translation in terms of the most rigorous exactitude.[43]

Walsh replied favorably, and Jefferson sent on the manuscript, referring to it this time in a new way.

I now enclose you Tracy's tract on the certainty of the operations of the human understanding. He rests them on our sensations, of which we are very certain, and on this basis erects demonstration irresistibly cogent, I think, against scepticism, a disease of the mind so incomfortable, that it is charity to exhibit its cure, if there exists one.[44]

[39] Thomas Jefferson to Destutt de Tracy, Monticello, December 26, 1820. Chinard, *Jefferson et les idéologues*, p. 202.
[40] *Ibid.*, p. 203.   [41] *Ibid.*, p. 194.
[42] Full title, *Principes logiques; ou, Recueil de faits relatifs à l'intelligence humaine.*
[43] Thomas Jefferson to Robert Walsh, Jr., Monticello, January 9, 1818. *Jefferson et les idéologues*, p. 174.
[44] *Ibid.*, p. 175.

Unfortunately for Jefferson's intentions, the *Register* was shortly thereafter suspended, and the project was entirely given up.

But Jefferson had shown repeatedly his interest in seeing the whole of the Ideology finished and set down for the enlightenment of thinkers and society.[45] Jefferson hoped that Tracy might "still be enabled to compleat the Encyclopedie Ideologique."

In his last letter to Tracy he reveals how he planned to use the finished work.

I hope it for the benefit of a child of my old age, the University of Virginia, on the buildings of which we have been five years engaged and hope in a year more, the patronage of our state continuing, to get it into operation. Its misfortune will be that identity of language will confine the choice of its professors to the countries speaking our own. But it will still be your science which we shall get thro' that medium.[46]

Considering this barrage of inquiry about the finishing of the "Ideological Circle," it is certainly unprovoked to imply that Jefferson was not interested in the entire theoretical structure of ideologic thought.[47] The predominance of interest did fall to the *Commentary* and the *Political Economy*, but there is, as indicated, indisputable evidence that Jefferson took the whole of ideology seriously and placed himself in the intellectual tradition of Tracy as a conscious philosopher.

[45] Cf. letter to Tracy, Monticello, May 15, 1817, which urges Tracy to work on, despite his blindness. "The completion of your circle of the moral sciences would have formed an epoch in the history of the human mind, much of which indeed you have effected, but while something more can be done, we never think we have enough. The unfinished part two 'de la Morale' is of the first degree of interest; but are we in the condition of those who grieve without hope?" *Jefferson et les idéologues*, p. 170.

[46] To Tracy, November 5, 1823; *ibid.*, pp. 215–16. He also explains here that no second edition of *Commentary* has yet appeared, because the owner of the copyright (Duane) had been in South America.

[47] Chinard seems at times to come close to this attitude; when, e.g., he says (in connection with the published suggestion on how to read the *Political Economy*): "Il n'était pas de ceux qui prenaient plaisir à ces hautes spéculations philosophiques et aux discussions abstraites . . . Jefferson, tout en étant salué par ses amis de France comme un 'philosophe,' ne se piquait pas d'enthousiasme pour les idées abstraites, surtout pour celles qui n'étaient pas susceptibles d'application immédiate." *Ibid.*, p. 144.

Chapter VIII

THE DOCTRINE OF IDEOLOGY

WHILE Jefferson's peculiar excitement about the philosophy called "ideology" has been current knowledge for some time,[1] not much attention has been given to the question of what this strange philosophy purported to be nor how those beliefs, once analyzed, managed to fit in with Jefferson's other known philosophic pronouncements.

What was ideology? It was a movement in philosophy, founded and so named by Tracy in France just at the close of the eighteenth century.[2] There is a broad usage of the term "ideologist," which refers to the continuous tradition of philosophers in France from the mid-eighteenth century, until well on in the nineteenth. This is the tradition which begins with Condillac and might be said to end with the generation *metaphysique et chrétienne*,[3] of thinkers like Biran and Ampère. It therefore includes within its generous development the thought of the *Encyclopédistes*, the *Philosophes*, and the *économistes*.[4] This usage is too broad; and for the purpose of this study it is proposed to restrict the meaning of "ideology" to that phase of eighteenth-

[1] Chinard's contribution of the volume of correspondence between Jefferson and Tracy and other philosophers is the single important source which makes available Jefferson's activities in behalf of ideology, as well as his judgments upon it. But Chinard discusses the political, personal, and business relationships in Jefferson's support of ideology more than he analyzes or evaluates ideology as a system of ideas, either in itself or through its hold upon Jefferson.

[2] The name "idéologie" was created by Tracy in 1796 at L'Institut National, and the followers of this doctrine were called "idéologistes." Cf. article "Idéologie" in *La Grande Encyclopédie*.

[3] *Ibid.*

[4] "En somme, l'idéologie est un moment dans le développement de cette philosophie scientifique qui, parfois unie au christianisme et à la métaphysique ancienne, parfois les combattant ou marchant seule, s'efforce de tirer, de la connaissance positive et systématisée de l'homme et de l'univers, les règles pratiques propres à diriger l'individu, à élever l'enfant, à organiser la société." *Ibid.*

century scientific philosophy or epistemology, which gave it fullest and most systematic expression—the work, in fact, of Cabanis and Tracy above all others. It was really in the volumes of Tracy's *Idéologie* that one found the encyclopaedic aim of the philosophers of the *Institut* most forthrightly presented. And it might well have been this encyclopaedic broadness of interest, disciplined by an almost affected precision and rigor of style, which Jefferson found so congenial to his own concept of philosophy.

We may place ideology in its traditional setting by calling the roll of Bacon, Condillac, and Locke. Bacon's views on scientific method, as well as his general division of the field of human knowledge, had already been explicitly adopted by the French *Encyclopédie*. This early form of "scientism" or "positivism" was joined with the epistemological sensationalism and psychology of Locke and Condillac. Tracy directly refers to himself as the continuator of his predecessors' work, and especially does he couple his philosophy with Condillac's. For no sooner has Tracy introduced the basic conception of ideology as a part of zoology [5] than he refers to Locke.

Locke est, je crois le premier des hommes qui ait tenté d'observer et de décrire l'intelligence humaine, comme l'on observe et l'on décrit une propriété d'un minéral ou d'un végétal, ou une circonstance remarquable de la vie d'un animal: aussi a-t-il fait de cette étude une partie de la physique. Ce n'est pas qu'avant lui on n'eût fait beaucoup d'hypothèses sur ce sujet, qu'on n'eût même dogmatisé avec une grande hardiesse sur la nature de notre âme; mais c'était toujours en vue non de découvrir la source de nos connaissances, leur certitude et leurs limites, mais de déterminer le principe et la fin de toutes choses, de deviner l'origine et la destination du monde.[6]

But Tracy reserves for Condillac the honor of really having founded the science of ideology.

Avant Condillac nous n'avions guère sur les opérations de l'esprit humain que des observations éparses plus ou moins fautives. Le premier il les a réunies, et en a fait un corps de doctrine; ainsi, ce n'est que depuis lui que l'idéologie est vraiment une science. Il l'aurait encore bien plus avancée si, au

[5] "On n'a qu'une connaissance incomplete d'un animal, si l'on ne connait pas ses facultés intellectuelles. L'idéologie est une partie de la zoologie, et c'est surtout dans l'Homme que cette partie est importante . . ." Destutt de Tracy, *Elémens d'idéologie*, I, xix. This reference will be given subsequently as *Elémens*.
[6] *Ibid.*, p. xxi.

lieu de disséminer ses principes dans plusieurs ouvrages, il les avait rassemblés dans un traité unique qui contînt, son systême tout entier; Mais, quoiqu'une mort prématurée l'ait empêché de rendre cet important service à la raison humaine, il n'en est pas moins le guide le plus généralement suivi par tous les bons esprits de nos jours, et il a la gloire d'avoir puissamment contribué à les former.[7]

It is clear from the above that Tracy conceived his own peculiar contribution to the advancement of the science of ideology to be that he had systematized and unified the scientific analysis of ideas and biologized the whole by placing it in the context of zoology.

Tracy's ready admission that ideology stemmed directly from Condillac should not be read as indicating that he had uncritically accepted everything in Condillac's doctrine; for Tracy criticized Condillac's position in several important points [8] and extended the implications far beyond what Condillac's works seem to have envisaged.

Ideology was conceived as a branch of the science of zoology for reasons far more weighty than that the classification was novel. The key to ranking ideology as a subclass of zoology is to be found in a very conscious and determined antimetaphysical polemic, which Tracy brought into prominence in his writing. The Preface to the Elémens d'idéologie is frank in its revolt against philosophy as metaphysics. Tracy wrote for his age, as others have for ours, the declaration of independence for philosophy—asserting that it is a science, freed from what was conceived as the barren tyranny of metaphysics. In continuing his statement, cited above, which disclaimed every intention of determining the "principle" and "end" of all things or of divining the origin and destination of the universe, Tracy commented: "C'est là l'objet de la métaphysique. Nous la rangerons au nombre des arts d'imagination, destinés à nous satisfaire, et non à nous instruire." [9] This is a remarkable statement of the thesis that has played so large a part in modern positivistic analysis.[10] Tracy was specifically associating

[7] Destutt de Tracy, Projet d'éléments d'idéologie: l'usage des écoles centrales de la République Française. Since this is 1801 under the Republic, the earlier title "Comte" has been abandoned for that of "Le Citoyen Destutt Tracy."
[8] See discussion following pp. 70–81 for specific departures from Condillac.
[9] Elémens . . . , I, xxi.
[10] For the explicit modern statement of this idea cf. A. J. Ayer, Language, Truth and Logic, chap. i.

metaphysical speculations with "emotive," rather than "cognitive," intent and classifying them with imaginative arts. The scientific philosopher is thus freed to investigate ideas without losing time in refuting or discussing metaphysical issues.

The point is driven home before the close of the Preface, with the statement that the ideological sciences (including the ideology of ethics and politics) are genuinely sciences—in Tracy's words—". . . qui, après tout, sont des sciences comme les autres, à la différence près que ceux qui ne les ont pas étudiées sont persuadés de si bonne foi de les savoir, qu'ils se croient en état d'en décider." [11] And the amusing explanation is tacked on, in a footnote, that "effectivement tous les hommes les savent plus ou moins, comme ils savent assez de mécanique pour s'appuyer sur une canne, et assez de physique pour souffler le feu." [12]

Almost every statement of the basic aim of ideology makes reference to the mission of freeing analysis from metaphysical tendencies; so much so that one might *define* ideology as a philosophy opposed to the mysteries of scholastic, rationalistic and idealistic metaphysics. The following statement of Tracy's bears strongly on such an impression.

L'étude de l'idéologie consiste tout entière en observations, et n'a rien de plus mystérieux ni de plus nébuleux que les autres parties de l'histoire naturelle. C'est donc bien différent de ce qu'on appelle la métaphysique; *ce qu'il fallait démonstrer:* ajoutez . . . que le seul moyen pour ne pas fair de la métaphysique nébuleuse . . . c'est de savoir l'idéologie.[13]

Ideology, recommended by Tracy as the "only safeguard" against hazy metaphysics,[14] approaches the mind as natural history, for which observation is a better instrument than a priori rationalizations. Ideology set itself a program, to consider philosophy as a natural science, devoted to the study of one normal human function, thinking, and its products, ideas. Tracy's radical approach, he rightly imagined, was more original with him than was the conception of a philosophy confined to analysis of "experience" (which after all, went back, not only

---

[11] *Elémens,* I, xxxiii.   [12] *Ibid.*   [13] *Projet d'éléments,* p. 355.

[14] Picavet, in *Les Idéologues,* offers further corroboration of the antimetaphysical character of ideology. He says: "A la fin de l'an IV et du commencement de l'an V, D. de Tracy lisait deux autres Mémoires sur l'analyse de la pensée ou plutôt sur la faculté de penser ou faculté de percevoir. Il demandait que la science résultant de cette analyse fût nommée *idéologie* ou science des idées, pour la distinguer de l'ancienne métaphysique." p. 306.

to Locke and Condillac, to the Encyclopaedists and Voltaire, but also beyond them to the seventeenth-century sceptics, and to Bacon).

For a better understanding of Tracy's more positive view of philosophy as ideology it is necessary to consult his major work, *Elémens d'idéologie*. The Preface to the *Elémens* offers an explicit statement of philosophic objective. Tracy there describes his aim quite simply. "J'ai essayé de faire une description exacte et circonstanciée de nos facultés intellectuelles, de leurs principaux phénomènes, et de leurs circonstances les plus remarquables, en un mot, des véritables élémens d'idéologie." [15] The manner of presentation must be suited to an elementary book of a science, the arguments being presented in clear, strict, logical, and systematic fashion.[16] The statement of the systematic ideal is undeniably reminiscent of the geometric method—"faire que toutes s'enchaînent et s'appuient réciproquement—" and the educational objective is stressed afresh in the express desire that the *Elémens* be understandable even to "les personnes les moins instruites."

This is only one half of Tracy's object: for his goal, and that of all genuine ideologists, is more than reformulation of knowledge, it is the discovery of new truths, "en un mot, il ne s'agit pas seulement d'exposer la vérité, mais de la découvrir. C'est ce que j'ai tâché de faire, sans me flatter d'y avoir toujours réussi." [17] In other words, the function of ideology was twofold, as is that of every science: there is the intellecual work of system building, of logical refinement and economy, and the experimental research which furnishes the hypotheses that are scientifically reliable for their time. Tracy's twofold aim is reflected in his metaphor for the new work: he apologizes for incompleteness of ideology by saying it is only a frame which can be stretched or shrunk as new vision or information may demand.[18] Tracy offered his work as merely the point of departure for further investigators. Thus there is no claim to finality or definitive settling of all philosophical problems, of the kind which is usually objected to as characteristic of philosophic systematizers. Accordingly, at least some of the criticism which has been leveled at Tracy's *Idéologie* is inappropriate.[19]

[15] *Elémens*, I, xxii. [16] *Ibid.*, I, xxiii. [17] *Ibid.*, I, xxiv. [18] *Ibid.*, p. xxvii.
[19] Picavet, for example, criticizes the ideologists in this way: "Ils ont insisté sur la nécessité de donner l'idéologie pour base a toutes les sciences, mais ils ont trop aisément cru qu'il suffisait, pour en faire une science indépendante, d'en tracer le plan et d'en indiquer la méthode." *Op. cit.*, p. 579.

But Tracy cannot fail to show, even in this first introduction to his work, that the logical ideal of system and the scientific ideal of research and speculation leading to new truth are supplemented by a social interest. Today *we* might call this the philosophic ideal of comprehensive reflection on the relations and interconnections among the various fields of knowledge, in terms of newly assigned roles for evidence and analysis. Psychologically Tracy was impressed with the primary importance of educational and moral conditioning as a propaedeutic to the advanced pursuit of ideology. This would have been sufficiently demonstrated in the large sections of the *Elémens* given over to education, morals, and the theory of society. But Tracy felt impelled to justify his aim in the Preface as well, to forestall possible charges of lack of rigor on the part of those whose conception of system and logic might be narrower than his own. He therefore confessed his desire to fight the superstitions and errors popularly accepted by the men of his age, even if this implied a relaxing of severe methodical progression in his argument. He remarks in the Preface that these psychological considerations must be recognized as departures from Condillac's advice about good logical writing but that, in this instance at least, Tracy is willing to depart from the attitude of the master. For, . . . il est pourtant vrai qu'on ne peut pas toujours construire, sans auparavant nettoyer le terrain; peut-être même ai-je trop négligé cette précaution . . .[20]

A glance at the divisions of ideology, as offered by Tracy, will now be useful, particularly in view of its avowed encyclopaedic aim.[21] Tracy used the word "ideology" in two different senses—a fact not generally appreciated. Ideology was (1) a generic term, referring to the whole scope of the analysis of ideas; and (2) a specific term, indicating the first part of the science of ideas, namely, that devoted to consideration of ideas as subject exclusively. In the second sense the other parts making up ideology are general grammar and logic; general grammar be-

---

[20] *Elémens*, I, xxv.

[21] This encyclopaedic aim of ideology was given concrete expression in the famous characterization of the *Institut* as the "Encyclopédie vivante" (a phrase of Daunou's), taken over by Lemontey, and apparently considered so apt that it stuck. Picavet, *op. cit.*, pp. 69–70.

ing the study of the expression of ideas (the "means") and logic of their deduction (the "end" or objective).[22] Apparently Tracy regarded epistemology, theory of signs,[23] and logic as the major domain of philosophy; [24] but to these must be added the subsidiary fields of human conduct (*de nos actions; ou, Traité de la volonte*), and Ethics. And although Tracy did not live to complete his plan, his published outline shows that he added to the foregoing subjects law, physics (or what amounts to a philosophy of physics, "des corps et de leurs propriétés"), geometry ("des propriétés de l'étendue"), and calculus (des propriétés de la quantité")—each subject listed for treatment in a separate volume. Although the moral and social sciences did not rank with respect to philosophical foundations with ideology proper, grammar, and logic, they were of great importance to Tracy,[25] and as motivation perhaps more important than any others. The inclusion of physics, geometry, and calculus in Tracy's table function purely as the intellectual completion of a system. Tracy never wrote or spoke about these subjects in any but the most casual fashion.

What are those elements of ideologic doctrine which lie at the heart of its philosophy? Following Tracy's division, we shall concentrate upon ideology "proprement dite" [26] (in its specific sense) and only mention the most important results which follow for the other aspects. In brief, the essential points appear to be: the interpretation given to the empirical method of analysis; the realistic modification of epistemological sensationalism; the significance of activity and will as the bridge between knowledge and society. There are, of course, other points of interest to philosophers, but these are sufficient to acquaint us with the solid outlines of ideologic thought and at the same time of special value in explaining Jefferson's preoccupation with ideology.

The whole direction of ideology derives from a resolution to adhere

[22] Tracy, *Elémens*, I, 4.
[23] Tracy said his conception of grammar was not at all that of "un art de parler; c'est un traité de la science des signes, continuation de celle des idées, introduction a celle du raisonnement." *Elémens*, II, 276.
[24] These constitute Section I of the *Elémens*. See the table, p. vii, for outline of entire projected study of ten parts, of which only the first five were written.
[25] Tracy's critical works, the *Review of Montesquieu*, *The Political Economy*, and the *Analyse de Dupuis*, can only be interpreted as evidence of this interest.
[26] This phrase qualifies the title of the first volume of *Elémens*.

to a definite philosophical method, by means of which unfounded speculations and dogmas can be weeded out from the field of authoritative
knowledge. The uncompromising rejection of metaphysics discussed
above is only understandable because of this, while the inclusion of
ideology as a subdivision of the science of zoology is explicable as a
further consequence of the empirical method adopted. The social motivation for discrediting religious orthodoxy (in line with the Encyclopaedic tradition) reënforces the argument for empirical method,
as does Tracy's desire to offset the reactionary writers and the Rous-
seauists who were engaged in robbing empiricism of its prestige in the
first few years of the nineteenth century.[27] From this point of view
Tracy's ideology is almost another defense of the traditions of French
encyclopaedism. Impressed with the vitality and progress of the experimental sciences in the seventeenth and eighteenth centuries and believing that the methods of Bacon and Newton and Locke were cen-
trally connected with the flowering of scientific knowledge, Tracy
hoped to convert philosophy into a science of methods. And philosophy,
conceived as the science of methods, was theoretically applicable to
every knowledgeable subject-matter, whether primarily intellectual or
social and practical.

That the conception of method was more important than the partial
reliance upon sensational philosophy is proven by Tracy's statement
that Condillac had no metaphysics or "system," but was significant
because of the method, the instrument for analysis, which he offered to
philosophy. In an interesting lecture delivered at the *Institut National*
Tracy compared the German adherence to the philosophy of Kant and
the reputed French adherence to the philosophy of Condillac. He
discovered this difference:

Quand les Allemands disent que nous sommes disciples de Condillac, comme
ils sont kantistes ou leibnitziens, ils oublient que Condillac n'a ni dogmatisé,
ni créé un système, ni résolu aucune des questions de psychologie, de cosmol-
ogie et de théologie dont les Allemands composent la métaphysique; qu'il
n'y a peut-être pas un seul de ceux qui, comme lui, se bornent à examiner
nos idées et leurs signes, à en chercher les propriétés, à en tirer quelques conséquences, qui adopte ses principes de grammaire, qui soit pleinement satisfait

[27] See Van Duzer, *The Contribution of the Ideologues to French Revolutionary
Thought*, p. 42.

de son analyse des facultés intellectuelles ou de ses théories sur le raisonnement. *On ne tient pas compte de ses décisions, mais de sa méthode.*[28]

Then Tracy discloses the features of this method.

Cette méthode conduit, d'un pas lent mais sûr, dans toutes les parties des
connaissances humaines, ceux qui observent scrupuleusement les faits; qui
n'en tirent qu'avec pleine assurances des conséquences, qui ne donnent jamais
à des simples suppositions la consistance des faits, qui ne lient entre elles que
les vérités qui s'enchaînent tout naturellement et sans lacune, qui avouent leur
ignorance et la préfèrent à toute assertion qui n'est que vraisemblable.[29]

On the basis of this simple description of the "slow but sure" method
of observation and inference leading to *evidenced* conclusions, one begins to appreciate why reactionaries in knowledge and spokesmen for
Church and State regarded the ideologists as their dangerous enemies.
Without even consulting the concrete applications of ideology in the
spheres of morality, economics, education, defenders of vested interests
at once feared this substitution of a method of analysis for a mysterious
but trusted "reason," [30] capable of revealing self-evident or transcendental knowledge, without benefit of every individual's potential review of "authoritative truths." In short, it was far from accidental that
Napoleon dissolved the second class of the *Institut* and banned the free
expression of the doctrine of ideology in the France of the Empire.[31]

Therefore ideology must be understood as a method, fashioned
chiefly for investigating the instruments and results of human knowledge. Going further, however, we see that ideological method, in so
far as it was more than the decomposition of general ideas into elementary ideas correlated with the surest "facts," emerges as a method of
treating ideas by reducing them to original feelings, activity, or sensation. Where this method succeeds there will be knowledge, and where
it fails, a careful methodologist refrains from speculative judgment.

[28] Quoted by Picavet, *Les Idéologues*, p. 348, from Tracy's lecture, "De la metaphysique de Kant."
[29] *Ibid.*
[30] For substantiation of this point see Boas, *French Philosophies of the Romantic
Period*, p. 31.
[31] See *ibid.*, p. 21, for an account of the closing of the ideologic *Ecoles Centrales*,
the dissolving of the "Second Class" in 1803, and the prohibition of discussion of
moral and political science save in relation to history, "especially very ancient history" within the *Institut*.

The broad structure of this argument is that of Condillac's sensationalist version of Lockean epistemology. Tracy agreed with Condillac on these basic points: (1) that all ideas are derived from sensations; (2) that any pure sensation is only a modification of our own being, containing neither a perception of relationship nor any interpretive judgment; and (3) that only the sensation of resistance can inform us about references to things outside ourselves.[32] This last item, emphasizing the notion of resistance, is made of primary importance in Tracy's epistemology.

In effect, resistance becomes the real efficient cause of knowledge, since without the sensation of resistance nothing resembling a judgment, whether of comparison in the present or of memory, can ever be made. Tracy distinguished in the sensation of resistance two aspects—movement and solidity. For such a conception of resistance, Condillac's hypothetical statue, with its postulated growth of knowledge from one sense to several, is totally useless. Nothing can be inferred about relationships between sensations on the part of a statue, which is deprived both of movement and of experience of bodies.[33] Thus it is quite incorrect to cover ideology with the tag of "sensationalism."

The primary philosophical importance of the sensation of resistance is really the key to Tracy's understanding of sensationalism. The tradition that Descartes established existence upon the inescapable act of thought it abandoned for the very different belief that feeling (actively experiencing sensations) acquaints us directly with our own existence. Here is Tracy's explicit substitute for Descartes's formula:

Il (Descartes) avait dit: *Je pense, donc j'existe;* il aurait du dire plus exactement; *Je sens, donc j'existe:* il aurait pu dire simplement: J'ai froid, j'ai chaud, j'ai faim, j'ai soif . . . donc j'existe; et cela eût été encore plus correct; et ensuite il aurait fallu qu'il montrât sans interruptions ni lacunes, comment de ce premier acte intellectuel se forment successivement toutes nos idées quelconques.[34]

Knowledge of our own existence is founded upon our specific biological feelings, relating us as moving and demanding organisms to a partially

---

[32] These three points are a free translation of Picavet, *Les Idéologues,* pp. 325–26.
[33] Picavet calls attention to this argument, *Les Idéologues,* p. 326.
[34] *Elémens,* III, 164.

obstructing environment: I am cold, I am hot, hungry, or thirsty—this is what informs me that I exist, that I am alive.

From the experience of resistance we progressively build not only knowledge of the self but also the existence of the external world. Tracy's section "De l'existence" points out that other philosophers, concerned to support their belief in the external world, had seized upon the sensation of touching; and Tracy agrees. However, the issue which must be clarified is: How can this be done? [35] In itself, the sense of touch produces one more internal sensation, no more trustworthy as an informant of external existence than the sensation of odor or sound. It is only when our movements have encountered the resistance of other bodies that we are entitled to assert the existence of things outside our own selves and the sensations or perceptions which reside within the self.

Movement of ourselves, however, further implies the will (or desire) [36] to move, and the three together are the source of any knowledge of other things, ideas, or people we may attain. Tracy gives this resumé:

. . . quand un être organisé de manière a vouloir et à agir sent en lui une volonté et une action et en même temps une résistance à cette action voulue et sentie, il est assuré de son éxistence et de l'éxistence de quelque chose qui n'est pas lui: *Action voulue et sentie* d'une part, et résistance de l'autre; voila le lien entre notre moi et les autres êtres, entre les êtres sentans et les êtres sentis.[37]

Thus, in the "reunion of our faculty of willing, with that of moving ourselves, and feeling [having a sensation of] it," [38] Tracy stems the tide of sceptical doubts about material existence and asserts that he has found an empirical answer to Berkeley and all other immaterialists who would allow spirit, but deny reality to matter.[39]

This form of reply gives us the biological setting which later develops into romantic voluntarism. Here Tracy is genuinely nearer Laromiguière and to Maine de Biran than he is to Condillac.[40] Even the more mystical voluntarism of Biran and Ampère keep Tracy's analysis of the

[35] *Elémens*, I, 83.
[36] Tracy defines the will as "la faculté de sentir des désirs"; *ibid.*, p. 284.
[37] *Elémens*, I, 291.   [38] *Ibid.*, p. 89.   [39] *Ibid.*, p. 94.
[40] See Lévy-Bruhl, *History of Modern Philosophy in France*, pp. 303–5.

active ego.[41] The simple matrix of sensation, which sufficed for Condillac, has been amplified and redirected to include the four fundamental faculties of the soul, sensibility, memory, judgment, and volition. These four types of operation are irreducible modes of sensation. And the mixture of willing and experiencing resistance against our planned movement, brings us the double "proof" of self-existence and the reality of otherness.

The foregoing account should have identified, if only *en route*, the different faculties which together form consciousness. They are: (1) sensibility, (2) memory, (3) judgment, and (4) will.[42] The last three faculties are the consequences of the first, and sensibility is therefore the essential faculty of thought. Nevertheless there is an interesting relation between sensibility and judgment, which also was implied in the discussion of resistance. The sensibility is the means of receiving impressions through our nerves, but the judgment is the instrument for sensing relations between perceptions.[43] The judgment alone can give us knowledge: "car si nous ne percevions aucuns rapports entre nos perceptions, si nous n'en portions aucuns jugemens, nous ne ferions éternellement qu'être affectés, et nous ne saurions jamais rien." [44] Sensations, as such, even though they are the ultimate and simple elements of all our ideas, never are knowledge. The judgment must intervene to "feel" identities, similarities, and every manner of connection between one idea and another,[45] before the simplest sensation can truly be said to be known. The second faculty, memory, is not developed with much care and is, roughly, nothing other than the sensation of being affected by memories of some experienced impression. The circularity and inconsistency of this description is sufficiently plain to need no comment.[46] The fourth faculty, the will, is given a more original interpretation, as we saw in the preceding analysis of the sensation of resistance. The will is thus, in Tracy's system, both more pervasive and more basic for the life of sense and knowledge than any early exposition of sensationalism had allowed.

[41] See Boas, *French Philosophies of the Romantic Period*, pp. 37, 39, 61.
[42] *Elémens*, I, 51.   [43] *Ibid.*, p. 34.   [44] *Ibid.*, p. 282.   [45] *Ibid.*, p. 34.
[46] Tracy's best statement about memory is: "Le souvenir est une sorte de sensation interne, mais . . . il est l'effet d'une certaine disposition demeurée dans le cerveau, et non celui d'une impression actuelle dans un autre organe." *Elémens*, I, 279.

There is some confusion in Tracy's treatment of the faculties of sensibility and judgment. In the first volume of the *Elémens* sensations, which are the logical ultimates of analysis and the original material of all ideas, are still not credited as knowledge; only when the judgment operates to perceive relations among sensations, does knowledge come about. In the third volume, however, the *Logic,* Tracy explains the kind of knowledge appropriate to each faculty. Certainty pertains to all sensations as such, and also to all isolated judgments, in so far as they are present perceptions (sensations) of relations between ideas. The faculty of judgment is regarded as nothing other than sensibility again, but it is applied simultaneously to two or more sensations. Error and the need to doubt, accordingly, can be attributed solely to the operation of memory; for our recollections of past sensations may be faulty.[47]

This means either that the memory is quite different from the sensibility (and judgment); or, if not, error cannot be applied to that faculty alone. If the tendency of the first volume to treat the sensibility and the judgment as two very different operations had been more consistently developed, Tracy would have been forsaking systematic sensationalism completely. He seems to remain true to sensationalism in his doctrine of certainty and error. The cost of this, for his system, is a severely limited role for judgment and a strangely overburdened one for memory, since memory must act as the receptacle of error, without enjoying any differential psychological or physiological status which might account for its unique failing.[48]

In a section supplementary to the *Logic* Tracy draws this specific corollary of his theory of error:

[47] To be more exact, Tracy claims that even our memories are certain in so far as they are present sensations; but when they cause us to impute a reference to previous experiences, they may be at fault. "Nos souvenirs sont de même certains en tant que perceptions actuelles: mais nous y joignons le jugement qu'ils sont la représentation fidèle d'une perception antérieure, et ce jugement peut être faux de plusieurs manières suivant l'espèce du souvenir." *Elémens,* III, 449.

[48] I believe that Tracy's difficulty in treating the four faculties of the mind is only one instance of a fairly persistent tendency in his system to move close to the kind of realism known as Scottish common-sense philosophy. It is difficult to resist the impression that ideology was a kind of half-way house between eighteenth-century sensationalism, and nineteenth-century realism and voluntarism; but a far more extended historical survey and comparison of the three positions would be needed to establish this opinion.

Que toutes nos erreurs viennent toujours du fond de nos idées, et non de la forme de nos raisonnemens; . . . Que toutes les règles que l'on peut prescrire à la forme de ces raisonnemens, ne peuvent servir de rien pour éviter l'erreur, ou du moins ne peuvent y servir qu'accidentellement.[49]

Thus epistemological inquiry into the formation of our ideas, our certainty and error, supplied Tracy his strongest ammunition against the formal scholastic logic which still reigned supreme in the schools and the colleges. The old logic, Tracy believed, tried to inculcate the art of reasoning, without ever having understood its own foundations as a science. Yet the principles discovered in the process of founding the science are actually of more value in teaching men how to avoid error than the supposed rules of syllogistic logic ever have been.

What, then, in a positive way, could be derived from the ideological account of knowledge? Tracy replies: "Nous n'avons donc pas d'autre moyen efficace pour éviter l'erreur, que de bien nous assurer de la compréhension de l'idée dont nous jugeons, c'est-à-dire des élémens qu'elle renferme." [50] And he adds the important "observation" that we can only be assured of the meaning of an idea after we have determined its extent. . . . car elle renferme beaucoup d'élémens dans certains degrés de cette extension qu'elle ne comporte pas dans d'autres; c'est-à-dire, qu'elle n'est pas . . . rigoureusement la même idée dans ces différens degrés d'extension.[51] This general means of avoiding error by establishing the complete extent of the component references of an idea includes several other devices, particularly the careful study of the object or objects from which the idea in question has come and safeguards against any emotional or habitual intrusions which might alter its independent form. These subsidiary aids to prevent human error are pointedly inconsistent with any ultimate phenomenalistic sensationalism. The impression grows that Tracy was only conventionally bound to sensationalism; that when he relied on it, for example, to establish certainty, he was thinking generally of intuitive principles (like Stewart) or logical identity.

One further step, and Tracy was ready to offer a theory of definition equally challenging to the old logical tradition. Tracy's logic made repeated reference to the priority of particular judgments over the

[49] *Elémens; supplément à la première section,* IV, 169.
[50] *Ibid.,* p. 170.   [51] *Ibid.*

more general, and this priority was both logical and historical.[52] The kinship of nominalist logic with sensationalist epistemology is again evident here; but the full import of this tendency is released in the section on definition. Tracy observes, on the basis of his reasoning on error and the devices for ensuring truth, that traditional logic defended a mistaken theory of definition. "Premièrement, ils croient qu'il y a des définitions de noms et des définitions de choses; et dans le vrai, il n'y a jamais que des définitions d'idées." [53]

No definitions are real definitions of things, because either we can explain the ideas we have attached to a word, or when we are referring to an existence (or any external thing) we can again only explain the idea we have of it, which is expressed in pronouncing its name. The failure to recognize that all definitions are only definitions of ideas resulted in the grave error of believing that definitions are principles and that principles are necessarily true. Tracy continues: "Secondement, ils établissent que les définitions sont des principes et qu'on ne peut pas disputer des définitions. Ces deux assertions sont contradictoires et pourtant fausses toutes deux." [54] And Tracy shows that definitions cannot be principles, for "the only true principles are facts," and definitions are not facts, but "simple explanations founded on facts," just as any other proposition is. Nor is one able to say that definitions cannot be disputed; for if a definition concerns a thing, one assumes that it is correctly applied to the thing (and this is arguable); and if a definition concerns a word, one implies that the employment of the word in this sense is both convenient and relevant.

The climax of the argument against traditional logic makes the author's positivistic convictions even plainer. Rejecting the Aristotelian brief for definition conceived *"per genus proximum et differentiam specificam,"* Tracy makes the interesting charge that the whole conception rests on an absurd belief that man's classifications are real reflections of nature. He refers contemptuously to "la doctrine fantastique en vertu de laquelle on croyait pouvoir partager toutes nos idées en différentes classes arbitraires appelées catégories." [55] Tracy sees that categories are nothing more than devices of order or indications of

[52] See the criticism of the Aristotelian position on the most general axioms and principles of knowledge, *Elémens*, III, 125–28.

[53] *Elémens*, IV, 171. [54] *Ibid.*, p. 172. [55] *Elémens*, IV, 173.

interests and purposes. He develops this criticism by pointing out that our ideas are susceptible to countless different classifications, depending upon the countless relations they bear to other ideas, and that therefore, strictly speaking, one can never find "le genre prochain ni la différence spécifique qui méritent exclusivement de caractériser une idée." [56]

Tracy's position on logic runs counter to Condillac's, particularly with respect to the latter's interpretation of judgments. For Condillac, reasoning is a series of judgments, and judgments are nothing other than the comparison of identical ideas; they can all be reduced to equations. While for Tracy, on the contrary, equations themselves were treated as a kind of judgment. And the terms or ideas which make up equations are not identical, they are only equivalent. [57] Apparently Tracy was anxious to resist the limitations of mechanical sensationalism in his logic just as much as those of formal scholastic ontology.

The volume on *Grammar* exhibits even more pointedly than does the *Logic* that Tracy's emphasis upon action and synthesis had actually changed the direction of his primary sensationalism. Tracy's thesis, in brief, is that propositions, not terms or ideas, are elementary in language, discussion, and argument. It therefore follows that if propositions are the "vrais élémens immédiats" [58] of discourse, not only all expression but also all knowledge must commence with a grouped judgmental action rather than with isolated sensations, or Locke's simple ideas. In Tracy's language:

Ce n'est point par le détail, mais par les masses, que commencent toutes nos expressions, ainsi que toutes nos connaissances. Si quelques langages possèdent des signes propres à exprimer des idées isolées, ce n'est donc que par l'effet de la décomposition qui s'est opérée dans ces langages; et ces signes, ou noms propres d'idées, ne sont, pour ainsi dire, que des débris, des fragmens, ou du moins des émanations de ceux qui d'abord exprimaient, bien ou mal, les propositions tout entières. [59]

Therefore, since it is the very nature of speech to be made up of propositions, these are the true "immediate" elements; the terms, which were incorrectly called the immediate elements in the past, are properly

[56] *Elémens*, IV, 173–74.
[57] For a discussion of this point see Lévy-Bruhl's *History of Modern Philosophy in France*, p. 305.
[58] *Elémens*, II, 24.   [59] *Ibid.*, p. 23.

inseparable parts of a proposition. Tracy then proceeds to devote his *Grammar* to a study of the proposition, especially to the proposition as it figures in "le langage articulé," because language at work is the richest and most realistic approach to the analysis of the proposition.[60]

The emphasis which Tracy places upon signs in his *Grammar* is the outcome of a theory that intelligence and reasoning are empirically characterized by the ability to fix clear and unequivocal signs for ideas. The highly complicated symbolic language of man is separated from "le langage d'action" of animals and of men, precisely because of this function of isolating ideas with fixed meanings.

Je pense qu c'est . . . cette capacité d'isoler une idée partielle, de détacher une circonstance d'une impression totale et composée, de séparer un sujet de son attribut, d'abstraire en un mot et d'analyser un certain point, qui manque aux animaux, qui fait que leur langage n'est jamais qu'une série d'interjections, qu'une suite de propositions implicites et qui constitue toute la différence entr'eux et nous; s'ils l'avaient, ils décomposeraient leurs perceptions; ils se créeraient des signes pour exprimer les idées résultantes de cette décomposition.[61]

It is not the formation of judgments; it is rather the ability to disentangle the terms of our judgments and to give them separate and distinct expression which Tracy calls characteristic of human reasoning. While animals and primitive men are just as beset by sensations and capable of indicating by gestures, cries, and even expressive sounds that their behavior has issued from implicit judgments, they do not ever employ "the proper noun of one isolated idea, separated from its attribute." Thus, while Tracy worked out the notion of a basic synthetic judgmental act and contended that this kind of intelligence was basic to thinking behavior, any extension of meaning, for example, thinking about thinking, or the more abstract mental operations, proceeds only by means of words with set meanings, separated from the living judgment. In short, Tracy thought of a continuum of language, ranging from the various languages of action to sophisticated and precise symbolic language.

In this way Tracy avoided both the atomism of sensationalistic empiricism and the artificial isolation of rationalism (whether scholastic

[60] *Ibid.*, p. 25.   [61] *Ibid.*, p. 24.

or Cartesian). This is additional proof that ideology is mid-way between eighteenth-century French "empiricism" and nineteenth-century "act philosophy," or voluntarism.[62] Thought and feeling are united in the *Grammar* in a way which neither sensationalism nor voluntarism could render plausible; and this achievement of Tracy's is more substantial than historians of philosophy have seemed to realize.

[62] It was highly illuminating to the writer to discover that William James was familiar with Tracy's *Ideology* and also with the works of Laromiguière. James quotes from Tracy and Laromiguière to substantiate his contention that they are among the "few honorable exceptions" among the "sensationalists" who have "explicitly contended for feelings of relation, consubstantial with our feelings or thoughts of the terms 'between' which they obtain. No other empiricists, nor the 'intellectualists' have accounted for our knowing relations through feeling." *Principles of Psychology*, I, 247.

Chapter IX

CABANIS AND THE ISSUE
OF "MATERIALISM"

ALTHOUGH only a few features of Tracy's *Idéologie* have been selected for discussion, the general methodological foundation of the school has been sufficiently described. In so far as "philosophy" implies a metaphysical position, however, the impression may have been created that the ideologists "had none" and that Jefferson in turn gave no thought to strictly metaphysical questions. In one sense this is true. Loyal to the principles set forth in the ideological methodology which we considered, the ideologists were cautious in philosophizing about any ultimates—whether cause, substance, goal, or "reality."

Despite this caution, the works of Cabanis have been regarded on the whole as illustrations of extreme "materialism." Tracy, of course, explicitly avowed agreement with the work of Cabanis and asserted that his own analysis presupposed the latter's physiological contribution. Therefore, if Cabanis is rightly described as a materialist, Tracy, by his own judgment, must also be considered one. Jefferson's views on this interesting question will be discussed later.

There are several metaphors in the *Rapports du physique et du moral de l'homme* which are very useful in establishing the claim that Cabanis was a materialist. The frequently quoted statement that the brain must be considered an organ specially made to produce ideas, as the stomach is made to digest,[1] leads on to the sensational formula that the brain secretes thought as the liver bile: "le cerveau digère en quelque sorte les impressions; qu'il fait organiquement la sécrétion de la pensée." [2] These are usually treated as if they constituted the

[1] Cabanis, *Rapports du physique et du moral de l'homme*, 2 vols., I, 133. Further references to this work will be given as *Rapports*.
[2] *Ibid.*, I, 134.

substance of Cabanis's position. In fact, they are misleading if read apart from the context in which Cabanis introduced them, because they are largely the dramatic media the author employs to translate his behaviorist account of nervous (including rational) activity.

Cabanis's entire work is founded on the belief that the mistaken tradition of philosophy which separated the metaphysical pursuit of mental and moral studies of human nature from the scientific study of physical man must be completely discarded. Locke and his successors found the right path when they brought together, in one inclusive method, the study of man under the double aspect of moral and physical nature. Cabanis wished to continue this work and carry it farther than Locke had conceived. The sole end of the *Rapports* is announced as the replacement of the moral sciences upon the solid base of physical nature.[3] In the Preface to his work Cabanis urged that human behavior, whether moral, purely mental, practical, or entirely physical, should be regarded as one unified science—the "natural history of man."

. . . le principe des sciences morales, et par conséquent ces sciences elles-mêmes, rentreraient dans le domaine de la physique; elles ne seraient plus qu'une branche de l'histoire naturelle de l'homme; l'art d'y vérifier les observations, d'y tenter les expériences, et d'en tirer tous les résultats certains qu'elles peuvent fournir, ne différerait en rien des moyens qui sont journellement employés avec la plus entière et la plus juste confiance, dans les sciences pratiques dont la certitude est le moins contestée: les principes fondamentaux des unes et des autres seraient également solides: elles se formeraient également par l'étude sévère et par la comparaison des faits; elles s'étendraient et se perfectionneraient par les mêmes méthodes de raisonnement.[4]

The description of this system as "materialism" must be judged as more willful than accurate when Cabanis's position on "first causes" is consulted. Cabanis very specifically disassociated his philosophy from anything related to metaphysics. The reasons he cites are even more in accordance with the idiom of contemporary positivisms than were the related passages in Tracy's *Idéologie*. Cabanis's argument is this. He calls attention to the fear, already expressed in certain quarters, that the object of his work, or if not the object then the effect, is to get rid of some regnant views on the nature of first causes and to put in their stead his own materialistic analyses. But Cabanis points out that this

[3] *Rapports*, I, xxvii.   [4] *Ibid.*, xii–xiii.

could never be his object, or effect, since "le lecteur verra souvent, dans le cours de l'ouvrage, que nous regardons ces causes comme placées hors de la sphère de nos recherches, et comme dérobées, pour toujours, aux moyens d'investigation que l'homme a reçus avec la vie." [5] In fact, Cabanis is so anxious to insist upon the limits of his undertaking that he hastens to make a "formal declaration" about traditional metaphysical speculations on first and ultimate causes. This declaration, too, is so appropriate to the positivistic spirit in favor of the supremacy of scientific method that it doubly deserves to be quoted.

Nous en faisons ici la déclaration le plus formelle; et s'il y avait quelque chose à dire encore sur des questions qui n'ont jamais été agitées impunément, rien ne serait plus facile que de prouver qu'elles ne peuvent être ni un objet d'examen, ni même un sujet de doute, et que l'ignorance la plus invincible est le seul résultat auquel nous conduise, à leur égard, le sage emploi de la raison. Nous laisserons donc à des esprits plus confians, ou si l'on veut, plus éclairés, le soin de rechercher, par des routes que nous reconnaissons impraticables pour nous, quelle est la nature du principe qui anime les corps vivans: car nous regardons la manifestation des phénomènes qui le distinguent des autres forces actives de la nature, ou les circonstances en vertu desquelles ont lieu ces phénomènes, comme confondues, en quelque sorte, avec les causes premières, ou comme immédiatement soumises aux lois qui président à leur action. [6]

This highly important statement precludes Cabanis from membership in any descriptive cosmological "ism," save "agnosticism"—not really an exception! Therefore, the "natural philosophy" of the ideologists (since it was largely left to Cabanis) is, technically speaking, nonexistent. The natural sciences are coaxed into the limelight instead. Where the sciences differ from the purely conventional Newtonian ones, they do so because of a shift in interest. Physiology, psychology, and the sociology of human nature are first in importance. The fundamental principle of all animal existence is still the faculty of sensing, or sensation; but Cabanis was eager to show its precise and multiform workings as internal impressions ("instincts," visceral processes, "unconscious" thoughts and desires). He also developed the theory of sensations as external impressions, from which ideas are derived, showing the modifications wrought by the state of the individual fac-

[5] *Ibid.*, p. xxviii.   [6] *Ibid.*, pp. xxix–xxx.

ulties receiving the impression. Therefore, although Cabanis said in one place that human nature was nothing but the functioning of the nervous system—"les nerfs—voila tout l'homme"—he was apparently not interested in physical sciences, per se, and was wholly unsympathetic to the idea of constructing a system of natural philosophy. Cabanis implied at least this when he chose Pope's "The proper study of mankind, is man" for the keynote quotation of the *Rapports.*

In the sense explained, then, it is true that Cabanis is not a conventional metaphysical materialist, but rather a methodological one. Proof of this contention is to be read in his repeated confessions of human ignorance of the ultimate nature or causes of things. Sceptical about such knowledge, Cabanis found materialistic methodology (positivism, phenomenalism) sufficient for his type of empirical philosophizing. He pointedly includes the legend wisely inscribed on an "ancient temple," "Je suis ce qui est, ce qui a été, ce qui sera; et n'a connu ma nature." [7] To which he appends the French version of *gnothe seauton:* "Connais-toi toi-même." The first kind of ignorance he regards as inevitable; the second

. . . est l'indication formelle et précise du but que doivent se tracer la philosophie rationnelle et la philosophie morale: elle est, en quelque sorte, l'abrégé de toutes les leçons de la sagesse sur ces deux grands sujets de nos méditations. [8]

With such decision does Cabanis assign these limits to human knowledge (stressing what in modern terminology would be labeled the "egocentric predicament") that all transcendent causes and agencies are legislated together into the realm of the unknowable. The small kernel of truth justifying the charge of materialism, however, consists in the development which comes after his summary execution of "ultimates" and nonempirical essences. Occasionally Cabanis strayed from the purist paths of self-conscious agnosticism to a confused empiricist dogmatism. For example, he says that since the only ideas of objects which we can have come through the observable phenomena which they present to us, "leur nature ou leur essence ne peut être pour nous que l'ensemble de ces phénomènes." [9] Since the character of observable phenomena, whether of nature solely or of the more intricate functionings of moral

---

[7] *Rapports,* p. 140.   [8] *Ibid.*   [9] *Ibid.,* p. 138.

nature, are systematically characterized in terms of material transformations (nerves, sensibility, and so forth), the outcome is to solidify our impressions of a materialistic philosophy. In all justice, however, we should observe that even in the unguarded statement quoted above Cabanis carefully inserted the qualifying phrase "pour nous" when he said the essence of phenomena can only be the collection of phenomenal appearances. The conclusion seems to be that practically all human investigations must end with materialistic, phenomenalistic statements, best illustrated in the sciences. Theoretically, speculatively, or as matter of faith other methods and beliefs may function, but not as knowledge.

In anticipation of the demur that a separation of the sort Cabanis effected amounts in fact to the same thing as metaphysical materialism, since the realm of non-empirical possibility (whether essence, nature, ultimate cause, or deity) must remain wholly inoperative, we must uphold Cabanis's distinction. Precisely because possibilities stand between Cabanis's methodological materialism and ultimate metaphysical dogmatism, Cabanis is able to retain the logical purity of his system. Interestingly enough, from a long-time point of view those possibilities may make a practical difference as they did in Cabanis's later development. Lévy-Bruhl pointed out that Cabanis, in his empirical treatment of what he called "instincts" was drawn on to admit final causes in the *Rapports,* but there he still refrained from inferring anything about the "Author" of these causes. However, Lévy-Bruhl points to the *Lettre à Faüriel sur les causes premières* as a departure from this abstinence: [10] yet surely a departure which could hardly have been credible without the carefully drawn distinctions and sceptical limitations of the *Rapports.* Indeed, there is enough margin of ambiguity in the *Rapports* to allow one critic, Alexis Bertrand, to maintain that there is no contradiction between the *Rapports* and the *Lettre à Faüriel.* His argument is illuminating and can be grasped from the following excerpt:

Remarquons d'abord la teinte de scepticisme ou plutôt de probabilisme répandue sur toute cette lettre; ce sont des rêves dont il s'enchante, non des vérités scientifiques qu'il enseigne. Il n'espère atteindre que des probabilités, mais les probabilités lui semblent être en faveur d'une âme spirituelle et d'un Dieu

[10] See Lévy-Bruhl, *History of Modern Philosophy in France,* p. 310.

intelligent et providentiel: quand on presse ces formules un peu flattantes et indécises, on s'aperçoit que Cabanis aboutit décidément à une sorte d'animisme universel ou de panthéisme a la manière des stoiciens, et que cette doctrine est précisément (sauf quelques phrases agressives, finalement atténuées ou expliquées) celle du livre des *Rapports*. Ceux qui ont vu dans la lettre à Fauriel une palinodie n'ont compris ni cette lettre, ni les autres ouvrages de Cabanis . . .[11]

Although this criticism is a bit too eagerly on the side of the angels, the remarks are not without foundation. Cabanis, like Tracy and other faculty members of the ideologic *Institut*, had decided to pay a good price to save positivism from the dogmas of materialism.

[11] See Alexis Bertrand's article "Cabanis," in *La Grande Encyclopédie*, p. 575.

Chapter X

JEFFERSON'S PHILOSOPHICAL BELIEFS

B Y AND LARGE we have already encountered Jefferson in his intellectual enthusiasm for the positivism of the French ideologists, and the "realism" of Dugald Stewart. Jefferson may have realized the complementary character of the two positions, which taken together make up a logical and almost natural practical philosophy. What the ideologists tended to refine away in the solvent of analysis, the Scottish dogmatists could more than reëstablish to their own satisfaction—and apparently to Jefferson's. Yet Jefferson was never the person to accept intellectual beliefs wholesale, without emending them by his own reflection and imagination. Therefore, in addition to the formal statements quoted earlier, in which Jefferson identified himself with the two movements mentioned, it will be interesting to see illustrations of Jefferson's philosophizing, taken from the practical context of personal and political affairs.

His lack of philosophic system, with which some charge Jefferson, he considered an accomplishment, sustained wittingly because estimates of human knowledge gave it sanction. The caution of scepticism was apparently commendable in Jefferson's eyes even before he had seen how ideologic positivism converted this caution into a methodological first principle. Therefore, in 1789 Jefferson explained his nonadherence to any one political party by this statement, which has obvious implications for ideas:

I am not a federalist, because I never submitted the whole system of my opinions to the creed of any party of men whatever, in religion, in philosophy, in politics or in anything else, where I was capable of thinking for myself. Such an addiction is the last degradation of a free and moral agent. If I could not go to heaven but with a party, I would not go there at all.[1]

[1] To Francis Hopkinson, Paris, March 13, 1789, M.E., VII, 300.

Independent criticism, therefore, extended to philosophical matters; and perhaps for this reason there is no evidence of philosophical system until Jefferson's late profession of loyalty to ideology. Philosophical problems were recognized only if they were genuine problems confronting Jefferson, bearing in some fashion upon his political, agricultural, moral, scientific, or religious affairs. It was characteristic of him to think his ideas through to their broadest foundations. In this piecemeal fashion he was able to clarify his own beliefs, but from the matrix of their particular settings. It is also in this sense that while his thinking was never formally or technically "philosophy," his intellectual habits and critical spirit were more philosophical (and Socratic) than many academic critics care to admit.

Jefferson was primarily a social and moral philosopher. Like most of the French encyclopaedists, materialists and ideologists, he found intellectual progress impeded everywhere by social and moral problems, and he judged that everything waited upon the solution of these problems. What Jefferson valued in knowledge, apart from his deep enjoyment of historical writing,[2] was scientific discovery and description. It is relevant to quote, as an example, Jefferson's concept of the connection between free society and the sciences. Referring to the generation of young men, Jefferson wrote:

We have spent the prime of our lives in procuring them the precious blessing of liberty. Let them spend theirs in showing that it is the great parent of *science* and of virtue; and that a nation will be great in both, always in proportion as it is free . . .[3]

Even while Jefferson found himself (despite his inclinations) [4] in the front ranks of republican and social engineering, he never seriously compromised the value of science and knowledge. In fact, it was to the cosmopolitanism inherent in ideas and reason that Jefferson looked for a practical demonstration of the poverty of moralities built upon exclusion and vested interest in ideas. There is one letter in which Jefferson

[2] To William Duance, April 4, 1813, M.E., XIII, 230.
[3] To Dr. Willard, Paris, March 24, 1789, M.E., VII, 329.
[4] Jefferson's disinclination for political and diplomatic life, and his desire for retirement to his farm, his books, and his family were, as everyone knows, frequently expressed.

tries to explore the peculiar role of ideas in surpassing the confines of normal property relationships.

If nature has made any one thing less susceptible than all others of exclusive property, it is the action of the thinking power called an idea, which an individual may exclusively possess as long as he keeps it to himself; but the moment it is divulged, it forces itself into the possession of every one, and the receiver cannot dispossess himself of it. Its peculiar character, too, is that no one possesses the less, because every other possesses the whole of it. He who receives an idea from me, receives instruction himself without lessening mine; as he who lights his taper at mine, receives light without darkening me. That ideas should freely spread from one to another over the globe, for the moral and mutual instruction of man, and improvement of his condition, seems to have been peculiarly and benevolently designed by nature, when she made them, like fire, expansible over all space, and like the air in which we breathe, move, and have our physical being, incapable of confinement or exclusive appropriation.[5]

With a background of free government linked reciprocally to free ideas and inventions, Jefferson had the "first principles" needed for his kind of "system."

The virtual use of a cautious scientific positivism is implicit in all Jefferson's serious thinking, but *Notes on Virginia*, written just before his mission to France, are individual and purely Jeffersonian. They are notes on Virginia because Jefferson considered himself a Virginia farmer; they are local, filled with descriptions of climate, flora and fauna, and native soil. But the accounts of grain and wheat and the measurement of typical rainfall somehow never manage to capture all the stage; they are real enough, but they are that on which the human scene must be acted. So we find Jefferson's brilliant discussions of freedom of religious worship, the refutation of the fictions of racial "inferiority and superiority," philosophy of education, theory of republican government, slavery, and numerous biological and geological

[5] To Isaac McPherson, Monticello, August 13, 1813, M.E., XIII, 334. The subject which gave rise to this passage is a question about the patenting of inventions. Jefferson's defense of the free career of ideas given above concludes with "Inventions then cannot, in nature, be a subject of property. Society may give an exclusive right to the profits arising from them, as an encouragement to men to pursue ideas which may produce utility . . ."

issues which were favored hypotheses at that time. Thus the *Notes on Virginia* really are striking symbols of what is meant by calling Jefferson a philosopher in the sense of *philosophe*—his themes are universal, his curiosity endless, his habit of reflection on all themes scientific and prudent.

While there is no technical philosophy in the *Notes,* the several indications of Jefferson's methodological preferences (startlingly close to the positivistic, scientific tradition of eighteenth- and early nineteenth-century France) are of real importance. The trend of Jefferson's agnosticism and of his conviction that hypotheses should be based upon preponderant evidence rather than upon transempirical "convictions" can be felt in the following illustrations.

(1) In a discussion of Voltaire's hypothesis about the formation of shells Jefferson urges considerations which make him discard it.

. . . we must be contented to acknowledge, that this great phenomenon is as yet unsolved. Ignorance is preferable to error; and he is less remote from the truth who believes nothing, than he who believes what is wrong.[6]

(2) In another context, where Voltaire assumes that "moisture is unfriendly to animal growth," Jefferson again is moved to question his hasty generalization. He makes this significant remark.

The truth of this is inscrutable to us by reasonings *a priori.* Nature has hidden from us her *modus agendi.* Our only appeal on such questions is to experience; and I think that experience is against the supposition. It is by the assistance of *heat* and *moisture* that vegetables are elaborated from the elements of earth, air, water, and fire. We accordingly see the more humid climates produce the greater quantity of vegetables. Vegetables are mediately or immediately the food of every animal; and in proportion to the quantity of food, we see animals not only multiplied in their numbers, but improved in their bulk, as far as the laws of their nature will admit . . .[7]

(3) Perhaps the most vigorous argument is launched concerning the question of the inferiority of the American Indians. Here Jefferson painstakingly and convincingly set himself against Buffon's assertion that they are, as a race, naturally inferior to the whites. From the point of view of practical anthropology Jefferson had far more observation and first-hand experience to his credit than Buffon did, and his criticisms

[6] *Notes on Virginia,* M.E., II, 43.   [7] *Ibid.,* p. 62.

were substantially more correct. Not content, however, with refuting Buffon, Jefferson introduced a more reliable comparative method in place of Buffon's "judgment . . . seduced by a glowing pen" [8]—the point of the comparative method being to insure that only those races which were in a *similar stage of development* would be evaluated with respect to each other. A little later, after having recounted with gusto a self-conducted "anthropological" experiment to determine the meaning of an Indian mound located on the banks of the Rivanna, Jefferson made one further constructive suggestion to help determine racial origins.

A knowledge of their several languages would be the most certain evidence of their derivation which could be produced. In fact, it is the best proof of the affinity of nations which ever can be referred to. How many ages have elapsed since the English, the Dutch, the Germans, the Swiss, the Norwegians, Danes and Swedes have separated from their common stock? Yet how many more must elapse before the proofs of their common origin which exist in their several languages, will disappear? It is to be lamented then, very much to be lamented that we have suffered so many of the Indian tribes already to extinguish, without our having previously collected and deposited in the records of literature, the general rudiments at least of the languages they spoke. [9]

Following out the hypothesis, for many years Jefferson patiently collected between "thirty and forty" Indian vocabularies, in order to determine at some future time whether linguistic similarities between Indian languages and the languages of Europe and Asia would justify any inferences about similar racial origins. [10] Proficient not only in the theoretical criticism of scientific hypotheses, Jefferson was also capable of offering constructive new hypotheses of his own and willing to prepare for them by direct observation and first-hand collection of data. In fact, Jefferson was ready to do this in every scientific or technical field in which he felt at home. As he said: "Law, medicine, chemistry, mathematics, every science has a language of its own . . ." [11] and Jefferson knew not only the languages mentioned, but those of agricul-

---

[8] *Ibid.*, p. 93.   [9] *Ibid.*, p. 140.
[10] To Dr. Peter Wilson, Monticello, January 20, 1816, M.E., XIV, 402. This collection was stolen from Jefferson one day in transit between Washington and Monticello.
[11] *Ibid.*, p. 403.

ture, botany, zoology, geology, political science, architecture in addition. Indeed, it is difficult to conceive of a single domain of pure or applied knowledge which failed to interest Jefferson at some time; an exhaustive list would have to include occasional excursions into *belles lettres*, prosody, and philology; serious study of ancient and modern history and the classical languages and literature; and minute practical knowledge of certain industries, for example, the manufacture of nails and textiles, on a homestead economy basis.

(4) The real gist of *Notes on Virginia* is found in its social philosophy, which is the subject of the following chapter. The specific recommendations made about the need for constitutional guarantees, the tendency of governors to consolidate power, the problem of slavery, the treatment of poverty in a republic are concrete but subsidiary supports for Jefferson's independent analysis of the relation of religion and authority. The doctrine of freedom of thought and belief is tested fully in the light of its personal and social implications and is found superior to the methods of coercion. The realistic, large-minded discussion closes with: "Reason and persuasion are the only practicable instruments. To make way for these free inquiry must be indulged . . ." [12]

While Jefferson's understanding of ideology, on its formal side (epistemological, logical), was complete, he did not offer any of those characteristic reformulations or applications which are evident in his treatment of moral and social philosophy. The significance of accepting ideology as a formal system of ideas, therefore, has more to do with the demonstration of what Jefferson believed his philosophy to be than with the exact understanding of knowledge and the universe which his own interpretation of that philosophy would provide. It is valuable, furthermore, as evidence that the trend of Jefferson's early and independent philosophical judgments is basically similar to the more elaborate system he later defended.

One important issue remains, however, which Jefferson was not content simply to accept as part of ideology—and was tempted to discuss in correspondence. This may be called, roughly, the question of materialism, a question which has already been reviewed in this study, but

[12] *Notes on Virginia*, M.E., II, 223.

only from the moral and religious viewpoint.[13] We might recall that despite Jefferson's repeated reference to himself as a materialist, in moral philosophy he was a deist. His metaphysical position, however, may furnish the explanation for his professed materialism.

Jefferson was reluctant to seize convenient metaphysical explanations as a matter of principle. As far back as *Notes on Virginia* he stated this explicitly. "A patient pursuit of facts, and cautious combination and comparison of them, is the drudgery to which man is subjected by his Maker, if he wishes to attain sure knowledge." [14] We may assume, therefore, that his version of materialism would be so fringed with caution and restraint that the dogmatic mechanistic metaphysics ordinarily connoted by that term would probably be absent. In this respect Jefferson's materialism cannot be confused with the extreme mechanistic materialism of philosophers like Baron d'Holbach and Helvetius, whose right to assert their position Jefferson was quick to defend. On the other hand, he did not share the intellectual impatience of his correspondent John Adams with regard to "these atheists." Adams's pen ran riot with sarcasm and irritation; in a letter to Jefferson he prepared himself to defend the idea of God by this prologue:

No man is more sensible than I am of the service to science and letters, Humanity, Fraternity and Liberty, that would have been rendered by the Encyclopedists and Economists, by Voltaire, D'Alembert, Buffon, Diderot, Rousseau, La Lande, Frederick and Catherine, if they had possessed common sense. But they were all totally destitute of it. They all seemed to think that all Christendom was convinced as they were, that all religion was "visions Judaiques," and that their effulgent lights had illuminated all the world. They seemed to believe, that whole nations and continents had been changed in their principles, opinions, habits, and feelings, by the sovereign grace of their almighty philosophy, almost as suddenly as Catholics and Calvinists believe in instantaneous conversion. They had not considered the force of early education on the millions of minds who had never heard of their philosophy. And what was their philosophy? Atheism; pure, unadulterated Atheism. Diderot, D'Alembert, Frederick, De La Lande and Grimm, were indubitable Atheists. The universe was matter only, and eternal; spirit was a word without a meaning; liberty was a word without a meaning. There was no liberty in the universe; liberty was a word void of sense. Every

[13] See Part I, chap. iv.   [14] *Notes on Virginia*, Query VI, M.E., II, 97.

thought, word, passion, sentiment, feeling, all motion, and action was necessary. All beings and attributes were of eternal necessity; conscience, morality, were all nothing but fate.[15]

. . . We all curse Robespierre and Bonaparte, but were they not both such restless, vain, extravagant animals as Diderot and Voltaire? Voltaire was the greatest literary character, and Bonaparte the greatest military character of the eighteenth century. There is all the difference between them. Both equally heroes and equally cowards.[16]

Jefferson replied to Adams in the mildest terms, but his reply seems purposely to have disregarded the tone and implications Adams had put there. Adams knew quite well that Jefferson counted himself at least a sympathizer with the company mentioned, and although the lapse of time and events had changed Jefferson's perspective somewhat, he was in no mood to concur with Adams's denunciation. Admitting, therefore, that some French philosophers had been atheistic materialists, Jefferson simply observes that the sociological conditions of Catholic countries tend to produce atheists when orthodoxy no longer works, while the Protestant countries tend to turn secessionists and critics into deists.[17] The civilized perspective behind this analysis makes Adams's vituperation against the French materialists seem like a fit of bad temper with the climate of every country other than his own. And while it is true that Jefferson did not take the final step with Holbach, for example, in denying all possible ideas of God, including the deistic,[18] his more sceptical positivism is still undoubtedly greatly indebted to the circle of encyclopaedists and materialists under discussion.

If we bear in mind the ideologic position of agnostic positivism described earlier and remember that Jefferson independently confirmed that position, while in his later role as apostle of ideology he officially associated himself with it, a brief comparison and contrast of Holbach's

[15] John Adams to Thomas Jefferson, Quincy, March 2, 1816, M.E., XIV, 439.
[16] *Ibid.*, p. 441.
[17] See letter to John Adams, Monticello, April 8, 1816, M.E., XIV, 468–71.
[18] Lange, in *The History of Materialism* (p. 116), points out that Holbach's *System of Nature* is distinguished by its outspoken attack on "the idea of God in every possible shape . . . Holbach is the first who appears to regard the cosmological doctrines as most important . . . [He] therefore pursues the deistic and pantheistic ideas of God, that were yet so dear to his age, with no less zeal than the ideas of the Church."

so-called "Bible of the Atheists" and Jefferson's views may throw light on the issue of materialism. A general statement of Holbach's philosophic orientation is readily given at the beginning of his book.

It is . . . to natural philosophy, and to experience, that man ought always to recur in his researches . . . These are what he ought to consult in his religion, in his morals, in his legislation, in political government, in the arts and sciences, in his pleasures, and in his fortunes. Experience enables us to know that nature acts by simple, uniform, and invariable laws. It is by our senses we are bound to universal nature: it is by our senses that we can experience and discover her secrets.[19]

There is some agreement here with relation to the basically physical interpretation of man or human nature, although the divergence of a mechanical and sensationalist physical interpretation, from a more subtle chemical, neurological and biological interpretation such as Cabanis began, is marked. "Man," Holbach asserts, with an air of certainty unlike Jefferson's, "is a being purely physical." [20] The suggestion of "purely physical" is precisely the kind of deduction Jefferson shied away from. This dogmatic mechano-materialism becomes even more pronounced in the sequel.

. . . the word man is only this physical being, considered under a certain point of view, that is to say, relatively to some of his modes of action, which are owing to his particular organization.[21]

. . . when they shall demand what is man? we say, that he is a material being, organized or conformed to a manner of thinking, of feeling, of being modified in certain modes peculiar to him alone, to his organization, *to the particular combinations of matter which find themselves assembled in him* [Italics mine]. . . . If they ask from whence man has come? we reply, that experience does not enable us to resolve this question, and that it cannot really interest us; it suffices for us to know that man exists, and that he is constituted in a manner to produce the effects of which we see him capable.[22]

The materialism which interested Jefferson partook more of the nature of empirical and experimental science than of the sweeping cosmological mechanism implied in Holbach's work. Cabanis, it should be recalled, actually started the study of materialistic physiology [23] and

---

[19] Holbach, *System of Nature*, p. 16.   [20] *Ibid.*, p. 14.   [21] *Ibid.*
[22] *Ibid.*, p. 83.   [23] Lange, *History of Materialism*, II, 93, 242.

was the first to emphasize the importance of somatic elements for the science of man.[24]

Cabanis's materialism is confined to his scientific hypotheses and research and is to this extent a *methodological scientific postulate*. There is doubt about his cosmological philosophy, since it fluctuates between vitalistic pantheism and materialism. Jefferson's materialism apparently meant methodology, in the former sense. We have already observed his enthusiasm about Cabanis's approach, but this might be reinforced by another instance.

The experimental work of Flourens in the physiology of the brain and the nervous system excited Jefferson profoundly. Lafayette, his friend, sent him a copy of Flourens's *Recherches sur le systeme nerveux dans les animaux vertebres*.[25] This was some eighteen months before Jefferson's death, and his comments on materialism and philosophy we may assume were given in all seriousness. He wrote first to John Adams about his discovery of Flourens, saying:

I have lately been reading the most extraordinary of all books, and at the same time the most demonstrative by numerous and unequivocal facts. It is Flourend's [26] experiments on the functions of the nervous system, in vertebrated animals. He takes out the cerebrum completely, leaving the cerebellum and other parts of the system uninjured. The animal loses all its senses of hearing, seeing, feeling, smelling, tasting, is totally deprived of will, intelligence, memory, perception, etc., yet lives for months in perfect health, with all its powers of motion, but without moving but on external excitement, starving even on a pile of grain, unless crammed down its throat; in short, in a state of the most absolute stupidity. He takes the cerebellum out of other, leaving the cerebrum untouched. The animal retains all its senses, faculties, and understanding, but loses the power of regulated motion, and exhibits all the symptoms of drunkenness. While he makes incisions in the cerebrum and cerebellum, lengthwise and crosswise, which heal and get well, a puncture in the medulla elongata is instant death; and many other most interesting things too long for a letter. Cabanis had proved

[24] In *History of Materialism*, II, 243. Lange adds: "Since Cabanis . . . the resolution of mental functions into the activity of the nervous system has kept its ground in physiology, whatever individual physiologists may have thought as to the ultimate grounds of all things."

[25] Jefferson describes the book, but does not mention it by name. However this is the one listed in his library catalog. See "Manuscript Catalogue of Second Library."

[26] "Flourend" is Jefferson's version of Flourens.

by the anatomical structure of certain portions of the human frame, that they might be capable of receiving from the hand of the Creator the faculty of thinking; Flourend proves that they have received it; that the cerebrum is the thinking organ; and that life and health may continue, and the animal be entirely without thought, if deprived of that organ. I wish to see what the spiritualists will say to this. Whether in this state the soul remains in the body, deprived of its essence of thought? or whether it leaves it, as in death, and where it goes? His memoirs and experiments have been reported on with approbation by a committee of the Institute, composed of Cuvier, Bertholet, Dumaril, Portal and Pinel. But all this, you and I shall know better when we meet again, in another place, and at no distant period. In the meantime, that the revived powers of your frame, and the anodyne of philosophy may preserve you from all suffering, is my sincere and affectionate prayer.[27]

A shorter letter to Lafayette, condenses the conclusions of the one above, after remarking that no other book had been as "gratifying" to read as that of Flourens. In this letter Jefferson finishes his appreciation of Flourens's contribution by speculating: "It will be curious to see what the immaterialists will oppose to this." [28]

These passages from Jefferson are of singular interest. They show that Jefferson's real concern with materialism is caused by his devotion to the hypothesis of specific faculties, and the progress of reliable knowledge about human events. This is the focus of attention; whatever prejudices or philosophies contrive to oppose scientific inquiry, are not only "mistaken," they are "evil." What Jefferson had detested about the "spiritualists" in the context of morals and ethics was the "mystification" they engendered, and the consequent distrust arising in each individual's mind when his own reason, intelligence, or conscience should have operated freely. Here, too, the spiritualists made blind obedience to the authority of some church or sect a condition of religious and, therefore, moral purity. As for the welfare of society or the genuine self-knowledge and virtue of the individual, these were of trifling value compared to God's Kingdom won. In fact, the more one recalls the source of Jefferson's irritation with the "mystifiers," the more one is enabled to see the meaning of his challenge to the metaphysical "spiritualists." The metaphysical spiritualists are, of course,

[27] To John Adams, Monticello, January 8, 1825, M.E., XVI, 90–92.
[28] To the Marquis de Lafayette, Monticello, January 16, 1825, M.E., XIX, 281.

as the letters cited indicate, the "immaterialists." "Immaterialism," from the doctrine of Plato to that of Descartes, Leibniz, and Berkeley, and in addition the whole tenor of scholasticism as the product of medieval theocracy, represented to Jefferson the denial of experience, individual and social, as the source and test of human knowledge. With the elusive abstractions of the immaterialists, Jefferson knew, truth and science would fare badly. Therefore he judged the danger of trans-empirical philosophy, whether rationalistic, idealistic, or vitalistic, in an unambiguous way: they were capable of substituting sophisms, myth, and nonsense for the patient but rewarding research which was the chosen "materialistic" method.

This, in Jefferson's eyes, would really make sacred philosophy (rightly viewed) profane. He saw no ignobility in the scientific materialism which connected thinking with the functions of a physical organ in relation to the nervous system, since however a body acted when thinking, the power, light, and mystery of thought remained the same. Jefferson's respect for truth and objective fact made it easy for him to accept the researches of pioneers like Cabanis and Flourens, with all their methodological materialism. Yet he could never make of his materialism a new metaphysics, he was too convinced of the correctness of positivist restraint for that. That metaphysical materialism was to Jefferson every bit as gratuitous and empirically unjustified as immaterialism emerges clearly enough in his letter to Adams, although the point is made lightly. Jefferson's empiricism had no room for cosmological formulae—first causes; necessary, universal law; essences; spiritual life after death—or in life, but not in body; revelation and theological paradox—none of these could break through into his philosophy when he was on guard.

The plainest evidence that Jefferson's philosophy was materialism only to the extent that it was sensationalistic positivism, is found in another letter to John Adams, which is the most direct statement of his philosophical "position" available. He asserts that he has been stirred up and bewildered by Adams's recent questions on "matter, spirit, motion, etc."

. . . I was obliged to recur ultimately to my habitual anodyne, "I feel, therefore I exist." I feel bodies which are not myself: there are other existences then. I call them *matter*. I feel them changing place. This gives me, *motion.* Where there is an absence of matter, I call it *void,* or *nothing,* or *immaterial space.* On the basis of sensation, of matter and motion, we may erect the fabric of all the certainties we can have or need. I can conceive *thought* to be an action of a particular organization of matter, formed for that purpose by its Creator, as well as that *attraction* is an action of matter, or *magnetism* of loadstone. When he who denies to the Creator the power of endowing matter with the mode of action called *thinking,* shall show how He could endow the sun with the mode of action called attraction, which reins the planets in the track of their orbits, or how an absence of matter can have a will, and by that will put matter into motion, then the Materialist may be lawfully required to explain the process by which matter exercises the faculty of thinking. When once we quit the basis of sensation, all is in the wind. To talk of *immaterial* existences, is to talk of *nothings.* To say that the human soul, angels, God, are immaterial, is to say, they are *nothings,* or that there is no God, no angels, no soul. I cannot reason otherwise; but I believe I am supported in my creed of materialism by the Lockes, the Tracys and the Stewarts.[29]

The first thing which comes to mind in reading this philosophic credo, is its apparent resemblance to Tracy's ideology. The analysis of the beginning of knowledge of the Self, is cruder in Jefferson's version. The positivist reduction of "immaterial" existences to "nothings" and the vigorous axiom *"when once we quit the basis of sensation, all is in the wind"* shows that Jefferson was at home in the Condillac tradition, if not in all the subtleties of Tracy's detailed analysis.

The second clarification furnished here regards the connotation of materialism for Jefferson: "I believe I am supported in my creed of materialism by the Lockes, the Tracys and the Stewarts." Notice that every "materialist" mentioned is really an empiricist, prepared in each case to admit that "matter exercises the faculty of thinking," if there is scientific evidence or indication that this is so. Not one of them, however, is a materialist in the radical sense, that is, dogmatic materialism which *denies* the existence of everything save material particles, grouped and combined according to the necessary, universal laws of physics. In fact, the conservative version of so-called materialism which Jefferson expresses leaves room for a deistic belief in the "Creator" and rejects the hypotheses of chance and blind necessity as cosmological first principles. What remains then? We see that mechanical metaphysical ma-

[29] To John Adams, Monticello, August 15, 1820, XV, M.E., 273-74.

terialism of the Holbachian type is not intended, and atheism is not intended. But the materialistic science of human nature, especially including the operations of the mind in thinking, is intended; and so is the outlawing of all philosophical systems and beliefs which are not founded upon inferences from sense experience and "proven" by the corroborative testimony of our senses and those of others.

Jefferson demonstrates this last qualification as an essential part of his philosophy when he concludes the letter referred to with these remarks:

Rejecting all organs of information, therefore, but my senses, I rid myself of all the pyrrhonisms with which an indulgence in speculations hyperphysical and antiphysical, so uselessly occupy and disquiet the mind. A single sense may indeed be sometimes deceived, but rarely; and never all our senses together, with their faculty of reasoning. They evidence realities, and there are enough of these for all the purposes of life, without plunging into the fathomless abyss of dreams and phantasms. I am satisfied, and sufficiently occupied with the things which are, without tormenting or troubling myself about those which may indeed be, but of which I have no evidence.[30]

A theory of valid evidence, therefore, based of course upon the famous "limitations of the human understanding," is the other integral feature of Jefferson's materialistic philosophy. The close connection between Jefferson's positivistic epistemology and his practical refusal to carry sceptical doubt too far, into "pyrrhonism," may be the explanation of his coupling Locke and Tracy with Stewart. Stewart's analysis of realism was compatible with Jefferson's fundamental need for a philosophy which made action possible, not action which had to be thought of as "irrational," or as with Hume based only on custom—action firmly grounded on reasonable assumptions. Stewart's theoretical confidence in uniform dictates of our mental faculties was a sturdier bridge to the sciences of man and society than were the other alternatives open to Jefferson. Faith in a workable philosophy for use in private and in public may have been conditioned in Jefferson's case, by earnest desire for one.[31] This quality in Jefferson, which James might have called "ten-

[30] To John Adams, Monticello, August 15, 1820, XV, M.E., 275–76.
[31] His constant references to resting his head on "the pillow of ignorance" when confronted with questions which exceeded human knowledge at the time, may re-

der-minded," made it natural for him to affirm something further, which is implied by faith in common sense, or rather *demanded* by it: the belief that man's reasoning faculty is a gift from the Creator and that its ability to bridge the chasm between man's thought and the objects outside is a part of the Divine intention and plan.

Jefferson's deistic reasonings are therefore to be accounted as one element in his intellectual make-up. However, from the viewpoint of his methodology of science this seems like a slip, possible only because his intellectual guard was down. Jefferson had written that he was an "empiric" in natural philosophy, "suffering my faith to go no further than my facts. I am pleased, however to see the efforts of hypothetical speculation, because by the collisions of different hypotheses, truth may be elicited and science advanced in the end . . ." [32] Either Jefferson did suffer his faith (in God) to go further than his facts, or he believed that the facts warranted his belief. The letter cited in another context, which presents the teleological argument for the existence of God, leans to the latter interpretation. After reviewing the atheists' arguments for an eternal universe, in "unceasing motion and circulation of matter through the animal, vegetable, and mineral kingdoms," Jefferson outlines the "theists' " reply, urging a first cause. And the theists, according to Jefferson, conceived this first cause as

possessing intelligence and power in the production, and intelligence in the design and constant preservation of the system; [they] urged the palpable existence of final causes; that the eye was made to see, and the ear to hear, and not that we see because we have eyes, and hear because we have ears.[33]

And at this point Jefferson makes the interesting comment: "an answer obvious to the senses, as that of walking across the room, was to the philosopher demonstrating the non-existence of motion." [34] If this comment be taken as a serious statement on Jefferson's part, it is diffi-

---

veal a constitutional unwillingness to remain long in the sphere of sceptical doubt. E.g., "When I meet with a proposition beyond finite comprehension, I abandon it as I do a weight which human strength cannot lift, and I think ignorance, in these cases, is truly the softest pillow on which I can lay my head." To John Adams, Monticello, March 14, 1820, M.E., XV, 239.

[32] To George F. Hopkins, Monticello, September 5, 1822, M.E., XV, 394.
[33] To John Adams, Monticello, April 8, 1816, XIV, M.E., 468–69.
[34] *Ibid.*

cult to see how the "facts" could have carried him so far; while it would be unwarranted to maintain that this positive statement was only thrown out as a speculative hypothesis, to engender others, and thus in time to stimulate the discovery of truth.

Jefferson did make one attempt to square his scientific materialism with his deism, by means of a highly venturesome argument on the nature of the soul. Since the notion of immaterial spirit or soul was unthinkable, Jefferson urged the materiality of the soul, claiming Locke as his authority in this particular. He then tried to prove that the early Christian theologians had urged this view of the soul, even applying it to God.

The fathers of the church of the three first centuries generally, if not universally, were materialists, extending it even to the Creator Himself; nor indeed do I know exactly [35] in what age of the Christian church the heresy of spiritualism was introduced.[36]

In support of this assertion Jefferson quotes from Huet's commentaries on Irigen, "St. Macari," in his discussion of angels, "St. Justin Martyr," Tertullian, "St. Augustin," and others.[37] Apparently what Jefferson would have liked to establish was a continuity between his most valued philosophical beliefs and his great personal and ethical ideal of divine and human benevolence. To reconcile "essential" Christianity with the most advanced scientific and social philosophy was Jefferson's actual, if not avowed, aim.

[35] Jefferson adds in a marginal note: "I believe by Athanasius and the Council of Nicea."
[36] To Dr. Thomas Cooper, Monticello, August 14, 1820, XV, M.E., 266. "Mr. Locke . . . openly maintained the materialism of the soul, and charged with blasphemy those who denied that it was in the power of an Almighty Creator to endow with the faculty of thought any composition of matter He might think fit."
[37] Ibid., pp. 266–67.

Chapter XI

CLASSIFICATION, WORDS, AND
KNOWLEDGE

JEFFERSON had occasion to think about the problem of the relationships between the sciences, or one might say of the classification of the realm of mind, on several occasions. One occasion was the humble task of classifying his two libraries on some significant division of subject matter; another was his plan for the curriculum of the University of Virginia, which he was in process of founding. But the impression remains that even if these specific occasions had not arisen, Jefferson would have been attracted to this problem quite naturally, because of the indisputable breadth of his interests and the persistence of his scientific inquiries. Therefore considerable value attaches to the seemingly modest fact that Bacon's classification of the faculties of the mind was employed by Jefferson in cataloguing his library.

Jefferson uses the Baconian division of the human mind into the following faculties: (1) memory; (2) reason; (3) imagination; and he carefully couples these with (1) history, (2) philosophy and (3) fine arts. Furthermore, it is interesting to see that philosophy, which Jefferson assigns exclusively to the faculty of reason, is in this classification made up of two parts: "mathematics" and "ethical." The expansion of these two subdivisions yields the specific sciences of mathematics and geometry in one group; ethics, religion, law, and politics in the other. If philosophy be understood as the inclusive study of mathematics, geometry, ethics, religion, law, and politics, it is certain that Jefferson philosophized extensively in this sense. But we must remember that the epistemological branch of philosophy and the "mental science" which occupied Jefferson must enter here partly under the category "ethics" and partly as a historical science ("zoology"), grouped with other "natural" as distinguished from "civil" sciences.

By "civil" science Jefferson understood only ancient and modern history.

Therefore the Baconian classification, while respected as the traditional order of the sciences, was employed to some extent, but was certainly not exempt from criticism.[1] An amusing commentary on the relative extent of English and French intellectual influence upon Jefferson is furnished by the latter's evident satisfaction in revealing that the famous Baconian classification really should be attributed to Charron. Since Jefferson establishes this point together with a criticism of the classification, we will quote an excerpt.

Lord Bacon founded his first great division on the faculties of the mind which have cognizance of these sciences. It does not seem to have been observed by any one that the origination of this division was not with him. It had been proposed by Charron more than twenty years before, in his book *de la Sagesse,* B.I., c. 14, and an imperfect ascription of the sciences to these respective faculties was there attempted. This excellent moral work was published in 1600. Lord Bacon is said not to have entered on his great work until his retirement from public office in 1621.[2]

The significance of Jefferson's catalogue lies in its revelation of Jefferson's professional and intellectual interests. Despite the fact that the general divisions "memory" and "imagination" include more headings, "reason" ranks second in quantitative importance.[3] Every single subdivision of reason (philosophy) was of special significance for Jefferson, and the mere mention of its subheadings sounds like the cross-section of the categories of his own thought: mathematics, ethics ("antient and modern"), religion, law, politics. What is even more significant about the distribution of books is that the separate subdivisions which swell the category of memory, enabling it to take first place nu-

[1] We might recall here Jefferson's suggestion of another system of classification (viz., one based on *professional interest*) for libraries, to replace that modeled on "the faculties of the mind."

[2] To Judge Augustus B. Woodward, Monticello, March 24, 1824, M.E., XVI, 17–18.

[3] This analysis is based on the second library collected by Jefferson, which was offered for sale at public auction, February 27, 1829 in Washington. "Memory" leads with approximately 372 titles; "Reason" is second with 342; and "Imagination" last with 206. The single headings of numerical importance are, in order: History (166); Politics (103); Philology (80); Ethics (76). See "Catalogue of Second Library," Library of Congress, Manuscript Division.

merically over reason, are the ones which complete the intellectual tendency manifested, that is, history ("antient and modern") and medicine, which round out philosophy, taken in Jefferson's frequent usage as the province of the sciences. In both senses, then, Jefferson's library catalogue suggests that his most important mental pursuits are "philosophy."

Additional light is thrown on the matter of classifying the sciences in the letter from which the above quotation was also drawn, when Jefferson follows up a pointed criticism of classifications which separates spirit from matter, since "the modern philosophers mostly consider thought as a function of our material organization . . ." [4] and "the materialists will perhaps criticize a basis one-half of which they will say is a non-existence . . . affirming that we can have no evidence of any existence which impresses no sense." [5] With this preparation, Jefferson discloses that his rearrangement of the sciences would make place for the increasing importance of the science of Ideology.

Were I to re-compose my tabular view of the sciences, I should certainly transpose a particular branch. The naturalists . . . distribute the history of nature into three kingdoms or departments: zoology, botany, mineralogy. Ideology or mind, however, occupies so much space in the field of science, that we might perhaps erect it into a fourth kingdom or department. But inasmuch as it makes a part of the animal construction only, it would be more proper to subdivide zoology into physical and moral. The latter including ideology, ethics, and mental science generally, in my catalogue, considering ethics, as well as religion, as supplements to law in the government of man, I had placed them in that sequence. But certainly the faculty of thought belongs to animal history, is an important portion of it, and should there find its place. [6]

The founding of the University of Virginia was another opportunity, which Jefferson did not slight, for reflection upon the realm of knowledge and the sciences. In view of the limitations of a new and poorly endowed university, Jefferson's plans for the college curriculum are not necessarily indexes of his general philosophical position, although they are good tokens of his educational philosophy put into practice. Moreover, there was considerable shift and change of policy in the

[4] To Augustus Woodward, Monticello, March 24, 1824, M.E., XVI, 19.
[5] Ibid., p. 18.   [6] Ibid., p. 19.

different reports to legislatures and in the discussions with educators and savants that Jefferson had to undertake; therefore it is necessary to state the general drift of his opinion, rather than to record its details.

First, we may observe that the familiar library classification reappears in Jefferson's first list of books for the library of the university.[7] Here, too, there is some correlation between his deep intellectual interests and the preponderance of books; they range, with allowance for pedagogy, from classics first, to jurisprudence, modern history, religion, pathology, philosophy and literature, "and lesser numbers on other subjects." [8]

What Jefferson regarded as essential to the intellectual life of even a small university can be gathered from his "Rockfish report," in which he outlines the basic "schools" within the contemplated university. Eight schools were actually established, and they were devoted to (1) ancient languages, (2) modern languages, (3) mathematics, (4) natural philosophy, (5) natural history, (6) anatomy and medicine, (7) moral philosophy, and (8) law. Two schools omitted from this list were included in the original plan, physico-mathematics and government. These were apparently eliminated because of limited resources, and redistributed in related schools.[9] Without pausing to consider the educational philosophy suggested by this division, the predominance of the sciences, natural and social, is a fact to be remembered.

The inclusion of two language schools is interesting, too; language training had played a very large role in Jefferson's education, and he never lost his pleasure in the study of languages or his respect for the importance of studying both classical and modern languages—the former for humanistic guidance, the latter for communications about the advancing sciences or as a prerequisite to international friendship and understanding. What is of more immediate interest, however, is that Jefferson's study of languages did not stop with grammar and literature. He was immensely interested in philology, and he liked to entertain ideas about theory of language. In this respect, he again resembles Tracy and the other ideologists, whose appreciation of the close dependence of ideas upon language developments and forms is

[7] Honeywell, *The Educational Work of Thomas Jefferson*, p. 86. See this book for a thorough discussion of these various educational plans.
[8] *Ibid.*   [9] *Ibid.*, p. 106.

one of the most characteristic features of their brand of empiricism.

One approach to Jefferson's views on language is furnished by his own style of writing and some questions arising from it. Jefferson had been criticized for using "neologisms"; his reply to this criticism took the form, not of denying the charge, but of emphatically accepting it at the same time that he offered a theoretical justification of neology.

I am a friend to neology. It is the only way to give to a language copiousness and euphony. Without it, we should still be held to the vocabulary of Alfred or of Ulphilas; and held to their state of science also: for I am sure they had no words which could have conveyed the ideas of oxygen, cotyledons, zoophytes, magnetism, electricity, hyaline, and thousands of others expressing ideas not then existing, nor of possible communication in the state of their language. What a language has the French become since the date of their revolution, by the free introduction of new words! The most copious and eloquent in the living world; and equal to the Greek, had not that been regularly modifiable almost *ad infinitum*. Their rule was, that whenever their language furnished or adopted a root, all its branches, in every part of speech, were legitimated by giving them their appropriate terminations. . . . And this should be the law of every language. Thus, having adopted the adjective *fraternal,* it is a root which should legitimate *fraternity, fraternation, fraternisation, fraternism, to fraternate, fraternise, fraternally.* And give the word *neologism* to our language, as a root, and it should give us its fellow substantives, *neology, neologist, neologisation;* its adjectives, *neologous, neological, neologistical;* its verb, *neologise;* and adverb, *neologically.* Dictionaries are but the depositories of words already legitimated by usage. Society is the workshop in which new ones are elaborated. When an individual uses a new word, if ill formed, it is rejected in society; if well formed, adopted, and after due time, laid up in the depository of dictionaries.[10]

Jefferson thus resolutely set himself against what he called "purism" in language-observance, precisely because the acceptance of purism would retard the growth of knowledge. The essential connection of language with the experiences of a particular society or with the fresh perception of shades of difference by a scientist or intellectual, are the conditions which he judged important. Each new social milieu naturally generates new word and language changes, and those bent upon outlawing them for the sake of purity simply fail to realize the function of language as a tool for communication and an instrument for record-

[10] To John Adams, Monticello, August 15, 1820, XV, 272–73.

ing new experiences and observations. Reënforcing Jefferson's recognition of the intermediary, instrumental role of language was an esthetic appreciation of the "strength, beauty, variety" of a language which would be "permitted freely to draw from all its legitimate sources." [11]

Applying his socio-utilitarian theory of language to the American scene, Jefferson found fault with the assumptions of the purists of the *Edinburgh Review*, who had expressed concern over the "adulteration" of the English language due to novelties of American style and speech. Jefferson remarked:

Certainly so great growing a population, spread over such an extent of country, with such a variety of climates, of productions, of arts, must enlarge their language, to make it answer its purpose of expressing all ideas, the new as well as the old. The new circumstances under which we are placed, call for new words, new phrases, and for the transfer of old words to new objects. An American dialect will therefore be formed; so will a West-Indian and Asiatic, as a Scotch and an Irish are already formed. But whether will these adulterate or enrich the English language? Has the beautiful poetry of Burns, or his Scottish dialect, disfigured it? Did the Athenians consider the Doric, the Ionian, the Aeolic, and other dialects, as disfiguring or as beautifying their language? Did they fastidiously disavow Herodotus, Pindar, Theocritus, Sappho, Alcaeus, or Grecian writers? On the contrary, they were sensible that the variety of dialects, still infinitely varied by poetical license, constituted the riches of their language, and made the Grecian Homer the first of poets, as he must ever remain, until a language equally ductile and copious shall again be spoken. [12]

Obviously Jefferson was sensitive to the practical and imaginative gains of a flexible as opposed to a rigid linguistic system. Only such a philosophy of language provides for the advancement of knowledge. Jefferson wrote to the publisher of Destutt de Tracy's treatise on *Political Economy* to apologize for the appearance of "Gallicisms" in the translation. These were necessary in order to catch the exact shade of meaning in the French manuscript. He is again moved to recommend neologism, with its technique of innovation and improvisation.

It is thus the English language has been brought to what it is; one-half of it having been innovations, made at different times, from the Greek, Latin,

[11] To John Waldo, Monticello, August 16, 1813, M.E., XIII, 344.
[12] *Ibid.*, pp. 340–41.

French and other languages. And is it the worse for these? Had the preposterous idea of fixing the language been adopted by our Saxon ancestors, of Pierce Plowman, of Chaucer, of Spenser, the progress of ideas must have stopped with that of the language. On the contrary, nothing is more evident than that as we advance in the knowledge of new things, and of new combinations of old ones, we must have new words to express them. Were Van Helmont, Stane, Scheele, to rise from the dead at this time, they would scarcely understand one word of their own science. Would it have been better, then, to have abandoned the science of Chemistry, rather than admit innovations in its terms? [13]

With this recognition that words are to be created at will whenever the one using them is ready to state what "new things" he intends to indicate by those words (that is, the process of definition), Jefferson consciously or unconsciously voiced the ideologic thesis. The probability that this was a conscious part of his positivist philosophy is increased by the fact that he took a very similar position regarding the nature of classification, in the natural sciences and in general. Jefferson asserts that the choice of features for classification is arbitrary, but more-or-less convenient. Classification is never the revelation of "essences," a theme recalling Tracy's familiar exposition in *L'Idéologie*. Jefferson's tendency toward particularism here, his emphasis on individuality, bespeaks the empiricist's suspicion of any theory of general terms other than that of "short-cut" expedience.

Nature has, in truth, produced units only through all her works. Classes, orders, genera, species, are not of her work. Her creation is individual. No two animals are exactly alike; no two plants, nor even two leaves or blades of grass; no two crystallizations. And if we may venture from what is within the cognizance of such organs as ours, to conclude on that beyond their powers, we must believe that no two particles of matter are of exact resemblance. This infinitude of units or individuals being far beyond the capacity of our memory, we are obliged, in aid of that, to distribute them into masses, throwing into each of these all the individuals which have a certain degree of resemblance; to subdivide these again into smaller groups, according to certain points of dissimilitude observable in them, and so on until we have formed what we call a system of classes, orders, genera and species . . .[14]

[13] To Mr. Joseph Milligan, Monticello, April 6, 1816, M.E., XIV, 463–64.
[14] To Dr. John Manners, Monticello, February 22, 1814, M.E., XIV, 97–98.

The net effect of these sentiments brings us more information about Jefferson than it does about a typical empirical tradition. We see that Jefferson is closer to the biological, individual approach to nature and the universe than to any mechanical or physical one. His interpretation of positivism and empiricism, therefore, starts from the center of human experience, but not without a suggestion of the uniqueness of each person's experience. The emergence of individuality as the basic reality has much to do with that genuine piety which made it impossible for Jefferson to conceive the universe, despite his keenest methodological cautions, as other than an "order" of Nature, issuing from the hand of the Creator. If one feels that Jefferson leaned toward a world in which he would have preferred to find that even any two atoms were unlike, one must acknowledge that his veneration for tolerance of difference in society was indeed deep-seated in his habitual thought.

PART THREE: THEORY
OF SOCIETY

Chapter XII

ON HUMAN NATURE

THE BIOLOGICAL slant of Jefferson's philosophy of nature and knowledge has been indicated in the preceding chapter. The slogan of the ideologists, philosophy, "a branch of zoology," is an emphatic reminder of this fact. The biological interest flowers into psychology in a way which is both natural and appropriate. While biology remains the ultimate terra firma of Jefferson's philosophy, his social philosophy draws upon a correspondingly more complex analysis of human nature.

Jefferson did little with any formal theory of human nature. In fact, he expressed himself so well satisfied with the ideologic analysis that this must be conceded to be the foundation of his psychology. In addition to the work of Tracy and Cabanis, that of Helvetius and D'Holbach was influential. So far the French philosophers, with their overt but modified materialism, appear to have captured Jefferson's support on the debated "science of man." He explicitly accepted materialism as a valid account of the human personality and soul, ranging himself, however, in the camp of "the Lockes, the Tracys, and the Stewarts." [1] While this points to his preference for a conservative materialism— compatible with a wisely created and planned universe—it is still true that the predominant influences in Jefferson's views on human nature come from eighteenth-century France. Positivism of the type sponsored by the ideologists is really a better description of Jefferson's thinking than the term "materialism," which he himself employed. Human thinking is explained, positivistically, as a "mode of action," of a "particular organization of matter." [2] It, like every human activity, is

[1] To John Adams, Monticello, August 15, 1820, M.E., XV, 274.
[2] *Ibid.*

only a form of feeling and action. Accordingly, the ideals and most far-reaching thoughts of human beings are knowable in the same way as other natural events, other material phenomena. The machinery of special revelation, of mystic intuition, of "divine" rules or superstitions is treated as antiquated nonsense or worse, the expensive impedimenta of ignorant ages. Jefferson will have nothing to do with speculations "hyperphysical and antiphysical." [3]

Jefferson's observations on human nature take place within this context, a context purely naturalistic and this-worldly for all practical purposes.

The most genuine scientific psychologist native to such an environment was the *idéologue* Cabanis. Jefferson entertained the highest opinion of that author's "most profound of all human compositions," [4] *Rapports du physique et du moral de l'homme*. This, therefore, furnishes the best clew to Jefferson's psychological beliefs. The distinguishing feature of Cabanis's work, taken historically, was that it first emphasized the thorough independence of psychology from metaphysics and interpreted psychology physiologically. Jefferson apparently appreciated this, for he wrote to Cabanis:

That thought may be a faculty of our material organization, has been believed in the gross; and thus the "modus operandi" of nature, in this, as in most other cases, can never be developed and demonstrated to beings limited as we are, yet I feel confident that you will have conducted us as far on the road as we can go, and have lodged us within reconnoitering distance of the citadel itself. [5]

Cabanis's lectures were devoted to exploring the relations between the physical organs and functions of man and the workings and results of his intelligence. Cabanis stated that his special interest was writing about

. . . des rapports . . . du développement systématique de ses organes avec le développement analogue de ses sentimens et de ses passions: rapports d'où il résulte clairement que la physiologie l'analyse des idées et la morale, ne

---

[3] To John Adams, Monticello, August 15, 1820, M.E., XV, 275–76.
[4] To Thomas Cooper, Monticello, July 10, 1812, M.E., XIII, 177.
[5] To Monsieur Cabanis, Washington, July 12, 1803, M.E., X, 404.

sont que les trois branches d'une seule et même science, qui peut s'appeler, à juste titre, *la science de l'homme*.[6]

With one "science of man" to include the study of physical constitution, rational behavior, and moral conduct, Cabanis was ready to analyse the particular influences of separate factors, such as temperament, age, sex, climate, and illness, upon human thought and conduct. Having determined the influence of the physical factors upon mental and moral behavior, Cabanis considers their influence upon the physical constitution. The entire work is characterized by biological tone, a tone which of necessity precludes elated generalizations about the reason, goodness, or progress of man, beliefs so commonly assigned to the eighteenth century. Jefferson was struck by this scientific tone; it was a principled, methodological extension of his own small scientific researches, his practices, his technological innovations, and especially his deep-rooted experimentalism.

When Jefferson applied himself to the problems of understanding human behavior, he was always more disposed toward *original* solutions, even if they were tentative or piecemeal in character. In addition, therefore, to Jefferson's formal views in psychology, which showed him to be a disciple of the French positivists, especially Cabanis, there are several illuminating discussions of his own reflections on human nature to consider. First, did Jefferson believe in an essential, fixed human nature, unchangeable by time and circumstance? There are at least two facts to support the belief that he did. One is Jefferson's enthusiasm for the literary and philosophical resources of antiquity. His love for Greek drama, his use of the Greek poets and the Greek and Roman historians, of the Roman political theorists (especially Cicero)—all point to an appreciation of their enduring truth.[7] Occasionally there is a genuine accent of regret that the excellencies of the Greek and Roman concepts of citizenship and statesmanship no longer operate in the modern world. Jefferson was particularly inclined to think so after Napoleon's rise to dictatorial power in France.

[6] Cabanis, *Rapports*, I, 7.
[7] "Greece was the first of civilized nations which presented examples of what man should be [in government]." To M. Coray, Monticello, October 31, 1823, M.E., XV, 480.

I feel a much greater interest in knowing what passed two or three thousand years ago than in what is passing now. I read nothing, therefore, but of the heroes of Troy, of the wars of Lacedaemon and Athens, of Pompey and Caesar, and of Augustus, too, the Bonaparte and parricide scoundrel of that day.[8]

Such keen appreciation for antiquity, argues a feeling for the ideal continuity of human nature.

The other inference which supports the hypothesis of a stable human nature is derived from Jefferson's theory of moral sense. Part of his firm belief in the moral sense "implanted" by the creator in "every breast" consists in the observable good morality (if not good sense) of ignorant men of all races (black and white), and even of "savages." This must not be interpreted to mean an equality of moral or mental condition, and indeed cannot be if we recall Jefferson's discussion of the development of the moral sense in different societies and of the differences in feeling and judgment of different individuals. However, the broad issues of right and wrong behavior can be grasped by all people, and to that extent human nature is constant, even though the specific objects of its perceptions may be altogether unlike.

An interesting illustration of Jefferson's belief in an essential human nature, shared by all men, is his position on the American Indians. After proving, in *Notes on Virginia*, that the superstitions about the Indians are unfounded, that they are as good a race of men as any, his letters and some of his presidential addresses to Indian "nations" are full of enthusiasm for them. A kind of Rousseauistic romantic naturalism is breathed in these letters, all in favor of the superior harmony, coöperation, and natural justice of their "uncivilized" organization and way of life. Their moral qualities, at any rate, are in some ways praised as a model for the civilized white Americans and Europeans.

Whether this "essential" human nature is morally good or bad, egoistic or altruistic, are the next questions that arise at this point. Is there any evidence to justify the assertion either that faith in, or distrust of "human nature" is more basic in Jefferson's estimate? While evidence on both sides can probably be made to balance, the systematic testimony in Jefferson's writings points to the more "hopeful" alternative. As Jefferson once said: "My theory has always been, that if we

[8] To Nathaniel Macon, Monticello, January 12, 1819, XV, 179.

are to dream, the flatteries of hope are as cheap, and pleasanter than the gloom of despair." [9] And given a chance to "dream" about mankind, Jefferson did usually manage to dream hopefully. When he was looking about him sharply, he was more likely to be on guard against self-interest and ruthlessness, but he was never willing to concede that these were the deepest or highest expressions of human nature. His hopefulness tended to take the form of faith in the educability of human beings, a recognition that they were not all they might be or all they may have been in an uncorrupted state originally, as they came from the hand of the Creator.

This amounts to a belief in progress, if by "progress" is understood the possible increase of well-being in society consequent upon the actual increase of scientific knowledge and general information. Some of man's natural goodness can be assumed to have been obscured by stupid conventions and inert institutions in society; but another kind of acquired, educated goodness awaits his effort. Those who would deny the reality of this kind of progress are "Gothic" thinkers, persuading men to return to superstition and orthodoxy, reinstating medievalism in effect.

The Gothic idea that we were to look backwards instead of forwards for the improvement of the human mind, and to recur to the annals of our ancestors for what is most perfect in government, in religion, and in learning, is worthy of those bigots in religion and government, by whom it has been recommended, and whose purposes it would answer.[10]

And, as Jefferson added, this was an idea which America would not "endure."

Jefferson's wish to emphasize the capacities for useful growth and coöperation in men was nothing of a heady idealism. He took issue, soberly, but reflectively, with Dupont de Nemours who was sceptical of the capacities of the common man. Dupont's theory of education and his consequent views on government were too conservative for Jefferson's complete agreement. The remainder of aristocratic preference, which made Dupont recommend the establishment of two distinct school systems, one for the sons of workingmen and one for the sons of gentlemen who presumably would alone have the leisure time to

[9] To M. Barbé de Marbois, Monticello, June 14, 1817, XV, 131.
[10] To Dr. Joseph Priestley, Philadelphia, January 27, 1800, M.E., X, 148.

pursue advanced studies of a nonvocational kind, was never shared by Jefferson, and all his educational plans show that he rejected the basic assumptions on which such a division rests.[11] He took issue similarly with Dupont's distrust of the people, with respect to their role in self-government. Jefferson thought Dupont regarded the people as "children" who had to be managed by more enlightened "adult" supervisors, whereas he himself knew their shortcomings well, but trusted education and self-interest to produce intelligent participation on the part of the majority. This reliance upon some measure of progress in society, the belief that all men might benefit from education, implies at least that degree of social progress. Jefferson wrote to Dupont to say that the human condition is in no sense forever fixed.

Of all those [provisions] which have been thought of for securing fidelity in the administration of the government, constant ralliance to the principles of the constitution, and progressive amendments with the progressive advances of the human mind, or changes in human affairs, it is the most effectual. Enlighten the people generally, and tyranny and oppressions of body and mind will vanish like evil spirits at the dawn of day. Altho' I do not, with some enthusiasts, believe that the human condition will ever advance to such a state of perfection as that there shall no longer be pain or vice in the world, yet I believe it susceptible of much improvement, and, most of all, in matters of government and religion; and that the diffusion of knowledge among the people is to be the instrument by which it is to be effected.[12]

There is an interesting letter to Condorcet in the Jefferson collection at the Library of Congress, which somehow appears to have been overlooked by the editors of the Memorial Edition.[13] In this letter Jefferson gives an enthusiastic description of the mathematical and architectural abilities of a free Negro citizen (Benjamin Banneker) who was also "a very worthy and respectable member of society." Jefferson continued:

I shall be delighted to see these instances of moral eminence so multiplied as to prove that the want of talents observed in them is merely the effect of

[11] Consider, for example, Jefferson's idea of the development of wards as educational units, devised to reach all people in every community.
[12] To Dupont de Nemours, Poplar Forest, April 24, 1816, M.E., XIV, 487.
[13] The Ford edition includes it, however (VI, 310–12).

their degraded condition, and not proceeding from any difference in the structure of the parts on which intellect depends.[14]

What is common to all human beings, no matter how organized or governed, is the *potentiality* of profiting from training and education. No natural inferiority or superiority of races, no "national" weakness or excellence is to be substituted as an excuse for failing to apply so much good discipline, or make available so much knowledge and science as a society may possess.

To assume, from this, that Jefferson was not suspicious of men, and aware of their capacities to exploit and injure others is quite unwarranted. Indeed, his way of putting the matter was neither reticent nor halting.

I do not believe with the Rochefoucaulds and Montaignes, that fourteen out of fifteen men are rogues; I believe a great abatement from that proportion may be made in favor of general honesty. But I have always found that rogues would be uppermost, and I do not know that the proportion is too strong for the higher orders, and for those who, rising above the swinish multitude, always contrive to nestle themselves into the places of power and profit. These rogues set out with stealing the people's good opinion, and then steal from them the right of withdrawing it, by contriving laws and associations against the power of the people themselves.[15]

Therefore, although not all men are rogues, the rogues are usually in power; so that "faith in human nature" by no means argues any abrogation of "eternal vigilance," nor is it a universalist faith in the goodness of each and every man either now or in the future.

We must conclude that although Jefferson measured the disposition to self-interest against natural benevolence, he found no reason therein for discouragement about improvement and progress. He could easily toss off a comment such as: "All know the influence of interest on the mind of man, and how unconsciously his judgment is warped by that influence." [16] This was obvious to Jefferson, but he preferred not to dwell upon it. The question for him was what can be done to minimize and to divert these tendencies in man.

[14] Thomas Jefferson to Condorcet, Philadelphia, August 30, 1791. Jefferson Papers, Library of Congress.
[15] To Mann Page, Monticello, August 30, 1795, IX, 306.
[16] *Autobiography*, M.E., I, 120.

A tract on education, which he apparently thought well of,[17] states the issue as Jefferson might well have stated it himself. James Ogilvie, its author, had this to suggest:

. . . the civilized world is at present divided into three great parties, the monopolists of power and property, the authors, inventors and participators of knowledge, and an almost infinite multitude of human creatures, destitute of independence, sensibility and knowledge, and disposed to throw the preponderance of force into the scale of one party or the other, as interest, passion or caprice shall prompt.[18]

This is clearly not the conventional "optimism" about human nature which romantic rationalism is supposed to hold. While ample allowance is made for monopoly of power and property, on the one hand, and gross stupidity and inertia, on the other, the hope of an energetic educational program, presented by "the authors, inventors and participators of knowledge" is still sustained.[19]

Psychologically, therefore, Jefferson was empirical, observant and particularistic, just as his philosophical positivism *in theory* inclined. Nothing could be more final proof of his realism about human nature than his inability to go along completely with those who looked to a gradual physical and moral perfecting of the human race. He was, for example, highly sceptical of the scientific possibility of eugenics. Cabanis was more sanguine than Jefferson in this matter. In his chapter on "Influence des tempéramens sur la formation des Idées" Cabanis holds that scientists can influence individual character in the future and can also influence the character of the whole human species. In fact, the indefinite existence of the race being granted, one would be permitted "de rapprocher sans cesse, de plus en plus, d'un type parfait, dont son

[17] Ogilvie's pamphlet, called *Cursory Reflections on Government, Philosophy and Education*, is bound in a volume with one of Tracy's manuscripts on *Education*, a pamphlet by Dupont, *Sur l'éducation nationale*, and another by Lancaster, *Improvements in Education*. Jefferson underlined sections of Ogilvie's essay. See his copy in Jefferson Collection, Rare Book Division, Library of Congress.

[18] Ogilvie, *Cursory Reflections on Government, Philosophy and Education*, p. 40.

[19] In Ogilvie's analysis the argument develops the socialistic ideal of equal economic status, without which education and free republicanism are impossible. Jefferson never developed this aspect of "liberty and equality," but there is reason to infer that he was informed concerning this kind of argument, and not unfriendly to it. His library catalogue shows as many as fifteen titles by the French socialist writer Mably. See *Catalogue of the Library of the United States*, 1815 (first library).

état primitif ne donnait même pas l'idée: il faut, en un mot, que l'hygiene aspire à perfectionner la nature humaine générale." [20] And in addition to recommending a hygiene which can perfect human nature, Cabanis presents a moral argument showing that we are obliged in decency to devote ourselves to the task. Mentioning the breeding of plants, domestic animals, flowers, and so forth he exclaims: "combien n'est il pas honteux de négliger totalement la race de l'homme!" [21]

However much Jefferson wished to respond to a program of such potential utility, he knew too much to overvalue the likelihood of such a development, while the "inevitability" of the perfectioning process was out of the question. An amusing letter to John Adams shows that this thesis is descended from Theognis, the Pythagoreans, and Ocellus: "as a principle . . . coition is not for the sake of pleasure," but for the sake of procreation, to continue the uninterrupted course of generation as God intended and to work for the improvement of the race. Jefferson disposes of undue moralistic optimism briefly by commenting:

But nature, not trusting to this moral and abstract motive, seems to have provided more securely for the perpetuation of the species, by making it the effect of the *oestrum* implanted in the constitution of both sexes. And not only has the commerce of love been indulged on this unhallowed impulse, but made subservient also to wealth and ambition by marriage, without regard to the beauty, the healthiness, the understanding, or virtue of the subject from which we are to breed. The selecting the best male for a harem of well chosen females also, which Theognis seems to recommend from the example of our sheep and asses, would doubtless improve the human, as it does the brute animal, and produce a race of veritable $\alpha\rho\iota\sigma\tau\iota$. For experience proves that the moral and physical qualities of man, whether good or evil, are transmissible in a certain degree from father to son. But I suspect that the equal rights of man will rise up against this privileged Solomon and his harem, and oblige us to continue acquiescence under the "$\alpha\mu\alpha\nu\rho\omega\sigma\iota\varsigma\ \gamma\epsilon\nu\epsilon o\varsigma\ \alpha\sigma\tau\omega\nu$" which Theognis complains of, and to content ourselves with the accidental $\alpha\rho\iota\sigma\tau o\iota$ produced by the fortuitous concourse of breeders.[22]

Despite the limited context, Jefferson is paying tribute to normal human indifference and the normal human need for spontaneous,

[20] Cabanis, *Rapports*, I, 480. [21] *Ibid.*
[22] To John Adams, Monticello, October 28, 1813, M.E., XIII, 394.

unpremeditated, preferential behavior. The scientific possibility of gradually transforming or bettering the race was nothing more than the most abstract possibility. This practical critique of an obvious "idealism" about human affairs is typical of Jefferson's approach to social questions, and however strong we may find his own faith in ideals, it is safe to assume that it will never be of the unquestioning kind commonly attributed to him and other "idealists."

Jefferson finds another route to general psychology—via the distinction between the basic and the culturally acquired in human nature. Jefferson could feel free to criticize the specific comportment of Europeans, as compared with Americans, on this ground. He wrote even of his favorite French, "Nourish peace with their persons, but war against their manners. Every step we take towards the adoption of their manners is a step to perfect misery." [23] "Persons" against "manners" is perhaps the best way to point up the intended contrast. While "manners" change, types of personality are fundamental and therefore not eradicable.

Jefferson's now-famous letter on the "natural" classification of Whig and Tory takes on fresh meaning in this light. In that letter Jefferson says that the political differences between Whig and Tory (or liberal and conservative, if one prefers) is more than an evanescent political division. Human beings are temperamentally inclined either to one belief or to the other, and this is due to the total personality of the individual, his "natural" physical structure and intellectual dispositions and habits, not to fragmentary "decisions" on isolated issues. Jefferson approaches here the Jamesian reduction of philosophical opposites to temperamental manifestations. He gives voice to this idea in several letters. To Joel Barlow, he wrote:

The division into Whig and Tory is founded in the nature of men; the weakly and nerveless, the rich and corrupt, seeing more safety and accessibility in a strong executive; the healthy, firm, and virtuous, feeling confidence in their physical and moral resources, and willing to part with only so much power as is necessary for their good government; and, therefore, to retain the rest in the hands of the many, the division will substantially be into Whig and Tory, as in England formerly. [24]

[23] To Mrs. Trist, Paris, August 18, 1785, M.E., V, 80.
[24] To Joel Barlow, Washington, May 3, 1802, M.E., X, 319.

In a letter to Lafayette, Jefferson expands the psychological attributes characteristic of the two types:

The parties of Whig and Tory are those of nature. They exist in all countries, whether called by these names, or by those of aristocrats and democrats, coté droite and coté gauche, ultras and radicals, serviles and liberals. The sickly, weakly, timid man fears the people, and is a Tory by nature. The healthy, strong and bold, cherishes them, and is formed a Whig by nature.[25]

There is nowhere in Jefferson's writings an explicit statement concerning the location of the fissures in the surface "manners" and where one may expect basic human dispositions to show through. But we do know that political affairs at least are in broad outlines and for many years determined primarily by natural temperamental differences. Many of the disputes and conflicts arising in any society are to that extent necessary and natural; not to be eradicated as unhealthy or destructive, but to be tolerated as one of the normal modes of human vitality contributing to the order of society.[26] Furthermore, such natural differences are productive of useful criticism in society. While one may honestly prefer the Whigs, the Tories help to watch and criticize their every mistake, and vice versa. The natural suspicion of the two human types, fundamentally different from each other, is elaborated with some originality into the grand theme that there should be popular watchfulness over the trustees delegated with power by the people.

[25] To Marquis de Lafayette, Monticello, November 24, 1823, M.E., XV, 490.
[26] When Jefferson became reflective about the *principles* behind Republicans and Federalists, he treated them as natural divergences of judgment colored by personality. As he said, "One fears most the ignorance of the people; the other, the selfishness of rulers independent of them." To Mrs. John Adams, Monticello, September 11, 1804, M.E., XI, 52.

Chapter XIII

HISTORY AND SOCIAL

PROGRESS

A CURIOUS source of information about Jefferson's notion of cause in society is the following unpublished note which he wrote on the flyleaf of one of his books,[1] *An Enquiry into the Life and Writings of Homer,* by Thomas Blackwell.

A man who would enquire why such a particular poet as Homer existed at such a place, in such a time, would throw himself headlong into chimaera, and could never treat of such a subject without a multitude of false subtleties and refinements. He might as well pretend to give a reason why such particular generals as Fabius and Scipio lived in Rome at such a time, and why Fabius came into the world before Scipio. For such incidents as those no other reason can be given but that of Horace

> Scit genius, natale comes, qui temperat estrum
> Naturae deus humanae, mortalis in unum—
> —Quodque caprit (?); vultu mutabilis, albus et ater.

In short, accident, chance, and circumstance are in Jefferson's sceptical view just as real factors as "good and sufficient reasons" are. History is not a chain of necessary, planned, and directed links—or if it is, our human minds can never know it. We are urged, therefore, to stop and admit the ultimate fact of genius and ability, treating them on the level of natural "miracles," if preferred, but never as mysterious, supernatural forces, planned by a superreason for earthly appearance at that particular time.

In his *Autobiography* Jefferson tried to account for the success of the "appeal to the rights of man" against its entrenched tyrannical op-

[1] This book of Blackwell's is in the Rare Book Collection in the Library of Congress. The present writer, in going through the entire collection of Jefferson's books which now remain, found this note and also several others. These seem not to be known.

ponents by the total effect of the small additions of each individual's revolt. The individual revolt, then becoming contagious, spread out to more and more people.

This is a wonderful instance of great events from small causes. So inscrutable is the arrangement of causes and consequences in this world, that a two-penny duty on tea, unjustly imposed in a sequestered part of it, changes the condition of all its inhabitants.[2]

Here is implied caution against applying overrationalized principles to history. Reason is not always relevant or adequate to explain the natural growth of events or movements.

To find the positive implications of these opinions is not too difficult. Jefferson is really arguing a faith in the powers of the individual; history is not made by large "interests," organizations, or classes alone. In his day Jefferson was apparently impatient with the numerous historians who approach material with a priori "causal" principles. Therefore, in this instance, too, Jefferson sides with the practiced agnostic or the empirical scientist. Even more than other fields of study, historical events must be appraised as unique, unexpected, humanly unpredictable. There is, accordingly, no substitute for intimate detailed knowledge of a particular epoch.

Undoubtedly Jefferson's approach to history was influenced by the passages of Bolingbroke's that we have already noticed in his *Commonplace Book* and by the consistent trend in English empiricism and French positivism to make careful distinctions between "necessary" truths, probable ones, and those not even probable. Jefferson was evidently not a closet-empiricist. The language and method of careful, practical science is seen in a slightly different, but allied context, in his letter to a friend, written in a rather gloomy vein, about the shortcomings of the current newspapers in America. Jefferson put the proposal that some conscientious editor "might begin a reformation"; and the reformation was to be modeled on these lines; he would "divide his paper into four chapters, heading the 1st, Truths. 2d Probabilities. 3d, Possibilities. 4th Lies." [3] Specific instructions follow. Anybody who urges such a program for newspapers, is likely to expect at least this

[2] *Autobiography*, M.E., I, 158.
[3] To John Norvell, Washington, June 11, 1807, M.E., XI, 224–25.

from the historian. Therefore, while Jefferson's version of history-making and historiography was somewhat personalized, it was not in the tradition of anecdote, gossip, or literary and speculative psychological introspection.

The uses of history, once history is actually captured by the historians, are many. Briefly, history provides for learning about society, particularly about the failures to achieve good society. "History, in general, only informs us what bad government is." [4] To this extent history is an elaborate and detailed warning. For specific institutions within one's own society, history is of positive value; for example, to understand "our laws, language, religion, politics and manners," [5] Jefferson recommends that we study their English foundations, in which our institutions are "so deeply laid." In the last analysis, however, the most important use of history is for the control of social programs for the future. In this sense the obtaining of historical truth is one of the most vital social pursuits imaginable. Its immediate influence upon men's opinions is tremendous, since it can inculcate political beliefs under the guise of simple information. This was what Jefferson held against Hume's *History of England*.[6] While he admitted the brilliance of the work, he accused Hume of starting with his Tory prejudices and reworking all the prior facts to fit his own reactionary political tendencies. He therefore urged Duane, on one occasion,[7] to publish an American edition of a revised, edited, and annotated version of the *History*, which he felt had not sufficiently reached the American public through its one small English edition; he thought this advisable in order to counteract the damage Hume had already done to the American public.

Yet there is no doubt that history, if truly presented (by which Jefferson meant not only scientific accuracy of verified fact, but more Whiggish in interpretation than Tory) was a most constructive social force. Anyone reading its dire lessons of unleashed ambition, corrupt power, and tyranny ("the Borgias") would be forewarned; ensuing

[4] To John Norvell, Washington, June 11, 1807, M.E., XI, 224–25.
[5] To William Duane, Monticello, August 12, 1810, M.E., XII, 405.
[6] See Jefferson's repeated explanation of the brilliance, but biased politics, of Hume's history, and its devastatingly bad Tory effect upon the younger generation. Letters of June 11, 1807 (to Norvell); August 12, 1810 (to Duane); November 25, 1816 (to John Adams); etc.
[7] To Wm. Duane, Monticello, August 12, 1810, M.E., XII, 404.

plans for the government of society would be so projected that the same mistakes, at least, might not recur. If we recall the history of people in slavery or of the dictators who enslave them (for example, Bonaparte, "the unprincipled tyrant who is deluging the continent of Europe with blood" [8]), we naturally wish to do everything possible to safeguard a free government. Knowledge in this case is already one degree of power. Or, as Jefferson framed it,

A word of truth to us is like the drop of water supplicated from the tip of Lazarus' finger. It is an observation of latitude and longitude to the mariner long enveloped in clouds, for correcting the ship's way. [9]

But Jefferson really extended this analysis of the directive power of "a word of truth" to the more comprehensive scale of the freedom of opinion, the progress of science, and the freedom, progress, and happiness of society in general.

Historical truth can be current only in a society where opinions are free; and wherever opinions are free there are discoveries made, facts multiply, and sciences take root and grow. [10] The causal chain continues, because where science is encouraged and knowledge is readily and quickly amassed, there prejudice, oppression, and tyranny cannot take root. It is exactly the development of knowledge and the spread of science and knowledge which makes man determined to preserve his freedom, and even to better it. [11] Enlightenment and tolerance of all diverse shades of opinion are the fruits of the most free and peaceful societies. While these are the terminus of the causative chain described, it may be noticed that there is more than a hint of circularity in a process which begins with free opinions and ends with them. Jefferson's circularity is in this case not vicious, since even occasional, accidental truth and piecemeal freedom in society may suffice to generate the causative process, whose terminus, notwithstanding, will be freedom and enlightenment.

Wherever knowledge has increased and mental habits have improved, we have a condition of progress which demands the further progress of objective institutions such as law, education, and so forth.

[8] To Dr. George Logan, Monticello, October 3, 1813, M.E., XII, 384.
[9] To John Quincy Adams, Monticello, November 1, 1817, M.E., XV, 144.
[10] To Benjamin Waring, Washington, March 23, 1801, M.E., X, 235.
[11] To General Kosciusko, Monticello, February 26, 1810, M.E., XII, 365.

Laws and institutions must go hand in hand with the progress of the human mind. As that becomes more developed, more enlightened, as new discoveries are made, new truths disclosed, and manners and opinions change with the change of circumstances, institutions must advance also, and keep pace with the times. We might as well require a man to wear still the coat which fitted him when a boy, as civilized society to remain ever under the regimen of their barbarous ancestors.[12]

It was also Jefferson's belief that should this natural accompaniment of mental progress be somehow stopped (he refers to the unyielding monarchs who have "lately deluged Europe in blood"), violence and blood will be the "rash and ruinous innovations" substituted for the peaceful, intelligent deliberations of a nation friendly to self-improvement. The progress of the mind thus appears to be the first condition in Jefferson's account, and social progress is considered its creation (while social waste and barbarity are the results of fixed mental and moral habits). The desirable encouragement of "progressive accommodation to progressive improvement" [13] provided by a good government is the only sensible attitude to strike in the face of our knowledge of history, society, and nature.

[12] To Samuel Kercheval, Monticello, July 12, 1816, M.E., XV, 41.   [13] *Ibid.*

Chapter XIV

POLITICAL RELATIVISM

"RELATIVISM" was a sophisticated social hypothesis which, unlike most eighteenth-century social philosophy, gave credit to the functions of time and local circumstance in the determination of the state of progress of any society. Intellectually, the influence must have been Montesquieu, under whose influence Jefferson had found himself since his student days. The *Commonplace Book* is well-supplied with passages from Montesquieu's *Spirit of the Laws*,[1] passages which reveal plainly enough that Jefferson had carefully familiarized himself with everything that Montesquieu had to suggest. Apart from specific ideas which Jefferson later borrowed,[2] Chinard points out that the fundamental idea that flexible moral codes vary with change of circumstance was quickly picked up by Jefferson and made his own.

Partout il a retrouvé cette idée, qu'il devait défendre toute sa vie, que les lois humaines sont variables et changeantes, qu'elles varient avec la nature des chôses et les moeurs, et, allant plus loin que Montesquieu, il ira jusqu'à proclamer qu'une génération d'hommes n'a pas le droit de légiférer pour les générations qui suivront.[3]

However, there is no reason to assume that Jefferson followed Montesquieu in all respects. On the contrary, as the concept of moral relativism attained explicit and practical import for Jefferson's thinking, it came to modify considerably the unimaginative, literal tendency of the *Spirit of the Laws*.

With regard to "principles," Jefferson clearly indicated that habits

[1] See Gilbert Chinard's *Pensées choisies de Montesquieu; tirées du "Common-Place Book" de Thomas Jefferson* . . . The years between 1764 and 1774 are, in Chinard's judgment, "l'étude approfondie de Montesquieu par Jefferson, en tout cas, avant la révision des statuts de la Virginie, avant la Déclaration d'Indépendance, avant la période vraiment active et féconde de sa vie politique" (p. 23).
[2] *Ibid.*, Chinard's Introduction, pp. 23-24.   [3] *Ibid.*

were equally important in determining the political form of a nation and that a blend of habits and principles decided the character of a government.

In other parts of our government I hope we shall be able by degrees to introduce sound principles and make them habitual. What is practicable must often control what is pure theory, and the habits of the governed determine in a great degree what is practicable. Hence the same original principles, modified in practice according to the different habits of different nations, present governments of very different aspects.[4]

It is in this form that Jefferson subscribed to the theory of political relativism. As he explained, the same principles might be applied to very different conditions, resulting in more or less political liberty; but this did not mean that the principles are not objective and continuous. Just as certainly, however, this excluded the possibility that any principles at all (for example, complete suffrage, self-government) might be forced upon a people in no matter what condition of development and receptivity they might be. For instance, referring to his own cautious judgment that prior to the French Revolution the French people were capable of nothing better than a constitutional monarchy, Jefferson, in 1801, tried to articulate the principle which had been his guide:

I am sensible how far I should fall short of effecting all the reformation which reason would suggest, and experience approve, were I free to do whatever I thought best; but when we reflect how difficult it is to move or inflect the great machine of society, how impossible to advance the notions of a whole people suddenly to ideal right we see the wisdom of Solon's remark, that no more good must be attempted than the nation can bear . . .[5]

On another occasion Jefferson made it a point to congratulate Dupont de Nemours for his work in behalf of a newly formed South American republic. "Like Solon to the Athenians, you have given to your Columbians, not the best possible government, but the best they can bear."[6]

Again and again one notices Jefferson's appreciation of the process of social acculturation, its close dependence upon the daily habits of a

[4] *The Correspondence of Jefferson and Dupont de Nemours,* edited by Gilbert Chinard, p. 37. Not in M.E.
[5] To Dr. Walter Jones, Washington, March 31, 1801, M.E., X, 256.
[6] To Dupont de Nemours, Poplar Forest, April 24, 1816, M.E., XIV, 492.

people, and the psychological expectations linked with them. Finally, in terms of this complex social orientation, the category of need becomes focal. It is always, then, in the light of the very specific needs of a nation that reforms or ideal principles must be adjusted and made suitable. Otherwise there will be violations of the genuine interests of a people—interests being defined by those same needs which custom, habit, expectation, and the comprehension which is based on these have forged. The best concrete illustration of this part of Jefferson's theory of social relativism can be found in his political recommendations offered to French patriots prior to and during the French Revolution. Years later he recalled his advice in a letter to Lafayette.

Possibly you may remember, at the date of the *jeu de paume*, how earnestly I urged yourself and the patriots of my acquaintance, to enter them into a compact with the king, securing freedom of the press, trial by jury, habeas corpus, and a national legislature, all of which it was known he would then yield, to go home, and let these work on the amelioration of the condition of the people, until they should have rendered them capable of more, when occasions would not fail to arise for communicating to them more. This was as much as I then thought them able to bear, soberly and usefully for themselves.[7]

With characteristic honesty, however, he concedes that Lafayette was right in estimating the capacity of the French for self-government a little more generously. "You thought otherwise, and that the dose might be still larger. And I found you were right; for subsequent events proved they were equal to the constitution of 1791 . . ." Unfortunately the patriots who were more radical than Lafayette made the "fatal error of the republicans," from which "flowed all the subsequent sufferings and crimes of the French Nation." To Jefferson, the scourge of Napoleon was a symbol of that error. But that scourge had at last been removed, and Jefferson knew that republican political principles had to be carefully guarded from extremism.

A full measure of liberty is not now perhaps to be expected by your nation, nor am I confident they are prepared to preserve it. More than a generation will be requisite, under the administration of reasonable laws favoring the progress of knowledge in the general mass of the people, and their habitua-

[7] To the Marquis de Lafayette, Monticello, February 14, 1815, M.E., XIV, 246.

tion to an independent security of person and property, before they will be capable of estimating the value of freedom, and the necessity of a sacred adherence to the principles on which it rests for preservation. Instead of that liberty which takes root and growth in the progress of reason, if recovered by mere force or accident, it becomes, with an unprepared people, a tyranny still, of the many, the few, or the one.[8]

Where Montesquieu would rely upon three fundamental forms of government, Jefferson sincerely believed that there is a "best" form of government, a limiting ideal toward which legislators, statesmen, and educators may look for inspiration and guidance. But the wise man would understand that this political ideal, like any other, needs careful and loyal tending—needs the appropriate time, place, and guidance to make it mature.

[8] To the Marquis de Lafayette, Monticello, February 14, 1815, M.E., XIV, 245.

Chapter XV

NATURAL RIGHTS

MANY people have assailed the "glittering generalities" of natural rights, without having discovered the full meaning beneath the phrase. Part of that meaning has always been only conventional; but sometimes deeper minds used the phrase, for want of a better, to express their most momentous perceptions of the needs or claims of men in society. Jefferson's interpretation of natural rights is not constant, nor is it clearly formulated, but rarely is it superficial.

To what extent is the doctrine of the American *Declaration of Independence* characteristic of Jefferson's version of the natural rights theory? Let us first recall Jefferson's original version of the *Declaration,* which, before Congress made its modifications, read:

. . . that all men are created equal; that they are endowed by their creator with *inherent and* inalienable rights; that among these are life, liberty and the pursuit of happiness; that whenever any form of government becomes destructive of these ends, it is the right of the people to alter or abolish it . . .[1] [Italics mine.]

And an entire passage concerned with slavery, which was later omitted, charged:

He has waged cruel war against human nature itself, violating its most sacred rights of life and liberty in the persons of a distant people who never offended him, captivating and carrying them into slavery in another hemisphere, or to incur miserable death in their transportation thither. This piratical warfare, the opprobium of *Infidel* powers, is the warfare of the *Christian* king of Great Britain. Determined to keep open a market where *Men* should be bought and sold, he has prostituted his negative for suppressing every legislative attempt to prohibit or to restrain this execrable commerce. And

[1] *Autobiography,* M.E., I, 29. For "inherent and" Jefferson substituted "certain" inalienable rights.

that this assemblage of horrors might want no fact of distinguished die, he is now exciting those very people to rise in arms against us, and to purchase that liberty of which he has deprived them, by murdering the people on whom he also obtruded them; thus paying off former crimes which he urges them to commit against the *Lives* of another.[2]

One other passage, also deleted from the final version, treats the terms of our "emigration and settlement here":

. . . that these were effected at the expense of our own blood and treasure, unassisted by the wealth or the strength of Great Britain: that in constituting indeed our several forms of government, we had adopted one common king, thereby laying a foundation for perpetual league and amity with them: but that submission to their parliament was no part of our constitution, nor ever in idea, if history may be credited.

These extremely interesting passages which Jefferson wrote into his version of the *Declaration* are (together with what we all know as the accepted final form) revelatory of Jefferson's belief about natural rights, in his first publicly held version of the theory.

There is one other source for this early version, not as generally referred to as the *Declaration*, but even a little earlier than it. Confirmation of the ideas in the *Declaration* and further theoretical support for them, is here available. This document is *A Summary View of the Rights of British America*, which Jefferson explicitly said "was not written for publication." He called it "a draft I had prepared for a petition to the King, which I meant to propose in my place as a member of the convention of 1774." Illness forced him to send on the draft to the Speaker, who found after submitting it to the members that "it was thought too strong for the times, and to become the act of the Convention, but was printed by subscription of the members." Jefferson comments: "If it had any merit, it was that of first taking our true ground, and that which was afterwards assumed and maintained."[3]

---

[2] *Autobiography*, M.E., I, 34–35. See also letter to Brissot de Warville, Paris, February 12, 1788, M.E., VI, 428, in which Jefferson declines membership in the Society for Abolition of Slave Trade: "I am here as a public servant and those whom I serve having never yet been able to give their voice against this practice, it is decent for me to avoid too public a demonstration of my wishes to see it abolished." This letter (press copy) in the Jefferson Collection, Library of Congress, is listed "February 11th."

[3] To John W. Campbell, Monticello, September 3, 1809, M.E., XII, 307.

In the *Summary* Jefferson made the following theoretical observations:

From the nature of things, every society must, at all times, possess within itself the sovereign powers of legislation. The feelings of human nature revolt against the supposition of a State so situated, as that it may not, in any emergency, provide against dangers which, perhaps, threaten immediate ruin.[4]

Jefferson reaches a climax of rhetorical and philosophical accent in his closing section of advice to the King:

. . . these are our grievances . . . laid before his Majesty, with that freedom of language and sentiment which becomes a free people, claiming their rights as derived from the laws of nature, and not as the gift of the Chief Magistrate. Let those flatter, who fear; it is not an American art. To give praise where it is not due might be well from the venal, but it would ill become those who are asserting the rights of human nature.[5]

A few lines later Jefferson concentrates on the moral theory behind natural rights.

The great principles of right and wrong are legible to every reader; to pursue them, requires not the aid of many counselors. The whole art of government consists in the art of being honest. Only aim to do your duty, and mankind will give you credit where you fail. No longer persevere in Sacrificing the rights of one part of the empire to the inordinate desires of another; but deal out to all, equal and impartial right . . .

This is followed by a plea for compromise and union, but ends with a significant warning:

But let them not think to exclude us from going to other markets to dispose of those commodities which they cannot use, nor to supply those wants which they cannot supply. Still less, let it be proposed, that our properties, within our territories, shall be taxed or regulated by any power on earth, but our own. The God who gave us life, gave us liberty at the same time; the hand of force may destroy, but cannot disjoin them.

The cumulative thought of these passages is as illuminating about Jefferson's version of natural rights, in its first form, as anything in his

---

[4] *Autobiography*, Appendix C, M.E., I, 204–5.
[5] *A Summary View of the Rights of British America*, M.E., II, 209–10.

writings. It appears that this version is reminiscent of other radical, secularized religious statements of compact theory.[6] "The God who gave us life, gave us liberty at the same time," and therefore all human beings, banded together in any association or society, are inherently above the lashings of force. No power on earth, legal or brute, can rightfully (this is what was meant) "disjoin" life from liberty.

Beginning, therefore, with the living individual creature who issues from the hand of the Maker with the right to live, to work, to realize and enjoy the fruits of his work, to govern himself by choosing his own type of government by law, which is to operate on the soil which he has made his own, Jefferson proceeds to deduce social corollaries from this set of assumptions. For instance there is: the right of revolution for victims of oppressive taxation and harsh legislation; the right to trade with any foreign nation; the right to own soil taken and remade by one's own toil; the right to expect "equal and impartial" treatment for every group within a nation or empire; the right to liberty and the pursuit of happiness, which makes slavery a "cruel war against human nature itself" and which makes the first and greatest mandate for any society that it shall "possess within itself the sovereign powers of legislation."

From piety and the Creator to human nature and thence to specific natural rights for society is a sequence made possible by the "moral sense" theory which Jefferson was using at that time.[7] As the tone of sarcasm in the passage on slavery shows ("This piratical warfare, the approbium of *Infidel* powers, is the warfare of the *Christian* king . . ."), Jefferson could hardly conceal his hatred for ceremonial, institutionalized Christianity.[8] Just as frankly, he found himself refer-

[6] See, e.g., the account of John Wise's version of Congregationalism in Schneider, *The Puritan Mind*, pp. 95–96; of left-wing English Puritans' "natural rights" theories in Pooke, *Fountain-Sources of American Political Theory*, p. 74; of "Separatist Theory of Compact," in McLaughlin, *Foundations of American Constitutionalism*.

[7] See section on Henry Home, Lord Kames, in Chapter I.

[8] That Jefferson never made peace with the Church until his very late acceptance of the liberal Unitarians is shown in numerous letters. See particularly: To John Adams, Monticello, April 11, 1823, M.E., XV, 425–30; to Dr. Thomas Cooper, Monticello, November 2, 1822, M.E., XV, 404; and to Horatio G. Spafford, Monticello, March 17, 1814, where Jefferson says: "In every country and in every age, the priest has been hostile to liberty. He is always in alliance with the despot, abetting his abuses

ring to what he knew was both more genuine religion and more trustworthy social policy, namely, "the great principles of right and wrong
. . . legible to every reader," the true morality to which human nature has been providently attuned.

Individual liberty and social freedom are the broadest "natural
rights," and to some degree symbolic of the indefinite number of
specific rights one can infer from them. Everything points to the conclusion that Jefferson's early, conventional form of "natural rights"
theory was purely in moral terms; his language is less the language
of history, even though he often makes much of historical precedent,[9]
or description, and more the language of what is morally becoming to
man as man. Notions like those of "inherent and inalienable" rights,
"equal and impartial right," "the God who gave us life, gave us
liberty,"—are all obviously moral terminology. There was good reason
for stating the argument for liberty in the moral mode. Many critics
have adverted unfavorably to the self-interest present in the case against
foreign rule, and in pointing it out they tend to suggest that the arguments are therefore suspect.[10] Whatever the case may be for other

---

in return for protection to his own . . . they have perverted the purest religion
ever preached to man into mystery and jargon, unintelligible to mankind, and therefore the safer engine for their purposes." M.E., XIV, 119–20. Unitarianism was
the most sensible and least artificial Christian religion Jefferson had encountered.
Channing's pronouncement that "the benevolent spirit of Jesus" had to be restored
to his "divided and afflicted Church" and that orthodoxy and creed were alien to a
genuine and moral Christianity was obviously congenial to Jefferson's outlook.
[9] See the passage in *A Summary View of the Rights of British America* (I, 206–7) on
property, where Jefferson develops the interesting argument that Saxon law, the basis
of common law, regarded all lands as held in absolute right; while later Norman
law, with feudal ties, asserted all lands in England were held "either mediately
or immediately of the Crown." Jefferson appeals to the tradition of Saxon laws,
therefore, for his denial that the King had any right to grant lands "of himself."
"From the nature and purpose of civil institutions, all the lands within the limits,
which any particular party has circumscribed around itself, are assumed by that
society, and subject to their allotment; this may be done by themselves assembled
collectively, or by their legislature, to whom they may have delegated sovereign authority; and, if they are alloted in neither of these ways, each individual of the
society, may appropriate to himself such lands as he finds vacant, and occupancy
will give him title." One should, incidentally, refer back to this passage for the
ultimate ground of Jefferson's dictum that "the earth belongs to the living." M.E.,
I, 206–7.
[10] Carl Becker, for instance, in *The Declaration of Independence*, says cleverly, but
with some misdirection: "That there is a 'natural order' of things in the world,

supporters of natural rights, Jefferson at least furnishes evidence that his own moral and religious beliefs were as genuine as his political theory would lead one to expect. For the doctrine of moral sense which he adhered to at this time is the genuine base of his political ideals. In fact, there is no other way to understand Jefferson's persistent opposition to Hobbes's reliance on self-interest as the efficient and final cause of social organization. Jefferson was profoundly convinced of the truth of the moral-sense doctrine, but he was a utilitarian in politics. In this he followed the Lockean tradition. We must keep in mind these two facets of Jefferson's political thought, or else his theory of natural rights looks wholly conventional, in the air, and purely expedient. The whole point of Jefferson's theory is different from Hume's radical utilitarianism. He regarded moral sense and natural rights as necessary allies. Moral-sense philosophy for Jefferson, as in the case of Locke and the earlier Scottish tradition, was defended as a basis for political liberty, not as a basis for theological intuition.

That "the whole art of government consists in the art of being honest" is unambiguous evidence that Jefferson opposed a "natural" moralism to the reputed "natural" rule of force.[11]

To a certain degree Jefferson never departed from this version of the natural rights theory; or rather, he restated the theory at different times, even late in his life, in this same form. One illustration will suffice. In a letter to Judge Johnson, written in 1823, just three years before Jefferson's death, he identified the aims and beliefs of his Republican party in the following fashion:

---

cleverly and expertly designed by God for the guidance of mankind; that the 'laws' of this natural order may be discovered by human reason; that these laws so discovered furnish a reliable and immutable standard for testing the ideas, the conduct, and the institutions of men—these were the accepted premises, the preconceptions, of most eighteenth century thinking, not only in America but also in England and France. They were, as Jefferson says, the 'sentiments of the day, whether expressed in conversation, in letters, printed essays, or the elementary books of public right.' Where Jefferson got his ideas is hardly so much a question as where he could have got away from them" (p. 27). There were many who managed quite easily to "get away from them," and there were many who accepted them without in any fashion making themselves responsible for the implications and basic principles from which these sentiments were derived. The nature of Jefferson's adherence is, therefore, worth ascertaining.

[11] Jefferson sees the issue much as Locke does in his second *Treatise of Civil Government*, when he answers Hobbes's argument.

Ours . . . was to maintain the will of the majority of the convention, and of the people themselves. We believed, with them, that man was a rational animal, endowed by nature with rights, and with an innate sense of justice; and that he could be restrained from wrong and protected in right, by moderate powers, confided to persons of his own choice, and held to their duties by dependence on his own will.[12]

But it is significant that Jefferson gave this account of the beliefs of the Republican party in opposition to the Federal party, which, he maintained, had devoted itself to recovering "in practise the powers which the nation had refused." The specific occasion for reviewing the history of the two parties in these terms was apparently Judge Johnson's intention of writing a history of the two parties. Jefferson wished to remind him that the charge that the Republicans had been merely an opposition party, "seeking for office," was quite false in the face of the principled difference in theory of power, sovereignty, and rights which existed between the two parties. In principle the Federalists looked to European writings and practices, "especially of England." This was enough to establish a cleavage, since

the doctrines of Europe were, that men in numerous associations cannot be restrained within the limits of order and justice, but by forces physical and moral, wielded over them by authorities independent of their will. Hence their organization of kings, hereditary nobles, and priests.[13]

In line with this European tradition, the Federalists "endeavored to draw the cords of power as tight as they could obtain them." [14]

The importance of this account must not be overlooked. It shows, first, that Jefferson retained his fundamental thesis about the opposition between two theories of society (one founded on force, bolstered by privilege, and administered by power-thirsty functionaries and orders independent of the will of the people; the other founded on reason and justice, marked by faith in natural rights, governed by deputies of the people, chosen by them and dependent on their will). While the basis of this account is to be found in Locke, as we noticed, and for that matter even earlier, in Hooker, Jefferson's elaboration of it is nevertheless his own, and has special significance in America. Indeed, he

[12] To Judge William Johnson, Monticello, June 12, 1823, M.E., XV, 441.
[13] *Ibid.*, p. 440.   [14] *Ibid.*, p. 441.

himself said, almost fifty years after writing the *Declaration of Independence:* "Neither aiming at originality of principle or sentiment, nor yet copied from any particular and previous writing, it was intended to be an expression of the American mind . . .[15] But unquestionably the *Declaration* owes more to European thought than does his late formulation of the two opposed theories of society. Placing the Whig theory of natural rights in the context of American republicanism and then narrowing down American republicanism to the views and practices of the Republican party, Jefferson makes Federalism synonymous with society founded on the subjection of the people instead of their independence.[16]

The second important implication can be derived from Jefferson's failure to mention explicitly the word "contract." This is not the only passage where the expectation of some form of contract theory is disappointed. Although Jefferson makes so much of natural rights, he rarely speaks directly of the social contract, and nowhere does he distinguish between different versions of the theory, despite his very full knowledge of Grotius, Pufendorf, Vattel, Montesquieu, Locke, Rousseau, Paine, and others.

The reason for this apparently mysterious omission lies in the interpretation Jefferson gave of "constitutions." When Jefferson did deal with contract, it appeared under the form of Constitutional theory. His ideas about contract theory, therefore, are at once more concrete and functional than those of his republican predecessors. But it should be understood that this aspect of Jefferson's thought did not emerge until 1789 and is an improved utilitarian extension of the natural rights theory in the *Declaration*. In a letter to Madison, from Paris, Jefferson produces his startling theory that constitutions and laws are essentially contracts with the living citizens of a country and that when the contracting generation no longer exists, the constitution and laws are no longer binding.[17] This famous letter, which is really an essay in political theory, is introduced with the query "whether one generation of men

---

[15] To Henry Lee, Monticello, May 8, 1825, M.E., XVI, 118. Jefferson further admitted that its sentiments were probably founded on those available in the "elementary books of public right, as Aristotle, Cicero, Locke, Sidney, etc."
[16] To Judge Wm. Johnson, Monticello, June 12, 1823, M.E., XV, 440.
[17] To Madison, Paris, Sept. 6, 1789, M.E., VII, 454-62.

has a right to bind another." The general form of the answer is contained in the powerful phrase, "the earth belongs in usufruct to the living." Since the Constitution is the fundamental law and only actual contract of society, the extremely short period [18] allowed for its rightful operation gives tremendous weight to the need for periodic self-criticism and revision of the Constitution. It is a literal expression of consent to the particular government each citizen must live by. Thus, Jefferson's treatment of contract is to be considered an attempt to give concrete value to the ideal "inalienable rights" and sovereignty of the people postulated in the American *Declaration*.[19] In this process of implementation the absolutist metaphysical character of natural rights and social compact disappear; and a more practical ideal is evolved, which conceives the basic right to self-government (the guarantor of the derivative rights of life, liberty, and pursuit of happiness) as a limited contract with the present members of society, formalized in a constitution.[20]

A further development, of extraordinary interest, is realized when Jefferson refines the notion of basic natural right still further. This is done by introducing the new language of reserved natural rights and acquired ones, or "fences." This more complete analysis of rights occurs in a letter to Noah Webster in 1790:

. . . the purposes of society do not require a surrender of all our rights to our ordinary governors; that there are certain portions of right not necessary to enable them to carry on an effective government, and which experience has nevertheless proved they will be constantly encroaching on, if submitted to them; that there are also certain fences which experience has proved peculiarly efficacious against wrong, and rarely obstructive of right, which yet the governing powers have ever since shown a disposition to weaken and remove. Of the first kind, for instance, is freedom of religion; of the

[18] In the first version of this theory, 34 years; later recomputed as 19 years. (See: To Samuel Kercheval, Monticello, July 12, 1816, M.E., XV, 42.)

[19] Also, see the version in *The Summary View of the Rights of British America:* "From the nature of things, every society must, at all times, possess within itself the sovereign powers of legislation. The feelings of human nature revolt against the supposition of a State so situated, as that it may not, in any emergency, provide against dangers which, perhaps, threaten immediate ruin."

[20] The relationship between this position and that of the Mayflower compact, e.g., is obviously close. But both of these are more contracts for a reasonable and desirable society than statements about the origin of society in general.

second, trial by jury, habeas corpus laws, free presses. These were the settled opinions of all the States . . .[21]

The context, of course, is changed in this letter, since the function of constitutions and bills of rights is considered under the broader topic of states' rights. The conclusion Jefferson reaches shows that the "fences against wrong" and the "unceded portions of right" were written into "instruments called declarations of right and constitutions." In this passage, in short, he makes no distinction between declarations of rights and constitutions, but regards both as instruments for safeguarding the rights not surrendered by the sovereign people to their governors. The implication is that natural rights are human potentialities for freedom and happiness, some of which are freely given over to society to ensure "effective government." Others, however, are specifically and expressly reserved, stated in declarations and constitutions, so that the potentialities for these freedoms may be actualized. The recognized power latent in fundamental manifestoes and laws of the land is necessary to make every individual's claim to "rights" a real privilege and a sturdy fence. Only the owners of the fences, incidentally, can arrange for their removal. "None of the reserved rights can be touched without resorting to the people to appoint another convention for the express purpose of permitting it . . ."[22] The compelling thoughts here are undoubtedly distrust and individualist resistance to "too much" power. The original nature of human rights, however, is not freshly investigated at this point, except in so far as the tendency of the doctrine of rights as reserved privileges and fences entails the revision of the theory contained in the *Declaration*. Rights are now seen to be so seducible by the encroaching governors of society that the primary problem in connection with them is to find instruments whereby they may be fenced off from aggression.

The third important perspective on natural rights used by Jefferson defies exact dating. He writes in his *Autobiography* [23] concerning his early fight in Virginia to abolish the law of primogeniture. The reasons he advanced against the opposition are of great interest for the natural rights theory. He said:

[21] To Noah Webster, Philadelphia, December 4, 1790, M.E., VIII, 112–13.
[22] *Ibid*.   [23] Written at the age of 77.

Mr. Pendleton wished to preserve the right of primogeniture, but seeing that that could not prevail, he proposed . . . a double portion to the elder son. I observed, that if the eldest son could eat twice as much, or do double work, it might be a natural evidence of his right to a double portion; but being on a par in his powers and wants, with his brothers and sisters, he should be on a par also in the partition of the patrimony . . .[24]

This is a remarkably clear-cut identification of "natural right" with "organic need" and with claims based proportionately upon an individual's capacity. The location of natural rights in needs is at once the least conventional and the most fruitful theoretical line Jefferson anywhere takes. It ties up with the biological and psychological emphasis present in Jefferson's philosophical approach and makes comprehensible the insistence upon natural rights as universal claims. Since Jefferson conceded a "fundamental human nature," despite acquired diversities of habit, "natural rights" can be the name for the common, basic needs that are manifest in all human beings—to live, to sustain life, and to have freedom of motion (including the rights of assemblage and expatriation), and, above all, of thought and expression. The strategical importance, consequently, of the right to self-government consists in its *sine qua non* function.[25] No other rights (life, property, happiness) can be realized in society unless one has the power to initiate, change, alter, abolish, or limit governing power.

When organic need is thus made the meaning of "natural right," one can also perceive the biological character of the demand for "equality" of rights. Equal rights were, in Jefferson's opinion, the foundation of republican government, and republican government (as we shall see) was the only form of government in harmony with natural rights. As Jefferson phrased it, "the equal right of every citizen, in his person and property" [26] are the firm basis of good republican government. Equal

[24] *Autobiography*, M.E., I, 64.

[25] This is apparent as early as 1779, when Jefferson wrote, in his *Bill for Proportioning Crimes and Punishments:* "Whereas, it frequently happens that wicked . . . men . . . commit violations on the lives, liberties, and property of others, *and, the secure enjoyment of these having principally induced men to enter into society,* government would be defective in its principal purpose, were it not to restrain such criminal acts . . ." (italics mine); Appendix to *Autobiography*, Note E, M.E., I, 218.

[26] To Samuel Kercheval, Monticello, July 12, 1816, M.E., XV, 36.

rights, as an argument, find support in the presupposed common human needs. The demands of each individual are consequently on a par with anyone else's. This explains the radically individualistic tone of some of Jefferson's writing about "rights." It is, for example, at the bottom of his theory of live sovereignty, which interprets "consent of the governed" in terms of immediate relationships with the living generation, approximated in the will of the majority. It makes clear other features of his political thinking as well: insistence upon the right of expatriation, of asylum, of freedom of the seas, complete theoretical condemnation of slavery; and, in truth, it is the cement of his entire theory of republican government.

The Law of Nature and Nations for Jefferson becomes another illustration of his theory of rights. The key to this is given in the view that each nation "forms a moral person" and every member of a nation is "personally responsible for his society." Jefferson resented the position that international affairs and political affairs are exempt from the demands of morality.

To say . . . that gratitude is never to enter into the motives of national conduct, is to revive a principle which has been buried for centuries with its kindred principles of the lawfulness of assassination, poison, perjury, etc. All of these were legitimate principles in the dark ages which intervened between ancient and modern civilization, but exploded and held in just horror in the eighteenth century. I know but one code of morality for men, whether acting singly or collectively. He who says I will be a rogue when I act in company with a hundred others, but an honest man when I act alone, will be believed in the former assertion, but not in the latter. . . . If the morality of one man produces a just line of conduct in him, acting individually, why should not the morality of 100 men produce a just line of conduct in them acting together? [27]

That the law of nature and nations is primarily a moral domain, dependent upon the same norms as individual behavior, is most clearly expressed in the context of an official paper discussing natural right, treaties, authority, and similar subjects.

The law of nations . . . is composed of three branches. 1. The moral law of our nature. 2. The usages of nations. 3. Their special conventions. The

[27] To James Madison, Paris, August 28, 1789, M.E., VII, 448–49.

first of these only concerns this question, that is to say the moral law to which man has been subjected by his creator, and of which his feelings or conscience, as it is sometimes called, are the evidence with which his creator has furnished him. The moral duties which exist between individual and individual in a state of nature, accompany them into a state of society, and the aggregate of the duties of all the individuals composing the society constitutes the duties of that society towards any other; so that between society and society the same moral duties exist as did between the individuals composing them, while in an unassociated state, and their maker not having released them from those duties on their forming themselves into a nation. Compacts then, between nation and nation, are obligatory on them by the same moral law which obliges individuals to observe their compacts.[28]

The limits upon the moral conduct of nations are the same as those upon relations between man and man. The only thing which outweighs the laws of nature and nations (conceived morally) is the transcendent and primeval right to resist self-destruction.

There are circumstances, which sometimes excuse the non-performance of contracts between man and man; so are there also between nation and nation. When performance, for instance, becomes *impossible*, non-performance is not immoral: so if performance becomes self-destructive to the party, the law of self-preservation overrules the laws of obligations in others.[29]

Jefferson claims that the sources from which these remarks are drawn are human reason and feeling. Indeed he insists that these are the only valid "evidences" for natural rights or law in general.

For the reality of these principles I appeal to the true fountains of evidence, the head and heart of every rational and honest man. It is there nature has written her moral laws, and where every man may read them for himself. He will never read there the permission to annul his obligations for a time, or forever, whenever they become dangerous, useless or disagreeable . . . And tho he may, under certain degrees of danger, yet the danger must be imminent, and the degree great. Of these, it is true, that nations are to be judges for themselves; since no one nation has a right to sit in judgment over another, but the tribunal of our consciences remains, and that also of the opinion of the world.[30]

In final analysis the "opinion of the world" substitutes for individual conscience in judging the acts of nations. The operation, of world-wide

---

[28] M.E., III, 227.   [29] *Ibid.*, p. 228.   [30] *Ibid.*

conscience, however, is slower than that of private conscience, and consequently less effective. Therefore, there is a corresponding degree of disorganization existing in the usages of nations and in the judgment of "mankind" upon those usages.

The cumulative implication of the passages cited brings out the moral dimension of the law of nature and nations. Wherever the interpretation of natural law weighs heavily on the side of justice, the cleavage between a theory of natural law and natural rights disappears. It is for this reason that Jefferson is able to maintain that he is "convinced man has no natural right in opposition to his social duties." [31] The law of nature and nations is thus part of moral philosophy, just as the theory of rights is, only not so fully. The second and third divisions of the law of nature and nations, namely, usages of nations and their special conventions, are more properly questions of law than right.

Although Jefferson was deeply interested in both aspects, his treatment of natural law is typically moral. The legal and historical material is used as documentation, illustration, or proof for the moral arguments. I believe this explains why Jefferson found such difficulty in deciding whether to classify the law of nature and nations with moral philosophy or with the department of law. His vacillations are on record in his reports on educational curricula for the proposed college, and they testify eloquently to the twofold connotation of the law of nature and nations in Jefferson's thought. [32]

The same combination of basic self-interest and need, tempered by coöperation and justice for others is consequently repeated for the supersociety of nations dealing with nations. That is the ground for the stated exception to international obligations and promises: self-preservation comes first for a country, as it does for a person. The needs of nations, considered in the analogical organismic sense, are once again the fundamental ones of person and property, the right to get enough for sustenance, to keep what is earned, to trade fairly and freely, to

[31] Reply to address of the Danbury Baptist Association, Washington, January 1, 1802, M.E., XVI, 281.
[32] See Honeywell, op. cit., p. 120: especially, "in 1779 the law of nature and nations was classed as moral philosophy, and at that time it partook more of the nature of philosophy than of law. In 1814 it was again classed as philosophy. In 1818 it was grouped with government and history, and continued with these in the School of Law in 1824."

prosper—in short, to pursue happiness. It is this persuasion that the basic demands of nations are alike in their simplicity and that the natural reason induces friendly coöperation as the only prudent course which governs Jefferson's treatment of intersocietal law. The vital issue of trade between nations is handled in terms of these same assumptions. In an exhaustive report on United States imports and exports, is the following declaration of law, natural and international:

Instead of embarrassing commerce under piles of regulating laws, duties and prohibitions, could it be relieved from all its shackles in all parts of the world, could every country be employed in producing that which nature has best fitted it to produce, and each be free to exchange with others mutual surpluses for mutual wants, the greatest mass possible would then be produced of those things which contribute to human life and human happiness; the numbers of mankind would be increased, and their condition bettered.[33]

Apart from the anticipation of free-trade economics, this is as unpretentious a recommendation to cosmic world economic socialism as one can find in print. The moral postulate on which it rests is largely borrowed from the above conception of natural law.

The formal tradition in which this part of Jefferson's philosophy is rooted is that of seventeenth- and eighteenth-century jurisprudence. He was thoroughly informed in the doctrines of the modern natural law school, Grotius, Pufendorf, Vattel, Wolf, Burlamaqui.[34] Grotius, using the older classical material on the law of nature in the Stoic and Ciceronic version [35] was easily the most sympathetic to Jefferson and the most influential. Incorporating the Stoic appeal to the inherent "sociableness" of man, Grotius rejects the universal rules of self-interest, force, and mere convention in society. This is in essence the perspective with which Jefferson works. His frequent denials of Hobbes's self-interest as sole interest are motivated, just as for Grotius, by the firm faith in man as a naturally social creature, to whom the actions of peace, good faith, and justice are intrinsically as agreeable as any move for direct self-aggrandizement. Men in a state of nature are supposed to

---

[33] M.E., III, 275.
[34] See, e.g., "Opinion on the Question Whether the United States Has a Right to Renounce Their Treaties with France . . ," M.E., III, 226–43 (April 28, 1793).
[35] Grotius, *De jure belli ac pacis*, Prolegomena, Sec. 6, p. 11. English translation in "The Classics of International Law," No. 3.

have these fundamental rights and mutual obligations, so that right and duty, for Jefferson, are both anterior to established society and government. The source for both natural rights and duties is, in the order of immediacy, the heart, the head, and the Creator. These "evidences" for Jefferson's theory of natural law are strikingly similar to Burlamaqui's three principles of morality: (1) "le sentiment moral," best understood as a kind of immediate, instinctive feeling; (2) reason; (3) the will of God.[36] The transfer of the modern natural-law theory into a theory of free republicanism is uppermost in the exposition of Grotius, as it is in that of Jefferson. The law of nature and nations envisages the world of states, in fair and friendly intercourse, only because the state itself is by his theory required to be of a certain kind. Such a state submits only to the natural rights and law; it is in republican rebellion against all vested authority.

In every age independent and wise and devout men . . . showed that . . . He [God] had drawn up certain laws not graven on tablets of bronze or stone but written in the minds and on the hearts of every individual, where even the unwilling and the refractory must read them. That these laws were binding on great and small alike; that kings have no more power against them than have the common people against the decrees of the magistrates, than have the magistrates against the edicts of the governors, than have the governors against the ordinances of the kings themselves; nay more, that those very laws themselves of each and every nation and city flow from the Divine Source, and from that source receive their sanctity and their majesty.[37]

Grotius's construction of the law of nature in this passage is almost a forecast of the theory of republicanism later to flower in America.

[36] Burlamaqui, *Principes du droit naturel*, p. 181.
[37] Grotius, introduction to *Mare liberum*. Quoted in *Law, the State, and the International Community*, by J. B. Scott, II, 80.

Chapter XVI

REPUBLICANISM

AS WE HAVE SEEN, Jefferson's system of republicanism rests upon the foundation of natural rights and natural law. The light of moral philosophy therefore goes far; it is even cast over the specific and realistic political elements which figure in the developed republican concept. This development is as true of Grotius and the other modern interpreters of natural law as it is of Milton and the seventeenth-century English republicans in general. Whether the fight was to be against the claims of churches to absolute authority and obedience or against the State's monarchical pretension to full and "divine" right, the rebellious secularizer would be sure to proceed under the banner of moral law and moral right.

Jefferson's interpretation is exceptional, however, in two respects. First, his elaboration of the full moral implications of republican theory went further than that of the continental or English writers. Second, his patience and inventiveness with the political devices necessary to the operation of republicanism were greater and, incidentally, more native to him and thus to America than derivative from the English or the French.

A good theoretical introduction to Jefferson's republican system is provided by his treatment of sovereignty. The radical individualism of basic equal needs and equal rights is the first premise. "The earth belongs to the living" is its second premise. The will of the majority, conceived literally, is the conclusion, and this gives the source of authority in the nation. Jefferson is thoroughly serious about his sovereign people and his reliance upon majority will. This is significant because it is a divergence from the Federalists, whose republicanism takes a form more related to Milton's version, that is, they express an active fear of the multitude or majority.[1]

[1] On this point see Parrington, *Main Currents in American Thought,* I, 285–86.

One looks in vain for any fear of the majority in Jefferson's writings. The deep fears he voices are all inspired by the menace of various organized minorities—the "Monarchomen," the aristocracy of wealth, the judiciary in their sometime role of "sappers and miners" (of the republican rights guaranteed in the Constitution); secret military societies, such as the Cincinnati; [2] political "schisms," [3] led by schemers who could be expected to "take part personally in . . . violent contests" and were primarily, in Jefferson's language, advocates of themselves.[4] In political theory this came to mean that any nation, like any individual, has the fundamental right to govern itself (liberty, independence); only, the individual "exercises" this right in his "single will," but a body of men do it through their majority. "For the law of the *majority* is the natural law of every society of men." [5] The law of the majority is, according to Jefferson, the fundamental law in any society which recognizes "equal rights"; it is therefore the "vital principle of republics." [6] Sometimes Jefferson refers to the *lex majoris partis* and asserts that it is founded in "common law as well as common right." [7] Taking account of this usage proves helpful. "Common law as well as common right" shows that the will of the majority is the only principle of government, of order in society, which does not involve the appeal to force. Jefferson clearly sees a dichotomy of this sort: either the will of the majority or force. In this sense the will of the majority is sacred, since it is the "natural," the legal, the habitual, and the just alternative to despotic societies.

Republicanism takes its objective structure from this base. It is in origin and in intention an anti-force society. That is, republicanism is from the start the political expression of reason, tolerance, arbitration, and the acceptance of the majority will, even if the majority's decision is not as each individual would have it, because it is the opposite of re-

---

Parrington regards Madison's entire theory of factions as a revolt against democratic reliance upon the will· of the majority.

[2] The story of Jefferson's principled objections to the organization of the *Cincinnati*, is worth investigating. See especially M.E., IV, 217–19; XVII, 84, 85, 89, 90.

[3] Jefferson's usual term of disfavor for political groups or parties which are self-interested solely, or further corrupt, is "schism."

[4] To John Adams, Monticello, June 27, 1813, M.E., XIII, 281.

[5] M.E., III, 60.   [6] *First Inaugural Address*, M.E., III, 317 (March 4, 1801).

[7] *Notes on Virginia*, Query XVIII Sec. 6, M.E., II, 172.

sorting to force. It is, of course, conceivable that the majority will might be "oppressive." Recognition of this fact caused Jefferson to introduce the notion of a *"fair* majority," [8] or the *"rightful* [9] will" of the majority. The reservation that even a society which is founded on majority rule and in process of enjoying it may be ignorant, prejudiced, and oppressive provides a much needed clarification of the previous statements. Not all majorities are automatically just or constructive in their actions; only those obedient to reason are genuinely mindful of equal rights for minorities. But more than half the battle is won, in Jefferson's opinion, if majority will rules, because majorities are on the whole, more reliable than minorities.[10]

The question of the reliability of majorities is a complex one. For Jefferson it is partly theoretical, partly practical, and partly a question of technology. The theory is that representative republics, which are large (therefore representation is necessary), are less liable to be torn by conflict than small societies are. This is an interesting feature of Jefferson's republican theory. In opposition to Montesquieu, Jefferson argues the contrary of the thesis that small countries alone are subjects for democracy. In large ones there is more chance of reconciling different demands and overcoming the pressure of partisan factions. Power, in short, will not be as easily captured and misused in large countries, and if it is misused, the abuses are rarely on such a wholesale scale. Localism and the atmosphere of heated, violent politics are typically the dangers of small republics.

It seems that the smaller the society the bitterer the dissensions into which it breaks. Perhaps this observation answers all the objections drawn by Mr. Adams from the small republic of Italy. I believe ours is to owe its permanence to its great extent, and the smaller portion comparatively, which can ever be convulsed at one time by local passions.[11]

Majority will, when made to speak through representatives from many local areas of a large country, is less likely to be emotional. Countries

[8] To President Washington, Monticello, Sept. 9, 1792, M.E., VIII, 397.
[9] To Thomas Seymour, Washington, February 7, 1807, M.E., XI, 154.
[10] This follows from his "faith" in the moral and practical qualities of men, from his theory of the spread of progress and enlightenment where society and therefore science are free—theories discussed earlier.
[11] To Robert Williams, November 1, 1807, M.E., XI, 389.

with extensive national boundaries may be favored with reason, law, and moderation.

This point is carefully cultivated by Jefferson. His great reliance upon Destutt de Tracy's *Commentary and Review of Montesquieu* in this case as in almost every question concerning political theory is evident. One of the major criticisms which Tracy launches against Montesquieu is this very championing of representative government for a great territory. His development of the idea touches off the same points we have observed in Jefferson's writing. He says:

> Representation, or representative government, may be considered as a new invention, unknown in Montesquieu's time; it was almost impossible to put it into practice before the invention of printing, which so much facilitates the communication between the constituents and the representative, and renders it so easy for the former to control, and the latter to account for his conduct; and above all, which averts those sudden storms, so often excited by the force of an impassioned and popular eloquence.[12]

To reinforce the theory that republicanism implies lawful governments based on majority will,[13] Jefferson turns to history and practice. From history he garners a negative answer; from practice (contemporary), a positive one. The negative result proven by history is the failure of "pure" democracy, meaning by "pure," direct, nonrepresentative rule by the people "in mass." The democracies of ancient Greece, for example, are criticized as having been unruly, swept by mob passion, chaotic—lacking proper law and principles—for example, Constitution, bill of rights, and so forth. But in truth the chief consideration is that they represent an entirely different political form than does representative democracy; history shows that when pure democracy ("the only pure republic, but impracticable beyond the limits of a town")[14] encountered obstacles, there was an immediate reversal to despotic gov-

---

[12] Destutt de Tracy, *A Commentary and Review of Montesquieu's Spirit of Laws*, p. 19. This title will be referred to subsequently as *A Commentary and Review*. . . .
[13] It is interesting to notice that Tracy, *A Commentary and Review* . . . , classifies all governments under two fundamental categories, "National" and "Special." "National" governments (a term preferred to "Republican" because of the latter's vagueness) are those in which "social rights are common to all" (p. 10); they are further characterized by the fact "that there is no one who can have any right to oppose the general will when manifested according to the established form" (p. 13).
[14] To Isaac H. Tiffany, Monticello, August 26, 1816, M.E., XV, 65–66.

ernment. ("An abandonment of themselves to an aristocracy, or a tyranny independent of the people.") [15]

Therefore, while "We of the United States . . . are constitutionally and conscientiously Democrats," [16] this is modified, representative democracy. The résumé of Jefferson's majoritarian society is set forth in his interesting letter to Dupont de Nemours, on April 2, 1816.

We consider society as one of the natural wants with which man has been created; that he has been endowed with faculties and qualities to effect its satisfaction by concurrence of others having the same want; that when by the exercise of these faculties he has procured a state of society, it is one of his acquisitions which he has a right to regulate and control, jointly indeed with all those who have concurred in the procurement, whom he cannot exclude from its use or direction more than they have him. We think experience has proved it safer, for the mass of individuals composing the society, to reserve to themselves personally the exercise of all rightful powers to which they are competent, and to delegate those to which they are not competent to deputies named, and removable for unfaithful conduct, by themselves immediately.

Jefferson goes on to say that "the people" are also considered competent to keep the functions of "judges of fact, under the name of jurors," but not being equally talented for public management, they use their good knowledge of "human character" to choose their representatives.

. . . And we believe that this proximate choice and power of removal is the best security which experience has sanctioned for ensuring an honest conduct in the functionaries of the society. Your three or four alembications have indeed a seducing appearance. We should conceive prima facie, that the last extract would be the pure alcohol of the substance, three or four times rectified, but in proportion as they are more and more sublimated, they are also farther and farther removed from the control of society, and human character, we believe, requires in general constant and immediate controul to prevent its being biassed from right by the seductions of self-love. [17]

In this letter Jefferson states briefly his definition of republicanism. He accepts Dupont's four cardinal moral values (liberty, truth, probity, and honor) and agrees that "morality, compassion, and generosity" are

[15] *Ibid.*
[16] To Dupont de Nemours, Poplar Forest, April 24, 1816, M.E., XIV, 487–88.
[17] *Ibid.*, pp. 488–89.

innate. He concludes, as does Dupont, that there is right independent of force, and he openly states that right to property is "founded in our natural wants." Justice is indeed the fundamental law of society,[18] and should a majority oppress any one person, it does not differ morally from any other oppressive brute force. But for climax Jefferson has this to say:

. . . that action by the citizens in person in affairs within their reach and competence, and in all others by representatives, chosen immediately and removable by themselves, constitutes the essence of a republic; that all governments are more or less republican in proportion as this principle enters more or less into their composition, and that a government by representation is capable of extension over a greater surface of country than one of any other form.

In this letter to Dupont we see the elements of theoretical republicanism beginning to merge with practical devices. As he says, these are the essentials. Genuine republicans will be bound to agree on most of these points. But it seemed quite possible to Jefferson that republicans might be "perplexed and divaricate, as to the structure of society most likely to secure them." His own form of "divarication" is both constructive and far-sighted, bringing us close to a technological consideration of the problems of government.

In approaching Jefferson's serious reflections on government, those written especially in the late years of his life, it is profitable to keep in mind Destutt de Tracy's *Commentary and Review of Montesquieu*.[19] While much of Jefferson's conception of natural rights and natural law shows it to be similar to Tracy's, his way of stating republicanism illuminates other features of Jefferson's social theory. Tracy makes much show of not taking sides, of strict neutrality. He states that his method will be to confine himself "wholly to the fundamental principles of po-

[18] Compare with "the law of the majority" as the fundamental law of society. This shows the moral complexion of Jefferson's "majority rule."

[19] Recall that Jefferson said about this book, to Dupont de Nemours, "I am not the author of that work . . . In truth I consider it as the most profound and logical work which has been presented to the present generation on the subject of government. Particularly, there is a purity and soundness of principle which renders it precious to our country particularly where I trust it will become the elementary work for the youth of our academies and colleges . . ." (November 29, 1813, M.E., XIX, 195).

litical society . . . neither censuring nor approving any." [20] He accordingly criticizes Montesquieu's division of governments into republican, monarchical, and despotic, and he urges the adoption of a basic twofold classification, national governments and *special* ones. National governments are defined as those "in which social rights are common to all"; special governments are recognized as the practice of "establishing or recognizing particular or unequal rights." [21] National governments may also be called "public," while special ones are "private"; because some governments "in all their deliberations affect publicity . . . others mystery." [22] The identification between governments founded on common and equal rights and their public character is very impressive as a clew to Jefferson's determined and zealous support of free speech, free press, open criticism of the government, written constitutions, and bills of rights,—the whole machinery of publicity. Republican governments are in origin and nature bound to respect the common. The origin of the term *in res publica,* commonwealth, is partial reënforcement of this point; there are common rights to property and the necessary extension of these rights to the means, open, public, and unobstructed, whereby they may be defended or revised as the occasion arises.

Tracy's "neutrality," however, is not conceivably justified by his work—unless by neutrality one means the approving judgment rendered after the best possible examination of evidence. In this sense, though, Tracy's aim not to censure or approve is too much influenced by the ideal of scientific mechanism, and it is interesting that his good sense breaks through his fashionable avowed aim. The objective accounts of pure democracy and representative democracy, or republicanism, show without any question to what Tracy's political beliefs incline, and they throw further light upon Jefferson's views.

The diatribes against pure democracy point to one difference between *The Commentary* and Jefferson's political philosophy. While Jefferson endorsed Tracy's book in every way (specifically as the soundest text in government ever written), he himself never felt so keenly about the shortcomings of the direct form of Greek democracy. Tracy speaks of "simple democracy" as a rude and almost uncivilized condition, quite unsuited to complex, interrelated modern national life. Of simple de-

[20] Tracy, *A Commentary and Review* . . . , p. 9.
[21] *Ibid.*, p. 12.   [22] *Ibid.*, p. 12*n.*

mocracy in general, Tracy says its existence is necessarily short and confined to "some insulated corner of the earth" where the bonds of society are not closer drawn than among savages.[23] Then he adds, just as Jefferson does: [24]

In every other circumstance, where the social relations are more intimate and multiform, it [simple democracy] cannot exist for any considerable time, and soon ends in anarchy, which brings on aristocracy or tyranny through the necessity of repose. History in all times confirms this truth.[25]

Simple democracy is really the "infancy of a state." [26] Despite the myth of idealized Greek democracies, Tracy regards them as aristocracies rather than pure democracies.

The democracies of Greece, so much boasted of, never existed by their own internal power, but through the protection of a confederation by which they were united; yet their duration was short; and besides, they were actually aristocracies in relation to the great mass of the population, and among them was a prodigious number of slaves who had no share in the government.[27]

For civilized people, therefore, simple democracy is neither possible nor desirable. Tracy's real enthusiasm reaches its peak in disclosing the virtues of representative democracy. Nothing else, not even an orderly and cunning monarchy, elicits the slightest overtone of moral praise. Not that he is unwilling to recommend the most effective measures for their successful operation (enthronement of religion as a primary state measure, conscious control and limitation of education, inculcation of deep respect for custom, venerable tradition, and authority),[28] but the aura of approval which suffuses the passages on representative democracy leaves no shade of question about his political tendencies. Even the most "neutral" description of representative democracy sets favorable cues before the reader.

[23] Tracy, *A Commentary and Review* . . . , p. 18.
[24] Letter to Isaac H. Tiffany, Monticello, August 26, 1816, M.E., XV, 65–66.
[25] Tracy, *A Commentary and Review* . . . , p. 18.   [26] *Ibid.*, p. 19.
[27] *Ibid.*, p. 18. Compare with this Jefferson's similar statement: "The government of Athens . . . was that of the people of one city making laws for the whole country subject to them. That of Lacedaemon was the rule of military monks over the laboring class of the people, reduced to abject slavery. These are not the doctrines of the present age." (To Monsieur A. Coray, Monticello, October 31, 1823, M.E., XV, 482.)
[28] Tracy, *A Commentary and Review* . . . , pp. 25–26.

. . . representative democracy . . . in which, according to forms expressed in an act or law freely deliberated, and agreed upon, and called a *Constitution*, all the associates called citizens, concur equally in choosing their representatives, define the authorities with which they are entrusted, and fix limits beyond which they must not trespass. This is democracy rendered practicable for a long time and over a great extent of territory. Simple democracy is the true state of nature; representative democracy is that of nature, in a perfect state, without having been sophisticated, and which acts neither by strategems nor expedients.[29]

Tracy's above account of representative democracy (republicanism) is more compendious than most such attempts, and in fact it is as good a definition of theoretical republicanism as one can find. The classic emphasis upon a fundamental rule by law and reason is there; and the modern democratic concept that this is a law "freely deliberated and agreed upon." The individuals who compose such a state are viewed as associates in a common enterprise (citizens), whose function is to share equally in selecting representatives and to define the offices they must fill and beyond which they "must not trespass." In another section Tracy calls attention to the principle of representative democracy expressed by the Parliament of Paris in October, 1788, by one of its members: "Magistrates as magistrates have only duties to perform; citizens alone have rights." [30] "Magistrate" is used here to include anyone invested with a public function.

It is when Tracy devotes himself to the climate of manners of such a society and the method of preserving it that some of the most familiar Jeffersonian themes are reënforced and placed in logical dependence upon the preliminary definitions and description of republicanism. He criticizes Montesquieu sharply for making republican virtue consist in "voluntary privations, in self-denials." Instead, he substitutes these virtues as typical of republican societies: "Simplicity, habits of industry, a contempt for frivolity, the love of independence so inherent in every being endowed with a rational will . . ." [31] Where these virtues take root in a citizenry, there one will find a society "naturally more engaged in preserving and enjoying what they already possess, than solicitous of acquiring what was not necessary to their security or happiness." The virus of invading the rights of others and of "improper appropriation of

---

[29] *Ibid.*, p. 19.   [30] *Ibid.*, p. 13.   [31] *Ibid.*, p. 20.

the public wealth" are presumably not favored by such a climate. The love of independence and the disposition to simplicity are therefore the cardinal safeguards of republican purity. Tracy has a new version, accordingly, of the "principle of preservation" for a representative democracy; he says: "It is evident that the principle of preservation, in this form of government, is love of country, and equality of rights, and if you will, the love of peace and justice." [32]

The elements of this free society are sound, because they conform to the eternal laws of nature. A surprising importance is given to the function of truth in society. Free and independent republics are founded on true principles, and their "goodness" and usefulness are only other facets of their basic truth. That is why representative democracies alone do not

call for nor need the constraint of the human mind, the modification of our natural sentiments, the forcing of our desires, nor the excitement of imaginary passions, rival interests, or seductive illusions; it should, on the contrary, allow a free course to all inclinations which are not depraved, and to every kind of industry which is not incompatible with good order and morals: being conformable to nature, it requires only to be left to act.[33]

But just as truth and freedom of science and opinion are the natural rights and fruits of democracies, they are also obligations. And here Tracy's doctrine is very closely linked to Jefferson's technological concern for the spread of education, its official encouragement, and its literal diffusion to the greatest possible portion of the population. Tracy's program is comprehensive.

. . . this form of government requires the general diffusion of the most correct and useful knowledge; information should be promulgated constantly, and error exposed and dissipated; popular and moral writers should be rewarded, not by engagement, but by such means as may be devised for exciting a general emulation, without rendering the reward of virtue a business of intrigue on one hand, or of patronage on the other . . .[34]

Tracy makes more of the social avenues for reaching the people on all political subjects than does Jefferson. Elementary works should be composed, "adapted wholly to the promotion of truth and virtue." He recommends supplementing these by

[32] Tracy, *A Commentary and Review* . . . , p. 19.
[33] *Ibid.*, p. 41.   [34] *Ibid.*, pp. 42–43.

almanacs and catechisms, moral allegories, pamphlets accordant with the spirit of public virtue . . . periodical journals should be instituted, which by multiplying the means of enquiry, should, through the medium of a bold or free criticism, perform those functions, which under other forms of government, are committed to the inspection of venal censors, or to indefinite restrictions; these would establish new shields for truth, and new incentives to genius and virtue. No one should be placed under any other restraint in the communication of his ideas or opinions, than the contract of moral sentiment, *fari quae sentiat,* for it is indisputable, that wherever opinion is left free with reason only to combat it, truth will ultimately predominate, since being founded in natural principles, it requires no support from remote means . . .[35]

To one not used to Tracy's system of thought there must appear to be some contradiction between the beginning of this passage and its end. For he starts out to argue for the creation and publication of a vast national literature devoted to "propaganda" of the virtues of republicanism, and he ends with a crashing condemnation of political censorship and intellectual suppression of any kind—in a passage, incidentally, reminiscent of Jefferson's own words. Tracy has in mind that the basic principles of representative democracy are true and that nothing which honors or describes them is to be considered artificial, forced, or warped. In short, truth can never be propaganda, if by propaganda is meant the influencing of political opinion without strict appeal to objective truth. The only censorship, therefore, which can rightfully operate in a free republican society is the restriction placed upon men's thoughts and speech by respect for truth. As Jefferson said, the only suppression necessary is to *restrain* the press to *truth.*[36]

The question of truth has more than incidental importance in Tracy's conception of republicanism. His most radical departure from Montesquieu, in fact, revolves around this issue. Tracy sketches the development of society from barbarism to representative democracy and finds three principles basic to modern democracy. They are: (1) Its first laws are "declared to be formed for the governed, not the governed for them." [37] (2) There should never be "a power in society which cannot

[35] *Ibid.,* p. 43.
[36] To William Short, September 6, 1818, M.E., XII, 169. ". . . restraining the press *to truth,* as the present laws do, is the only way of making it useful."
[37] *Ibid.,* p. 154.

be changed without violence, nor any such that when it is changed all must change with it." (3) A rational government will always aim at conserving "the independence of the nation, the liberty of its members, and such security for every individual as to supersede the idea of fear internal or external." Apart from the inherent interest of these three principles, we must notice that they are, after proper development and defense, declared to be externally true and universally so. Montesquieu's political pluralism, while not banished from the realm of differentiated political superstructure, operates only in the restricted area of secondary political devices and customs: it does not extend to basic political principles at all.[38]

. . . these alone are the real fundamental principles of government, inasmuch as they alone are unchangeable, and should always exist; for all others can and should be changed, when the members of the society will it . . . so that the laws we speak of are not properly positive laws, but those of our nature, the declaration of principles, the enunciation of eternal truth; they should be placed at the head of all constitutions, instead of those declarations of rights which of late years have prefaced them . . .[39]

The reason Tracy advocated placing his principles at the head of constitutions, instead of declarations of rights, is that the latter "argue a long forgetfulness in which these rights have been left" and testify to the long warfare "that everywhere existed between the governed and governing." [40] Rather than start constitutions, therefore, with manifestoes, calling implicit attention to past oppression, Tracy advocates a more positive beginning by reminding men of the principles drawn from the great truths about the nature of man, which are the foundation of the constitution now being placed before them. These principles are the real reminder of eternal justice,[41] freedom, and independence.

---

[38] The discussion seems to work towards the distinction between a set of political principles and the specific customs and habits and rules which surround them.
[39] Tracy, *A Commentary and Review* . . . , p. 155.   [40] *Ibid.*, p. 156.
[41] Condorcet also complains about Montesquieu's failure to face the issue of justice. See his "Observations on the 29th Book of the Spirit of Law," appended to the *Commentary and Review* . . . , pp. 261–82. Note: "Why has not Montesquieu spoken of the justice and of the injustice of the laws he quotes, and the motives which he attributes to the laws? Why has he not laid down some principles which would enable us to discriminate among the laws flowing from a legitimate power, those which are unjust, and those which are conformable to justice?" P. 263.

While Jefferson's instrumentality in causing the Bill of Rights to be added to the constitution should not be forgotten, it does not imply disagreement with Tracy. The Constitution was written in his absence, and the addition of the Bill of Rights was merely precautionary and second best. When Jefferson himself did write political manifestoes, they always did begin with principles. The opening of the *Declaration* is the foremost illustration of Jefferson's partiality to a statement of principles; the preamble to the Virginia constitution of 1776, and the famous "Statute of Virginia for Religious Freedom" are other substantial examples of this practice.

Chapter XVII

WARDS

JEFFERSON's theory of "wards," [1] one of his most significant and original ideas for implementing representative democracy, is a blend of "principles" and shrewd "realism." The anxiety Jefferson manifested in his educational projects to ensure the spread of knowledge to every small, however remote, locale in America is elevated into a political principle of the first magnitude in the concept of wards.

Wards are units of local government, constructed to bring political management and administration straight to the people who are being "represented." They are the bulwark against all attempts at "mining and sapping" the liberties of the people. As political machinery, they are the heart of pure republicanism, because through a system of wards the government keeps in touch with the needs of the people and is sensitive to their criticism. Instead of advocating extensive polls of "public opinion," Jefferson interested himself in setting up this kind of local self-government, to do on a small scale what national government does on a large scale. At the same time that wards would be keeping people alive to their share in the immediate neighborhood politics, citizens would be in process of perpetual training for extending their experience and participation to the arena of national or Federal affairs. Wards were therefore to perform a dual role, checking the petty tyrants at home in the immediate community and educating and "activizing" people in their function as vigilant and intelligent performers in the democratic rule of an extensive federated union. The political flavor of Jefferson's feeling about wards is well presented in his famous letter to Joseph Cabell, which is a brief but first-rate political treatise in itself.

[1] See: To J. C. Cabell, Dec. 25, 1820. Missing from M.E., but quoted by Honeywell, *Educational Work of Thomas Jefferson*, p. 152.

No, my friend, the way to have good and safe government, is not to trust it all to one: but to divide it among the many, distributing to every one exactly the functions he is competent to let the National government be entrusted with the defence of the nation, and its foreign and federal relations; the state governments with the civil rights, laws, police and administration of what concerns the state generally; the counties with the local concerns of the counties; and each Ward direct the interests within itself. It is by dividing and subdividing these republics from the great National one down thro' all its subordinations, until it ends in the administration of every man's farm and affairs by himself; by placing under every one what his own eye may superintend, that all will be done for the best.[2]

Nothing shows more clearly than this, that Jefferson's political theory is basically unified and consistent in its tendency. The radical individualistic starting point of his theory of sovereignty and republicanism inspires the entire concept of wards. In fact, wards are the token of good faith in Jefferson's political vocabulary. They are the proof that he took seriously the principle of majority rule and that he thought the wards would be the most workable medium for effecting it.

In terms of physical characteristics a ward is simply a territory about six miles square, answering to "the hundreds of your Saxon Alfred." [3] The business to be transacted within the province of the ward is a mixture of education and politics.

In each of these might be, first, an elementary school; second, a company of militia, with its officers; third, a justice of the peace and constable; fourth, each ward should take care of their own poor; fifth, their own roads; sixth, their own police; seventh, elect within themselves one or more jurors to attend the courts of justice; and eight, give in at their folk-house, their votes for all functionaries reserved to their election.[4]

And Jefferson's hopeful conclusion is that "each ward would thus be a small republic within itself," where each person would be behaving as a functioning member of his common government, "transacting in person a great portion of its rights and duties."

Stating the theory of wards in a different way, Jefferson said he

[2] To Joseph Cabell, Monticello, Feb. 2, 1816, M.E., XIV, 420.
[3] To Major John Cartwright, Monticello, June 5, 1824, M.E., XVI, 46.
[4] *Ibid.*, p. 46.

had two measures at heart, both of which were necessary to the maintenance of republics. The first was general education; the second was his plan to "divide every county into hundreds, of such size that all the children of each will be within reach of a central school in it." [5] He then describes the political and social duties of the hundreds in much the same fashion as in his account of wards. But before leaving his subject Jefferson shows that the workability of these small units has made a deep impression upon him.

We owe to them the vigor given to our revolution in its commencement in the Eastern States, and by them the Eastern States were enabled to repeal the embargo in opposition to the Middle, Southern and Western States, and their large and lubberly division into counties which can never be assembled. General orders are given out from a centre to the foreman of every hundred, as to the sergeants of an army, and the whole nation is thrown into energetic action, in the same direction in one instant and as one man, and becomes absolutely irresistible. [6]

Thus, for Jefferson, if for no other republican theoretician of his time, the notion of direct democracy, purified by criticism and made to work coördinately with the more complicated conditions of modern representative government, is retained and absorbed. His species of republicanism must be identified with a pyramid, starting from wards, nestled directly in the midst of the people, to counties, states, and the central Federal Government. The democratic impulse, starting with its home-made lessons in the "pure republics" at the base, travels up the various levels of the pyramid, its strength at each successive level depending upon the purity and force of the original impulse.

Jefferson's famous case against the judiciary, his fight against Federalist revivals of aristocratic theory and practices, his warfare with all political groups ("cabals," "Juntos") which encroached upon reserved or democratically recognized rights of the people are in fact but the reverse side of his positive theory of wards. What Jefferson is aiming at with his device of wards is very plain in his most direct "definition" of republicanism; why republicanism will need wards as a unit of "small republic" is implied in what he says about the term "republic" in a letter to John Taylor.

[5] To Governor John Tyler, Monticello, May 26, 1810, M.E., XII, 393.
[6] *Ibid.*, p. 394.

Were I to assign to this term a precise and definite idea, I would say, purely and simply, it means a government by its citizens in mass, acting directly and personally, according to rules established by the majority; and that every other government is more or less republican, in proportion as it has in its composition more or less of this ingredient of the direct action of the citizens. Such a government is evidently restrained to very narrow limits of space and population. I doubt if it would be practicable beyond the extent of a New England township. The first shade from this pure element, which, like that of pure vital air, cannot sustain life of itself, would be where the powers of the government, being divided, should be exercised each by representatives chosen either *pro hac vice*, or for such short terms as should render secure the duty of expressing the will of their constituents. This I should consider as the nearest approach to a pure republic, which is practicable on a large scale of country or population.[7]

According to this view, countries are never completely republican, for republicanism, being a limiting ideal, can be approached only in degree. Trust in the people as participants in government is the *sine qua non*. His summary of the discussion recalls his fundamental distrust of interested egos and organized minorities, which the popular control attainable in wards would be designed to thwart.

. . . governments are more or less republican, as they have more or less of the element of popular election and control in their composition; and believing, as I do, that the mass of the citizens is the safest depository of their own rights and especially, that the evils flowing from the duperies of the people, are less injurious than those from the egoism of their agents, I am a friend to that composition of government which has in it the most of this ingredient.[8]

[7] To John Taylor, Monticello, May 28, 1816, M.E., XV, 19.
[8] *Ibid.*, p. 23.

Chapter XVIII

EDUCATION

J EFFERSON's desire to see the light of education brought into the county, the village, and the hamlet is a detail of his governmental theory which is far more dynamic and more charged with implications than one might suppose. Governments founded on such principled recognition of truth must find their justification in their plans for education. Jefferson did not "develop" an interest in education in his old age; he always had it, and it was always the center of his vision of good government, of orderly, happy society. As a social engineer, Jefferson demonstrated by his work in the educational field his will to fashion the practical devices demanded by his pure political principles. He knew as well as anyone knows today that "what is practicable must often control what is pure theory." [1] His recommendations for educational policy, directions for reading to numerous friends, his early *Bill for the More General Diffusion of Knowledge*, "for the amending the constitution of the College of William and Mary" and "for establishing a public library," are only parts of a long-range enterprise.

Tracy's book gives the reason for the genuine democrat's consecration to education. Enlightened governments (that is, representative democracies) are founded upon knowledge of truths and will last as long as those truths are appreciated. The system of public education and the intellectual climate encouraged by freedom of speech and press therefore furnish the real standing army of the functioning republic. A maxim of Beccaria's prefaces Tracy's *Commentary and Review* and emphasizes the theme of the ensuing essay. Beccaria wrote: "The most certain means of rendering a people free and happy, is to establish a perfect method of education."

Jefferson and Tracy are completely in accord on this point; but

[1] To Dupont de Nemours, Washington, January 18, 1802. Missing from M.E., but given in Chinard's *Correspondence of Jefferson and Dupont de Nemours*, p. 37.

Jefferson was able to leave the realm of theory without reluctance, while Tracy's whole genius was as a theoretician. Jefferson's progress was in action; his theoretical aptitude, as we have seen, was present very early and grew with the years. But in the late years of his life, when he was released from a heavy schedule of public duty, he pruned his theory of education to fit the needs of an actual university and went through the spadework of arranging for funds from the Legislature of Virginia, drawing up the architectural plans for the university, making its curriculum, and even providing for its faculty. He also was most anxious to introduce the "honor system" of self-government for the student body. But safeguarding the tolerant spirit at the university did not encourage him to lose sight of the smallest sign of danger to republicanism. The one condition which had to be guaranteed if education and all other social benefits were to continue was a citizenry bred in the knowledge of their own principles of government. One textbook is therefore not to be left to the choice of the individual instructors—the text on government.[2] There "we are the best judges," and our duty is to present the best principles of government without ambiguity. Jefferson felt a special reverence for this task, and it is the essence of the famous trilogy of deeds written in his epitaph.[3]

Jefferson's general argument for popular education as the only safeguard of democracy is too familiar in its outlines to need restatement. His faith in the progress of knowledge, the thriving of the sciences under a free society, and the reciprocal influences which they exert to perpetuate that freedom have already been described. The strength of his belief that ignorant people would never merit, and therefore never achieve, a free society is lyricized in his exclamation, "Where the press is free, and every man able to read, all is safe." [4]

There is one less familiar aspect of Jefferson's respect for knowledge which did not appear in his thought until some of the disillusionments of politics had given him occasion to reflect on the concrete, local menace which confronts a community, unarmed because of its ignorance and at the mercy of corrupt peanut tyrants in public office. County

[2] To —— (address lost), Monticello, February 3, 1825, M.E., XVI, 114.
[3] "Here was Buried Thomas Jefferson Author of the Declaration of American Independence of the Statute of Virginia for Religious Freedom and Father of the University of Virginia."
[4] To Colonel Yancey, January 6, 1816, M.E., XIV, 379.

courts and county administration in general were the causes of serious alarm to Jefferson when he reflected on the "monopolies" which controlled them and the difficulties of finding "some means of breaking up a cabal, when such a one gets possession of the bench." [5] He mentions one county whose court is of thirty members, twenty of them Federalists.

There are large and populous districts in it without a justice, because without a federalist for appointment; the militia are as disproportionably under federal officers. And there is no authority on earth which can break up this junto, short of a general convention. The remaining one thousand four hundred and forty, free, fighting, and paying citizens, are governed by men neither of their choice nor confidence, and without a hope of relief. They are certainly excluded from the blessings of a free government for life, and indefinitely, for aught the Constitution has provided. This solecism may be called anything but republican, and ought undoubtedly to be corrected.[6]

The suggestion which is contained in this letter to John Taylor is pushed further in two interesting letters to Joseph C. Cabell, neither of which have found their way into the "Definitive Edition" of Jefferson's writings. In these letters Jefferson develops the idea that knowledge and education are "political power" and accordingly indispensable on that, if on no other, count. In one letter Jefferson shows signs of impatience with the official attitude of negligence toward education in Virginia and says:

All the States but our own are sensible that knowledge is power. The Missouri question is for power. The efforts now generally making through the States to advance their science, is for power; and while we are sinking into the barbarism of our Indian Aborigines, and expect, like them, to oppose by ignorance the overwhelming mass of light and science by which we shall be surrounded. It is a comfort that I am not to live to see this.[7]

Pursuing this same theme, Jefferson put on record his admiration for the educational achievements of Massachusetts.

[5] To John Taylor, Monticello, July 16, 1816, M.E., XV, 45.
[6] Ibid., p. 45–46.
[7] To J. C. Cabell, January 22, 1820, quoted in Honeywell, *The Educational Work of Thomas Jefferson*, p. 151.

I lately saw in a newspaper an estimate in square miles of the area of . . . the states, of which the following is an extract: "Virginia 70,000 square miles, Massachusetts 7,250, Connecticut 4,764, Delaware 2,120, Rhode Island 1,520." By this it appears that there are but three states smaller than Massachuetts; that she is the twenty-first only in the scale of size, and but one-tenth of that of Virginia; yet it is unquestionable that she has more influence in our confederacy than any other State in it. Whence this ascendency? From her attention to education, unquestionably. There can be no stronger proof that knowledge is power, and that ignorance is weakness. *Iuousque tandem* will the Legislature be dead to this truth?

While it would be absurd to overemphasize this element of Jefferson's philosophy of education, it is so natural a complement to his practical, scientific bent that its exclusion leaves the story of his constantly regenerating enthusiasm for education incomplete.

Chapter XIX

POLITICAL ECONOMY

JEFFERSON's belief that the only "legitimate objects of government" in the present age are "the equal rights of man and the happiness of every individual" [1] was admittedly an expression of mixed desire and fact. That Jefferson wished, however, to think about the "realistic" subsoil for such a society is evidenced by his pursuit of clarity in the chaos of political economy. The good society which Jefferson kept in mind throughout his social philosophy was never utopian in the sense of ignoring economic foundations. While the ends of republican government were to be happiness, freedom, and enlightenment, the means were strenuous ones: industry, frugality, peace. It is true that Jefferson had such strong inclinations in the direction of "republican virtue" that the duties and the means often are colored by aesthetic preference, thus becoming self-justifying ends.

His sense of class conflict was sharpest in his pre-Presidential years, but while it diminishes on occasion, it can never be fully discounted. The two great economic classes, for Jefferson, are the "landed and laboring" class and the manufacturing, commercial, and banking interests. In his early years the cleavage was simpler: it was between the agricultural interests, on the one side, and the urban inhabitants, on the other. Jefferson had no hesitation to classify himself with the first group, bound to oppose the other, with its attendant evil and corruption, for life.

Although much has been made by certain critics of Jefferson's landed wealth, his sentiments are consistently in favor of the "laboring classes." While this was partly sentimental with him, it was also common sense and obvious republican necessity. If laborers are turned into a pauper class by their aristocratic overlords, the destruction of their self-respect and their general fatigue will make them unfit for political and moral

[1] To Monsieur A. Coray, Monticello, October 31, 1823, M.E., XV, 482.

responsibility. Jefferson's criticisms of European conditions are couched more in terms of the conflict between the "pauperized yeomanry" [2] and the aristocracy than in terms of agricultural against urban classes. These older European societies are the ones in which "every man must be pike or gudgeon, hammer or anvil," and that is the real reason for the bankrupt social and political condition of France, for example. Looking back in later years on the causes of the French Revolution, Jefferson explained the pressure of the people for a constitution by saying:

Nor should we wonder at this pressure, when we consider the monstrous abuses of power under which this people were ground to powder; when we pass in review the weight of their taxes, and the inequality of their distribution; the oppressions of the tithes, the tailles, the corvees, the gabelles, the farms and the barriers; the shackles on commerce by monopolies; on industry, by guilds and corporations; on the freedom of conscience, of thought, and of speech; on the freedom of the press by the Censure; and of the person by Lettres de Cachet; the cruelty of the Criminal code generally; the atrocities of the Rack; the venality of the judges, and their partiality to the rich; the monopoly of military honors by the Noblesse; the enormous expenses of the Queen, the Princes and the Court; the prodigalities of pensions; and the riches, luxury, indolence and immorality of the Clergy. Surely under such a mass of misrule and oppression, a people might justly press for a thorough reformation, and might even dismount their rough-shod riders, and leave them to walk on their own legs . . . [3]

When he turned from the European to the American scene, there was less need to reckon with "rank and birth, and tinsel-aristocracy." [4] Here wealth and commerce were grouped against free farmers and landholders. He openly championed the latter, and when his political hostilities were aroused, usually identified his enemies with the immoral aristocracy of capital, whose interests were knifelike at the throat of the people. In the seventeen-eighties he wrote about the "cultivators of the earth" and the corruption of the manufacturing, commercial, and other classes. When he wrote to John Jay from Paris, in 1785, that "Cultivators of the earth are the most valuable citizens," [5] he con-

[2] To Dr. Thomas Cooper, Monticello, September 10, 1814, M.E., XIV, 181.
[3] *Autobiography*, M.E., I, 127.
[4] To John Adams, Monticello, Oct. 28, 1813, M.E., XIII, 402.
[5] To John Jay, Paris, Aug. 23, 1785, M.E., V, 93.

fessed that if he could have his way in the development of America
he would not countenance converting the citizens into "mariners, arti-
sans or anything else." The reasons were uncompromising. Cultivators
of the earth

are the most vigorous, the most independent, the most virtuous, and they are
tied to their country and wedded to its liberty and interests, by the most
lasting bonds.

I consider the class of artificers as the panders of vice, and the instruments
by which the liberties of a country are generally overturned.[6]

In this period Jefferson was capable of saying:

You ask what I think on the expediency of encouraging our States to be
commercial? Were I to indulge my own theory, I should wish them to
practise neither commerce nor navigation, but to stand with respect to
Europe, precisely on the footing of China. We should thus avoid wars, and
all our citizens would be husbandmen.[7]

However, he found himself recognizing the probability of other patterns of economic life and providing that those who desired it be fairly
represented and guarded by "their servants." His wish to see America
remain a purely agricultural country, keeping its workmen in Europe
and in turn supplying Europe with "rough materials and even sub-
sistence," he admits, is "theory only, and a theory which the servants
of America are not at liberty to follow." He adds, a bit ruefully, "Our
people have a decided taste for navigation and commerce. They take
this from their mother country; and their servants are in duty bound
to calculate all their measures on this datum . . ." [8]

During the years of his Presidency and afterward Jefferson's con-
cessions to navigation, commerce, and industry were somewhat less
grudging. He never lost his love and respect for the life of agriculture,
and he worked his own farm experimentally, trying to make it produce
everything it needed, from nails to the cloth used in the clothing of
his household. But, his First Inaugural Address, intended to heal the
mutual *calomnie* of the preceding campaign of the Federalist and Re-

[6] To John Jay, Paris, Aug. 23, 1785, M.E., V, 93.
[7] To Comte de Hogendorp, Paris, October 13, 1785, M.E., V, 183.   [8] *Ibid.*

publican parties, proclaimed the fundamental unity of all Americans. "We have called by different names brethren of the same principle. We are all republicans—we are federalists." [9]

At various points thereafter Jefferson defended manufacturers; [10] he wished to encourage manufacturing interests so that domestic raw materials could be used. He then changed the composition of his class warfare to include the laboring classes against the navigation interests and excessive commercialism, which were threatening to make of America "an Amsterdam, a Hamburg, or a city of London." [11]

But this capitulation, motivated as it was to accommodate the obvious needs of expanding national America, was always bordering on distrust. In 1804 a letter to J. B. Say is much less sweeping in its case against manufacture and for agriculture than earlier; but while Jefferson here advances his position to a reflective attitude about the mutual benefits of both occupations, he still maintained that one should give a slight edge to the proposition that "all our laborers should be employed in agriculture." [12] However, his reasons are not as sure at this point, and he resorts to weighting them, finally, with his old preference. "In solving this question, too, we should allow its just weight to the moral and physical preference of the agricultural, over the manufacturing, man."

His most forthright defense of manufactures, however, is found in a letter to Benjamin Austin in 1806, and in a letter to J. B. Say. To Austin, Jefferson says:

Manufacturers are now as necessary to our independence as to our comfort —and if those who quote me as to a different opinion, will keep pace with me in purchasing nothing foreign, where an equivalent of domestic fabric can be obtained, without regard to difference of price, it will not be our fault if we do not have a supply at home equal to our demand, and wrest that weapon of distress from the hand which has so long wantonly wielded it. If it shall be proposed to go beyond our own supply, the question of '85 will then recur, viz: Will our *surplus* labor be then more beneficially employed

[9] Inaugural Address, March 4, 1801, M.E., III, 319.
[10] See Dorfman, "The Economic Philosophy of Thomas Jefferson," *Political Science Quarterly*, LV (March, 1940), 98–121.
[11] To William H. Crawford, Monticello, June 20, 1816, M.E., XV, 28.
[12] To Jean Baptiste Say, Washington, February 1, 1804, M.E., XI, 2–3.

in the culture of the earth, or in the fabrications of art? . . . the maxim to be applied will depend on the circumstances which shall then exist.[13]

Peace, and order, and economy were what Jefferson was interested in preserving—and prosperity was the stable reward hoped for from their conjunction. The generalized form of class opposition is perhaps the most fundamental argument in Jefferson's artillery. It is the continuous background of his various complaints about bureaucracy and privilege. Its importance cannot be minimized, since it is wholly in accord with the theory of republicanism of the populist form to which Jefferson adhered. Good republican society must avoid above all "the general prey of the rich on the poor." [14] This, in Jefferson's opinion, is exactly what ruined the "governments of Europe," which had adopted the terrible practice of dividing their subjects into a sheeplike majority, while the governors, the wealthy, and the priests were the wolves who fed upon them.[15]

Modern republics, while founded upon "the guarantee to everyone of a free exercise of his industry and the fruits acquired by it," [16] were bound to injure themselves if the poor were to be virtually enslaved. The impression given is almost like an Aristotelian recommendation for a large and sound middle class, to prevent the extremes of wealth and poverty from throttling the republic. America has a future, in Jefferson's eyes, because there is enough homogeneity of work and the incomes are moderate enough not to tear it into the "orders" of Europe.

First, we have no paupers, the old and crippled among us, who possess nothing and have no families to take care of them, being too few to merit notice as a separate section of society, or to affect a general estimate. The great mass of our population is of laborers; our rich, who can live without labor, either manual or professional, being few, and of moderate wealth. Most of the laboring classes possess property, cultivate their own lands, have families, and from the demand for their labor are enabled to exact from the rich and the competent such prices as enable them to be fed abundantly, clothed above mere decency, to labor moderately and raise their families. . . . The

[13] To Benjamin Austin, Monticello, January 9, 1816, M.E., XIV, 387.
[14] To Col. Edward Carrington, Paris, January 16, 1787, M.E., VI, 58.
[15] *Ibid.*
[16] See Dorfman, "The Economic Philosophy of Thomas Jefferson," *Political Science Quarterly*, LV (March, 1940), 120.

wealthy, on the other hand, know nothing of what the Europeans call luxury. They have only somewhat more of the comforts and decencies of life than those who furnish them. Can any condition of society be more desirable than this? [17]

Although there is ample proof, therefore, for Jefferson's recognition of the right to property as a basic "natural" right in republican societies [18] ("that a right to property is founded in our natural wants, in the means with which we were endowed to satisfy these wants, and the right to what we acquire by those means without violating the similar rights of other sensible beings" [19]), he is severely opposed to its concentration in the hands of a minority. Land is the great barrier against this excessive concentration, since a nation of freeholders, living in peace, under the protection of a friendly government, is the genuine alternative to pauperism and economic exploitation on a large scale.[20] Even taxation should be guided by this consideration; for a taxation policy can be so arranged that the poor will not be ground under its burdens or the rich grow dangerously powerful. Jefferson was proud for many years of having given "the death blow" to excise taxes, "the most vexatious and unproductive of all taxes." [21] His attitude is best shown in the following statement, made about import taxes:

We are all the more reconciled to the tax on importations, because it falls exclusively on the rich, and with the equal partition of intestates' estates, constitutes the best agrarian law. In fact, the poor man in this country who uses nothing but what is made within his own farm or family, or within the United States, pays not a farthing of tax to the general government, but on his salt . . .[22]

[17] To Dr. Thomas Cooper, Monticello, September 10, 1814, M.E., XIV, 182.
[18] This is so, despite the famous omission of the right to property in the *Declaration of Independence*, and the story told by Chinard that Jefferson struck out the word "propriété" from Lafayette's draft of the French *Declaration of the Rights of Man*, Article II (see Chinard's Introduction to *Jefferson and Dupont de Nemours*, pp. lxii–lxiii).
[19] To Dupont de Nemours, Poplar Forest, April 24, 1816, M.E., XIV, 487.
[20] To Mr. Lithson, Washington, January 4, 1805, M.E., XI, 55. Jefferson's reasons for revising Query XIX of *Notes on Virginia* contribute to a general understanding of his ideas on political economy.
[21] To M. Dupont de Nemours, Monticello, April 15, 1811, M.E., XIII, 37.
[22] *Ibid.*

This populist conception of landed prosperity was paralleled, on another level, in the ideal of a "pay as you go" government.[23] Almost the same recommendations that Jefferson would have made to a group of citizens are entertained for the financial policy of the government. "I have cherished . . . peace, economy, and riddance of public debt, believing that these were the high road to public as well as to private prosperity and happiness."[24] Jefferson was pleased to think that in his own administration the government had managed to free itself from public debt and thus to put itself in a position where its surplus could be

applied to canals, roads, schools, etc., and the farmer will see his government supported, his children educated, and the face of his country made a paradise by the contributions of the rich alone, without his being called on to spare a cent from his earnings.[25]

A government which pursues an economic policy of this kind will avoid bankruptcy and therefore will presumably not be troubled by revolution.

The Louisiana Purchase seems to be the one magnificent exception to Jefferson's rule of frugality. While it was an extraordinary expenditure, the estimate Jefferson had made of its potential value to the developing United States justified his decision to have his agents purchase the territory. But even this fortification did not forestall a fervent *examen de conscience* on Jefferson's part, for acting in an "unconstitutional" manner. Tom Paine sent Jefferson a strong letter of encouragement, setting forth the arguments in favor of the purchase with his customary logical acumen. This extremely important letter, which is in the Jefferson collection,[26] has been ignored in the literature revolving about the Louisiana Purchase question, and is not published in any editions of Jefferson's works. Paine wrote:

It appears to me to be one of those cases with which the constitution had nothing to do and which can be judged of only by the circumstances of the

[23] To John W. Eppes, Monticello, June 24, 1813, M.E., XI, 269–70; and see, in general, letters to Albert Gallatin.
[24] To Henry Middleton, Esq., Monticello, January 8, 1813, M.E., XIII, 202.
[25] To Dupont de Nemours, Monticello, April 15, 1811, M.E., XIII, 39.
[26] Thomas Paine to Thomas Jefferson, Connecticut, September 23, 1803. Jefferson Papers, Library of Congress.

times when such a case shall occur . . . The cession makes no alteration in the constitution; it only extends the principles of it over a larger territory, and this certainly is within the morality of the Constitution, and not contrary to, nor beyond, the expression or intention of any of its articles.

In the end Jefferson did not regret his original move, nor did it prove to contradict his policy of national economy.

When Jefferson advocated "laissez faire" as a principle for international commerce, he was again thinking in terms of his recommendations for free and unshackled individual producers. Although he was forced to modify his opinion here on many occasions, there is no doubt about what principles he would have liked for commerce among nations:

. . . could every country be employed in producing that which nature has best fitted it to produce, and each be free to exchange with others mutual surpluses for mutual wants, the greatest mass possible would then be produced of those things which contribute to human life and human happiness . . .[27]

[27] "Report on the privileges and restrictions on the commerce of the United States in foreign countries," December 16, 1793, M.E., III, 275.

Chapter XX

JEFFERSON AND TRACY'S "A TREATISE ON
POLITICAL ECONOMY"

I
F IN THE course of these remarks about political economy it seems
difficult to discover whether Jefferson believed in a "natural
order" and a theory of rent such as the *economistes* and physiocrats
in France held, or whether he was a follower of Adam Smith, or a
Mercantilist, the difficulties are justified by the material.[1] Perhaps the
most clarifying remark is one which Jefferson made himself about the
"science" of political economy: " . . . in so complicated a science as
political economy, no one axiom can be laid down as wise and expedient
for all times and circumstances." [2]

However, in political economy, as in government, if there is any
single systematic work which Jefferson is inclined to accept, it is that
of Destutt de Tracy. It is true that John Taylor has been called "the
economist of Jeffersonian democracy," but there is less evidence for
Jefferson's complete theoretical accord with Taylor than with Tracy.
In fact, Taylor's "pragmatic point of view" has been remarked, and
while Jefferson certainly shared in this, his desire for a thorough ra-
tionalized review of the theory of political economy was better satisfied
by Destutt de Tracy's *A Treatise on Political Economy*. While Taylor's
independent and often original criticism won unstinting praise from
Jefferson, it was largely directed toward local American problems, for
example, Hamiltonian fiscal policies, the nationalist construction of

[1] See Dorfman, "The Economic Philosophy of Thomas Jefferson," *Political Science
Quarterly*, LV (March, 1940), 107, for the point that Jefferson "depending on
circumstances . . . utilized the doctrines of mercantilists, physiocrats or Adam
Smith, and sometimes all three at once. But what may appear as inconsistency in
Jefferson may after all merely serve to raise the question as to whether the differences between the various schools are as substantial as is thought."
[2] To Benjamin Austin, Monticello, January 9, 1816, M.E., XIV, 388.

the Constitution by Marshall, the protective tariff, and so forth.[3] Jefferson had spent so much time in France and had kept up his friendships with the physiocrats so long, especially through Dupont de Nemours and Destutt de Tracy, that his interest in the more sophisticated methodological and logical approach of "political economists" as such appealed to him.

Jefferson's enthusiasm carried him into an unqualified endorsement of the *Commentary and Review of Montesquieu,* and likewise of the *Political Economy,* which he virtually translated,[4] adding various notes and advices, and saw through publication. Jefferson, anxious to interest Duane in publishing it, describes the book thus.

The present volume is a work of great ability. It may be considered as a review of the principles of the Economists, of Smith and of Say, or rather an elementary book on the same subject. As Smith had corrected some principles of the Economists, and Say some of Smith's, so Tracy has done as to the whole. He has, in my opinion, corrected fundamental errors in all of them, and by simplifying principles, has brought the subject within a narrow compass.[5]

As he said when writing to the author, an interesting science, "heretofore voluminous and embarrassed," has now been "happily simplified and brought within a very moderate compass." [6]

More specifically, one understands what Jefferson valued in the *Political Economy* by consulting his prefatory letter to the book. Jefferson expresses the hope that it will find its way to every reader in the country.

By diffusing sound principles of Political Economy, it will protect the public industry from the parasite institutions now consuming it, and lead us to that just and regular distribution of the public burthens from which we have sometimes strayed. It goes forth therefore with my hearty prayers, that while the Review of Montesquieu, by the same author, is made with us the elementary book of instruction in the principles of civil government, so the present work may be in the particular branch of Political Economy.

[3] See Eugene T. Mudge, "The Social Philosophy of John Taylor of Caroline," p. 7.
[4] Jefferson's complaint about the inadequate translation and his offer to correct it are in letter to Mr. Joseph Milligan, Monticello, April 6, 1816, M.E., XIV, 456–66.
[5] To Col. William Duane, Monticello, January 22, 1813, M.E., XIII, 214–15.
[6] To Destutt de Tracy, January 26, 1811, M.E., XIII, 11.

These are the points to which he then drew attention in a careful "Prospectus." Political economy as a science started with the economists of France. They made it part of a system, regarding the matrix as the "natural order of society." Jefferson mentions the names "Quesnia [*sic*], Gournay, Le Trosne, Turgot and Dupont de Nemours" for the *economistes* and grants that criticisms have been made of their work, particularly of their treatment of production and taxation. He refuses to discuss the "merit of their principle of taxation," because he feels that the *correctness* of the principle is not relevant so much as whether the proposals are acceptable to the people, "whose will must be the supreme law." This is most crucial, here, because

taxation is, in fact, the most difficult function of government, and that against which, their citizens are most apt to be refractory. The general aim is, therefore, to adapt the mode most consonant with the circumstances and sentiments of the country.[7]

The very first theoretical point that Jefferson has to make is thus a rejection of universal "principles" in practical economic policy for governments, and a reminder of his belief in the consent of the governed to the measures of their government. He then continues with his brief sketch of the development of political economy and mentions Adam Smith, some of whose corrections of the doctrine of the *economistes* were well taken and whose system at the time it was launched was highly honored for its novelty. But Jefferson thinks that Smith's truths are so well accepted by that time (1816) that his book appears "prolix and tedious." So that Jefferson's second contribution raises questions of formal simplicity and clarity of style in the emerging science of political economy.

He writes with greater appreciation of the "very superior work" of John Baptist Say, in France, for whom clarity and systematic arrangement of ideas, plus a "style perspicuous," are natural gifts. And to cap all this, Say has "the whole subject brought within half the volume of Smith's work; add to this, considerable advances in correctness and extension of principles." [8]

[7] Tracy, *A Treatise on Political Economy*, Prospectus, p. iii. Also given in letter of T. Jefferson to Milligan, Monticello, April 6, 1816, M.E., XIV, 456–66.
[8] *Ibid.*

This repeated emphasis of Jefferson's upon methodological matters —arrangement and system, clarity of ideas, economy—is too persistent to be ignored. A glance at J. B. Say's book confirms the impression that these are serious and sophisticated objections, based upon a conception of the rigors of a so-called "science." Jefferson most likely concurred with Say when the latter said, in his introduction,[9] that political economy would never become a science until it (1) confined itself "to the results of inductive investigation" and (2) developed as a logical system of ideas, presented as in a deductive science, with the "results . . . so complete and well arranged, as to afford to each other mutual support." [10] In effect, Say argues very well that while the general principles of political economy must be "strictly deduced from observation," [11] not manufactured a priori or treated purely mathematically and arithmetically, neither is political economy to be haphazard as in the "compilation of an almanac." [12] He then offers penetrating criticisms of the *economistes* and Adam Smith, which are in a similar vein, although more specific, than Jefferson's.[13]

But, as one might expect, Tracy's work wins highest honors. Jefferson introduces it by saying: "The work of Senator Tracy . . . comes forward with all the lights of his predecessors in the science, and comes with the advantages of further experience, more discussion, and greater maturity of subject." [14] He commends Tracy for the cogency of his logic, the "rigorous enchainment of ideas" in his work, and for the spirit of "fearless pursuit of truth, whithersoever it leads"—a tribute to the republican honesty of a philosopher under the Napoleonic dictatorship and under the Bourbon restoration.

Jefferson dutifully outlines the place of the *Political Economy* in Tracy's *Elements of Ideology* and says that before Tracy turns to the proper subject of his inquiry—"the formation, distribution, and employment of property" he discusses the origin of the rights of property and personality, "a question not new indeed, yet one which has not hitherto been satisfactorily settled."

Jefferson concludes by explaining why the original French work is

[9] Say, *A Treatise on Political Economy*, p. xxxvii.
[10] *Ibid.*, p. xliv.   [11] *Ibid.*, p. xxviii.   [12] *Ibid.*, p. xxiv.
[13] The entire book, especially the Introduction, is worth reading for a critique of the early history of political economy.   [14] *Ibid.*, p. v.

first to be published in America: "A manuscript copy communicated to a friend here has enabled him to give it to a country which is afraid to read nothing, and which may be trusted with anything, so long as its reason remains unfettered by law." [15]

Tracy's consecutive reasoning is highly suggestive when it is brought to bear upon what is already known of Jefferson's ideas about political economy. The first link is given in the section Jefferson referred to as the "origin of the rights of property and personality," a subject, Jefferson assures the reader, which will now be satisfactorily settled. Tracy makes feeling basic to personal existence, saying that it is the "same thing as ourselves." [16] The same genetic method applies to the social institution of property, for, Tracy says, "as long as we do not see the natural model of an artificial institution which we examine we may be sure we have not discovered its generation, and consequently we do not know it completely." [17] Turning this genetic method upon property, Tracy discovers the simple "thine" and "mine" as a necessary distinction in any group of men; derived from the fact of their individual existence, "they are individuals feeling, willing, and acting distinctly the one from the other, they have each one the inalienable, incommutable, and inevitable property, in their individuality and its faculties." [18] The idea of property follows, therefore, from the individual privacy of faculties and feelings, likings and aversions. Property is dependent upon the primary category of personality, and self, whether the property be goods or wants and sentiments.

Tracy has thus set the stage for an hypothesis about the relation between labor, rights to property, and the essentially active personality.

. . . nature . . . has given him [man] nothing as his own but his individual and personal faculties, as well physical as intellectual. This is his sole endowment, his only original wealth, and the only source of all which he procures for himself. In effect, if even we should admit that all those beings, by which we are surrounded, have been created for us . . . it would not be less true that we could not appropriate one of those beings . . . but by our action on them and by the employment of our faculties to this effect.[19]

[15] Say, *A Treatise on Political Economy*, p. vi.
[16] Tracy, *A Treatise on Political Economy*, p. 42.
[17] *Ibid.*, p. 48.   [18] *Ibid.*, p. 53.   [19] *Ibid.*, p. 60.

If this passage is taken in connection with Jefferson's stress upon the individual throughout his social theory, it supplies the organizing rationalization for his positions. For example, the radical theory that society and government are a contract with a living generation and that the earth is their property, the fundamental laws of their choosing, financial obligations their own to make and to recognize, is but the expanded social implication of ascribing property rights to the individual self.

Society is formed by insensible and gradual steps, to increase the power and thus the liberty of individual men. Tracy believes that society is in essence a set of conventions, and conventions are really exchanges. It is the nature of exchange to be useful to both the contracting parties, and therefore the advantages of society "are to produce a concurrence of force, the increase and preservation of knowledge, and the division of labor." [20] But individual force is "our only primitive riches"; this force, our labor, is consequently the sole cause of all other values.

Inequality is inevitable in a society thus conceived, since personality and property are its substructure. It is true that men in society are united, since they all have wants and are all consumers, and they all have means and are all proprietors. But they are naturally unequal, and some "have property in advance, and many others have not." [21] Two great classes of men are created by this difference in society; the hired and the hirers. Tracy, describing these classes in terms of economics, sounds prophetic. The hired and the hirers are "opposed in interest in the respect, that the one selling their labor wishes to sell dear, and the other buying it wishes to buy cheap."

This opposition of interests among men is necessary, and Tracy believes it wise to recognize that we must submit to it. He does not believe that any form of "revolution" or re-making of society can erase it, but this is no excuse for blindly believing that all inequalities are "inevitable." He therefore suggests: "The conclusion which I should draw from it . . . is, that the laws should always endeavor to protect weakness; while too frequently they incline to favour power." [22] Society should try to lessen inequality—"always by gentle, and never by violent, means." The condition to be avoided is a society with possessors

[20] *Ibid.*, p. 250.   [21] *Ibid.*, p. 251.   [22] *Ibid.*, p. 113.

of great fortunes, because these are idle men, who do not augment their riches "and pay no labour but for their pleasure." Tracy is moved to say,

Thus the more there are of great fortunes, the more national riches tend to decay and population to diminish. The example of all times, and all places, supports this theory. For wherever you see exaggerated fortunes, you there see the greatest misery and the greatest stagnation of industry.[23]

Here, once more, is a noticeable convergence of Jefferson's and Tracy's ideas. All Jefferson's distrust of the big banking interests, of excessive "feudal" estates, of concentration of wealth; all his feeling that virtue centers in economy, frugality, simplicity, and industry for the lives of citizens and their government—are comprehended in this argument. The ideal of prosperity, which is one of Jefferson's republican rewards, is announced by Tracy too, when he asserts that perfection of society would be "to increase our riches greatly, avoiding their extreme inequality." [24]

For students of Jefferson the final points of interest in Tracy's book are his theory of government economy and his view of the respective merits of agriculture, manufacture, and commerce.

"Of the Revenues and Expenses of Government," Tracy has one message to read; they are to be the smallest possible. Governments are great consumers, "living not on . . . profits, but on . . . revenues." [25] The expenses of government are necessary but "sterile." Good advice for government is not to contract debts; when they wield the power of contracting debts, euphemistically called "public credit," they are speedily conducted to their ruin.[26] As for taxes,

The best taxes are, first, the most moderate, because they compel fewer sacrifices and occasion less violence. Secondly, the most varied, because they produce an equilibrium amongst themselves. Thirdly, the most ancient, because they have already mixed with all prices, and everything is arranged in consequence.

The strong bias in favor of agriculture, so marked in Jefferson, is distinctly not one of the features of Tracy's analysis. Jefferson's praise of agriculture, when it is fervent, bears the mark of physiocratic [27]

---

[23] Tracy, *A Treatise on Political Economy*, p. 159.
[24] *Ibid.*   [25] *Ibid.*, p. xvi.   [26] *Ibid.*, p. xxvii.
[27] It frequently sounds like a republican application of Quesnay's famous formula: "Pauvres paysans, pauvre royaume; pauvre royaume, pauvre roi," which was the motto to his *Tableau économique*.

theory more than it does of Tracy's. Also, it is on the whole less intellectual and more the result of experience with Virginia life than is generally recognized. There is one important influence, however, that was much older than the physiocrats—that is, the influence of classical antiquity, particularly Cicero. But Jefferson's broader view about manufactures and commerce, which is observable in some of his later writings, is a new tendency, possibly due to the operation of local conditions, such as the war and the embargo. In any case, it is revealing to see that Jefferson accepts with enthusiasm a work which gives no special place to agriculture, but classifies it with the "manufacturing and fabricating industry" generally. Tracy seems to be quite aware of the interdependence and mutual relatedness of the different occupations, and his account is worth hearing:

Since the whole of society is but a continual succession of exchanges, we are all more or less commercial. In like manner, since the result of all our labours is never but the production of utility, and since the ultimate effect of all our manufacturers is always to produce utility, we are all producers or manufacturers,—because there is no person so unfortunate as never to do anything useful. But by the effect of social combinations, and by the separation of the different kinds of occupation which is its consequence, every one devotes himself to a particular kind of industry. That which has for its object the fashioning and modifying all the beings which surround us, to fit them for our use, we call specifically manufacturing or fabricating industry . . .[28]

Society, republican or otherwise, divides its labor as need dictates; and it is only the objective and the use that is made of any given occupation which entitles it to moral approval or censure.

[28] Tracy, *A Treatise on Political Economy*, p. 35.

Conclusion

THE PERENNIAL SIGNIFICANCE OF
JEFFERSON'S THOUGHT

ANYONE who reads Jefferson seriously today is likely to come away with an inescapable impression of the *actualité* of this thought; and the experience is more likely with Jefferson's writings than with the writings of any other political figure in America, including Lincoln. It is almost a duty, therefore, to try to crystallize out from his thought those features which are of perennial significance—understanding by "perennial," not *sub specie aeternitatis*, but persisting and deep traits with respect to our culture.

First, one is struck by Jefferson's belief that American political procedures represent something novel in the history of civilization. Jefferson appreciated fully "the American experiment," crediting it partly to the spontaneous adaptation of immigrants of Scottish and English ancestry to a new soil and fresh problems, but tending to view the "experiment" with the eyes of a classicist and a scholar. The resulting amalgam, formed of first-hand experience and reflection upon the "sages" of Greece and Rome and the thinking men of his time in England and France, is both instructive and refreshing. One is led to imagine Jefferson, the son of a surveyor, looking keenly at the American Indian tribes, the rugged white freeholders in his neighboring states, the frontiersmen already beginning to explore further West, but seeing them as if they might become the future citizenry of an ideal Ciceronian republic. The philosophical significance of this approach is that it prepared Jefferson to receive the empirical, positivist philosophies without hesitation.

This way of keeping himself in the midst of "reality" and fact, and training upon that daily life his wise learning, actually gave the American experiment, at its very start, the proportion of dignity and bearing.

Jefferson never forgot that what America did would have great influence upon the world. He wrote of the fact that America, as an influential example, was cited again and again in the French National Assembly, treated quite as though it were "the bible." [1] America had a political mission to fulfill, for itself and before the eyes of the world: to prove that reason, order, and law are the genuine fruits of an educated people governing themselves. He said it in so many words.

. . . the eyes of the virtuous all over the earth are turned with anxiety on us, as the only depositories of the sacred fire of liberty, and that our falling into anarchy would decide forever the destinies of mankind, and seal the political heresy that man is incapable of self-government. [2]

But Jefferson never allowed his grave sense of America's dual importance, as a native achievement and a world-wide example and symbol, to verge on the fanatic or foster the parochial. He was so filled with knowledge of the varieties of possible political experience that he shied clear of political eternities. He showed himself aware that in the nature of the case, sooner or later the restraining bonds which are necessary in any society, will be broken through by the succeeding society. Therefore he refers unsolved problems to "the future generations," which will see them, and also some which the present generation considers solved, in a thoroughly new light. His defense of revolutions, so frequently misinterpreted as literal advice to nourish the tree of liberty with bloodshed every twenty years, is really part of his desire to provide a framework of freedom and liberty for social changes. He evidently was convinced that it was not humanly possible to excommunicate revolutions or to be so wise that they would forever be rendered unnecessary. Society will have its revolutions. Why not build society, then, in a manner which would encourage only those political revolutions which are in accord with consent—the people's consent, majority revolutions? Jefferson took very deep pleasure in "bloodless revolutions," hailing those profound changes in society which are engineered by reason and persuasion instead of the "blind" machines of force. Quite clearly the ideal is "that of changing our form of government under the authority of reason only, without bloodshed." [3]

[1] To James Madison, Paris, August 28, 1789, M.E., VII, 448.
[2] To John Hollins, Esq., Monticello, May 5, 1811, XIII, 58.
[3] To Mr. Izard, Paris, July 17, 1788, M.E., VII, 72.

It may seem that reason and persuasion are too slow. Let us grant, said Jefferson, that they require patience; but "the ground of liberty is to be gained by inches . . . we must be contented to secure what we can get, from time to time, and eternally press forward for what is yet to get. It takes time to persuade men to do even what is for their own good." [4]

At certain dire epochs in the development of societies reason is swept aside. The French Revolution was one such mighty struggle, which "I deplore as much as anybody"; but posterity "will be enjoying that very liberty" for which their ancestors gave up their lives. Indeed, "the liberty of the whole earth was depending on the issue of the contest," [5] and when this is in the balance, Jefferson has no mood for reluctance. "I would have seen half the earth desolated," he wrote Short, "were there but an Adam and an Eve left in every country, and left free, it would be better than it is now." But Jefferson repeatedly warned that this was wisdom only for supreme emergency, when the highest law of all becomes the need for "saving our country when in danger." [6]

The best permanent method of keeping social mechanisms flexible is to be forewarned against the arteriosclerosis of the body politic— "bureaucracy." Peace, freedom, and happiness will have a chance for survival and stability only when citizens learn to hinder the sabotaging of "the rights of mankind" by factions and aristocracies, local judges and kings, or violently, at times, on a grand scale by a "Cartouche or a Bluebeard." [7] The vigilance of the people is to be directed against unprincipled bureaucracies, since these have always been prepared "to sell them [the people] for a mess of pottage." [8] That is the meaning, in principle, of Jefferson's fight against the judges and against his great political opponents, the Federalists. Jefferson hated the Federalists only when he saw in them incipient "monarchists." One tendency of the Federalists he could never come to terms with was their design "to lessen the dependence of the Executive and of one branch of the Legislature on the people, some by making them hold for life, some heredi-

[4] To the Rev. Charles Clay, Monticello, January 27, 1790, M.E., VIII, 4.
[5] To William Short, Philadelphia, January 3, 1793, M.E., IX, 9.
[6] To J. B. Colvin, Monticello, September 20, 1810, M.E., XII, 418.
[7] To Col. William Duane, Monticello, April 4, 1813, M.E., XIII, 230.
[8] Ibid., July 25, 1811, M.E., XIII, 67.

tary, and some even for giving the Executive an influence by patronage or corruption over the remaining popular branch, so as to reduce the elective franchise to its minimum." [9]

Attacking the same thing from another angle, Jefferson conducted an elaborate campaign of exhorting caution about power. The crux of liberty is the "restraint" of too much power; therefore, in free or republican society power must always "revert" to the people. Governments are as likely to be captured by hungry "hierarchies" as are religions. There is little to choose between a hierarchy of "emperors, kings, princes, and nobles" and one of "popes, cardinals, archbishops, bishops, and priests." Free men must work like heroes to protect themselves from the unscrupulous and the cunning, whose hunt for power is endless. "In short, cannibals are not to be found in the wilds of America only, but are reveling on the blood of every living people." [10] People who are deaf to this lesson and yield themselves as the "willing dupes and drudges" of these creatures will live to weep over their own irremediable follies and fate.

One final word about Jefferson, the man, is in place and may serve to correct the focus with which to view his thought. After a lengthy and curious *Autobiography*, written at the age of seventy-seven and with less indulgence in personalities than any other *Autobiography* in the world, Jefferson appended a note.[11] In this note he asked a simple question: "Is my Country the Better for my Having Lived at All?" The question is striking; most people, even if the question would occur to them, would hesitate to express it, to bring forth into the light of print and of day the results of a lifetime's activity. Jefferson's sincerity is so great that his simplicity disarms, and one reads on to see what the man has to say in defense of himself. The list is precious: The river Rivanna, never before navigable, through his labors is now in use, "fully for carrying down all our produce." Then comes the flat statement, "The Declaration of Independence." Then he mentions work for the freedom of religion; the act of putting an end to entail; the act prohibiting the importation of slaves; the act concerning citizens and establishing "the natural right of man to expatriate himself, at will"; the act "giving

[9] To John F. Mercer, Esq., Washington, October 9, 1804, M.E., XI, 54.
[10] To Charles Clay, Esq., Monticello, January 29, 1815, M.E., XIV, 234.
[11] Appendix to *Autobiography*, Note G, M.E., I, 256–58.

the inheritance to all the children"; the act for apportioning crimes and punishments. The modest enumeration is much what we expect of Jefferson. The last two acts, however, are surprising. He mentions with utter gravity that in 1789 he had "a great number of olive plants, of the best kind, sent from Marseilles to Charleston, for South Carolina and Georgia. They are planted and are all flourishing." In 1790, "I got a cask of heavy upland rice, from the river Denbigh, in Africa . . . which I sent to Charleston, in hopes it might supersede the culture of the wet rice, which renders South Carolina and Georgia so pestilential through the summer." And as if in explanation, Jefferson adds: "The greatest service which can be rendered any country is, to add an useful plant to its culture." [12]

The olive trees, the heavy rice, and the opening of the "river Rivanna" are eloquent symbols of Jefferson's great plan to improve the material estate of mankind. His intellectual life is close to this purpose, too; it is primarily practical, drawing upon the basic source of human experience. Loving ideas dearly, Jefferson was not an "Ideologue" in the Napoleonic sense of the intellectual dreamer whose abstractions carry him beyond this society and this life. Similarly, Jefferson's understanding of ideology was not a speculative discipline for its own sake at all. He tried to put ideology into practice, and throughout his vigorous life of ideas one senses a matrix of immediacy, a kind of local grain. For Jefferson those ideas were significant which related to the needs, the sweat, and the labor of human life. He never quite lost the farmer's sense that the products of the orchard, the garden, and the fields are born of arduous labor.

The significance of this study consists in this: it is apparent that ideology functioned in Jefferson's mind as a conscious program of action; he was, in fact, an ideologist in our sense of the word. The implications of this conclusion are many and have been explored in their political, social, and philosophic expression.

It is hoped that now the principle of integration has been made evident. For Jefferson ideology is a tool which, handled resourcefully, ensures steady conquest of the recalcitrant forces in society, man's home.

[12] Appendix to *Autobiography*, Note G, M.E., I, 259.

Bibliography

I. JEFFERSON MANUSCRIPTS

The Jefferson Collection, Library of Congress. There are reputed to be upwards of 50,000 of Jefferson's letters extant, of which the largest collection is owned by the Library of Congress. This collection is indexed in the Calendar of the Correspondence of Thomas Jefferson. Washington, Department of State, 1894–1903. Part I: Letters from Jefferson. Part II: Letters to Jefferson. Part III: Supplementary.

The Massachusetts Historical Society has the second largest Jefferson collection, totaling some 7,000 pieces.

The University of Virginia has about 1,400 pieces.

The Missouri Historical Society estimates that it has 1,100 pieces.

There are sizable collections, moreover, in the Virginia State Library and in the National Archives, but the number in these collections has not been ascertained by the libraries.

General confusion about the location and quantity of Jefferson letters in public and private collections has prevailed up to the present time, and no inclusive checklist has ever been compiled. This confusion may be dispelled by the forthcoming publication by the University of Virginia of an extensive checklist of all Jefferson papers in the country. See Helen Duprey Bullock, "The Papers of Thomas Jefferson," in *The American Archivist*, IV (October, 1941), 4.

II. JEFFERSON'S PRINTED WORKS

Albert Ellery Bergh, ed. The Writings of Thomas Jefferson. "Definitive Edition containing his Autobiography, Notes on Virginia, Parliamentary Manual, Official Papers, Messages and Addresses, and other writings, official and private, now collected and published in their entirety for the first time. Issued under the auspices of the Jefferson Memorial Association of the United States. Washington, D.C., 1903. 20 volumes." This is referred to in the footnotes as the "Memorial Edition."

Chinard, Gilbert, ed. The Commonplace Book of Thomas Jefferson; a Repertory of His Ideas on Government. Baltimore, 1926.

Chinard, Gilbert, ed. The Correspondence of Jefferson and Du Pont de Nemours. Paris and Baltimore, 1931.

—— The Letters of Lafayette and Jefferson. Baltimore, 1929.

—— The Literary Bible of Thomas Jefferson: His Commonplace Book of Philosophers and Poets. Baltimore, 1928.

—— Trois amitiés françaises de Jefferson, d'après sa correspondance inédite avec Madame de Bréhan, Madame de Tessé et Madame de Corny. Paris, 1927.

—— Les Amitiés américaines de Madame d'Houdétot d'après sa correspondance inédite avec Benjamin Franklin et Thomas Jefferson. Paris, 1924.

Ford, P. L., ed. The Writings of Thomas Jefferson. 10 vols. New York and London, 1892–99.

Ford, W. C., ed. Thomas Jefferson Correspondence. Printed from the originals in the Collections of William K. Bixby. Boston, 1916.

Jefferson Papers, The, in Massachusetts Historical Society, *Collections,* Boston, 1900, Ser. 7, Vol. I.

III. SOURCE MATERIALS USED BY JEFFERSON, INCLUDING THOSE IN HIS OWN LIBRARY WHICH ARE IN THE JEFFERSON COLLECTION, RARE BOOK DIVISION, LIBRARY OF CONGRESS.

Jefferson's Library (Rare Book Division, Library of Congress). After the burning of the old Library of Congress, Jefferson offered his library for sale to the government. In 1815 the transaction was completed; Jefferson received $23,950. A second fire in the Library of Congress destroyed a considerable part of the Jefferson Collection. After Jefferson had sold his fine library to the United States government, he started to collect another one, which was sold at public auction after his death. Catalogues for both libraries are available. For specific items see:

Catalogue of the Library of the United States, Jonathan Eliot, Washington, 1815.

Catalogue. President Jefferson's library. A catalogue of the extensive and valuable library of the late President Jefferson, to be sold at auction . . . Feb. 27, 1829. Washington, 1829. Miscellaneous pamphlets, Vol. CCMLIX, No. 14. (Original MSS in Jefferson Collection.)

The author has found it fruitful to consult Jefferson's own books for clues to his reaction as indicated by marginalia and occasional notes. Titles followed by an asterisk are in the Jefferson Library Collection.

Blackwell, Thomas. An Enquiry into the Life and Writings of Homer.* 3d ed. London, 1757.

Bolingbroke, Henry St. John, 1st Viscount. Reflections concerning Innate Moral Principles.* London, 1752.

—— The Philosophical Works of Bolingbroke.* 5 vols. London, 1754.

Burlamaqui, J. J. Principes du droit naturel.* Genève, 1756.

Cabanis, P. J. G. Rapports du physique et du Moral de L'Homme. 2 vols. Paris, 1824.

Charron, Pierre. De La Sagesse; trois livres.* Leyde, 1656.

Condillac, E. B. de. The Logic of Condillac; trans. by Joseph Neef.* Philadelphia, 1809.

Condorçet, M. J. A. N. C., marquis de [M. Schwartz, pseud.]. Réflexions sur l'esclavage des nègres.* Paris, 1788.

Cooper, Thomas. The Scripture Doctrine of Materialism. Philadelphia, 1823.

Destutt de Tracy, Antoine Louis Claude, comte. A Commentary and Review of Montesquieu's Spirit of Laws; to which are annexed observations on the Thirty-First Book by the late M. Condorcet and two letters of Helvetius on the merits of the same work. Philadelphia, 1811.

—— Analyse raisonnée de l'origine de tous les cultes; ou, Religion universelle. Paris, 1804.

—— A Treatise on Political Economy; to which is prefixed a supplement to a preceding work on the understanding, or Elements of Ideology. Georgetown, D.C., 1817. Trans. from the then unpublished French original.

—— Élémens d'idéologie. 5 vols. Paris, 1827.

—— Observations sur le système actuel d'instruction publique.* Paris, n.d.

—— Principes logiques; ou, Recueil de faits relatifs à l'intelligence humaine. Paris, 1817.

—— Projet d'élémens d'idéologie à l'usage des écoles centrales de la République Française.* Paris, 1801.

Du Pont de Nemours, Pierre Samuel. Sur l'éducation nationale dans les États-Unis d'Amérique.* MSS copy, June 15, 1800.

—— National Education in the United States of America. Newark, 1923. Translation of the preceding item.

—— Philosophie de l'univers.* Paris, 1796.

Federalist, The.* 2 vols. New York, 1788.

Franklin, Benjamin. Political, Miscellaneous and Philosophical Pieces.* London, 1779.

Gassendi, Pierre. Opera omnia. 6 vols. Lyons, 1658.

Godwin, William. Political Justice. 2 vols. 1st Amer. ed. Philadelphia, 1796.

Grotius, Hugo. De jure belli ac pacis.* 2 vols. Amsterdam, 1724. Trans. by Kelsey in The Classics of International Law. Washington, 1913–25.

Helvetius, Claude Adrien. De l'homme.* Londres, 1781.

Holbach, P.H.T., baron d'. System of Nature; or, The Laws of the Moral and Physical World.* Philadelphia, 1808.

Home, H., see Kames, H. H., Lord.

Hume, David. Philosophical Essays on Morals, Literature and Politics.* 2 vols. 1st Amer. ed. Georgetown, D.C., 1817.

Hutcheson, Francis. An Inquiry into the Original of Our Ideas of Beauty and Virtue.* London, 1753.

—— A Short Introduction to Moral Philosophy. 3 vols. Philadelphia, 1788.

Kames, H. H., Lord. Essays on the Principles of Morality and Natural Religion.* Edinburgh, 1751.

—— Elements of Criticism.* 3d ed. Edinburgh, 1765.

Lancaster, Joseph. Improvements in Education.* New York, 1804.

Lolme, Jean Louis de. Constitution de l'Angleterre; ou, Etat du gouvernement anglais, comparé avec la forme républicaine et avec les autres monarchies de l'Europe.* Amsterdam, 1771.

—— The Constitution of England, London, 1853. The most recent English translation of the preceding item.

Ogilvie, James. Cursory Reflections on Government, Philosophy and Education.* Alexandria, Va., 1802.

Peel, Joshua. Truth and Reason.* Virginia, 1805.

Priestley, Joseph. A Harmony of the Evangelists in Greek; to which are prefixed critical dissertations in English.* 2 vols. London, 1777.

—— An History of the Corruptions of Christianity.* 2 vols. Birmingham, 1782.

—— An History of Early Opinions concerning Jesus Christ. Birmingham, 1776.

—— Socrates and Jesus Compared. Philadelphia, 1803.

—— Disquisitions relating to Matter and Spirit. Birmingham, 1782.

—— A Free Discussion of the Doctrines of Materialism; a correspondence between Dr. Price and Dr. Priestley. London, 1778.

Say, Jean-Baptiste. A Treatise on Political Economy; or, The Production, Distribution and Consumption of Wealth. Philadelphia, 1830.

Shaftesbury, Anthony Ashley Cooper, 3d earl of. Characteristics of Man, Manners, Opinions, Times. 3 vols. [London, 1900.]

Sidney, Algernon. Discourses concerning Government.* London, 1763.

Stewart, Dugald. Elements of the Philosophy of the Human Mind.* 3 vols. London, 1792.

—— Amer. ed. revised and abridged. 1 vol. Boston, 1864.

—— Esquisses de philosophie morale. Paris, 1826.

—— Works. 7 vols. Cambridge, 1829.

Tracy, Antoine Destutt de, see Destutt de Tracy, Antoine.

Wollaston, William. The Religion of Nature Delineated.* Glasgow, 1746.

IV. SECONDARY SOURCES

Adams, Henry. History of the United States of America during the Administration of Thomas Jefferson. 2 vols. New York, 1930.

Ayer, A. J. Language, Truth and Logic. London, 1936.

Beard, Charles Austin. Economic Origins of Jeffersonian Democracy. New York, 1915.

Becker, Carl Lotus. The Declaration of Independence; a Study in the History of Political Ideas. New York, 1922.

Boas, George. French Philosophies of the Romantic Period. Baltimore, 1925.

Carpenter, William Seal. The Development of American Political Thought. Princeton, 1930.

Chinard, Gilbert. "Jefferson and the Physiocrats," University of California Chronicle, XXXIII (1931), 18–31.

Crist, Clifford Mortimer. The Dictionnaire philosophique portatif and the Early French Deists. Brooklyn, 1934.

Dorfman, Joseph. "The Economic Philosophy of Thomas Jefferson," Political Science Quarterly, LV (March, 1940), 98–121.

Fisher, G. P. "Jefferson and the Social Compact Theory," in American Historical Association, Annual Report for 1893, Washington, 1894, pp. 165–77.

Ford, P. L. "Jefferson's Notes on Virginia," Nation, LVIII (1894), 80–81, 98–99.

Ford, W. C. "Jefferson and the Newspapers," Columbia Historical Society, Records, VIII (1905), 78–111.

Galbreath, C. B. "Thomas Jefferson's Views on Slavery," Ohio Archeological and Historical Quarterly, XXXIV (1925), 184–202.

Gide, Charles, and Charles Rist. A History of Economic Doctrines. Boston, 1915.

Gierke, Otto Friedrich von. The Development of Political Theory. Trans. by Bernard Freyd. New York, 1939.

Gould, W. D. "The Religious Opinions of Thomas Jefferson," Mississippi Valley Historical Review, XX (1933), 191–209.

Grossman, Mordecai. The Philosophy of Helvetius. New York, 1926.

Hall, J. Leslie. "The Religious Opinions of Thomas Jefferson," The Sewanee Review, XXI (1913), 164–76.

Higgs, Henry. The Physiocrats; Six Lectures on the French Economistes of the 18th Century. London, 1897.

Holt, Raymond V. The Unitarian Contribution to Social Progress in England. London, 1938.

Honeywell, R. J. The Educational Work of Thomas Jefferson. Cambridge, Mass., 1931.

James, William. Principles of Psychology. 2 vols. New York, 1890.

Kean, R. G. H. "Thomas Jefferson as a Legislator," Virginia Law Journal, XI (December, 1887), 705–24.

Lange, Friedrich Albert. The History of Materialism. New York, 1925.

Lévy-Bruhl, Lucien. History of Modern Philosophy in France. Chicago, 1899.

Lewis, Joseph. Jefferson the Freethinker. New York, 1925.

Locke, John. An Essay concerning Human Understanding. 2 vols. Oxford, 1894.

—— Of Civil Government; two treatises. New York, 1924.

McKee, G. H. Thomas Jefferson—Ami de la Revolution Française. Lorient, 1928.

McKeon, R. "The Development of the Concept of Property in Political Philosophy; a Study of the Background of the Constitution," *Ethics*, XLVIII (April, 1938), 297–366.

McLaughlin, Andrew C. Foundations of American Constitutionalism. New York, 1932.

Mayo, Thomas Franklin. Epicurus in England (1650–1725). Dallas, Texas, The Southwest Press, 1934.

Merriam, C. E. A History of American Political Theories. New York, 1926.

Morais, H. Deism in 18th Century America. New York, 1934.

Mossner, Ernest Campbell. Bishop Butler and the Age of Reason. New York, 1936.

Mott, R. J. "Sources of Jefferson's Ecclesiastical Views," *Church History*, III (No. 4, December, 1934), 267–84.

Mudge, Eugene T. The Social Philosophy of John Taylor of Caroline. New York, 1939.

Parker, Harold Talbot. The Cult of Antiquity and the French Revolutionaries. Chicago, 1937.

Parrington, V. L. Main Currents in American Thought. 3 vols. New York, 1927.

Parton, James. Life of Thomas Jefferson. Boston, 1894.

Patton, John Shelton. Jefferson, Cabell and the University of Virginia. New York and Washington, 1906.

Picavet, François Joseph. Les Idéologues. Paris, 1891.

Pooke, Florence A. Fountain-Sources of American Political Theory. New York, 1930.

Rand, Benjamin. Philosophical Instruction in Harvard University, from 1636 to 1906. Cambridge, Mass., 1929.

Randall, H. S. The Life of Thomas Jefferson. 3 vols. Philadelphia, 1871.

Rogers, A. K. English and American Philosophy since 1800. New York, 1922.

Schapiro, Jacob Salwyn. Condorcet and the Rise of Liberalism. New York, 1934.

Ruyssen, Theodore. "Epicurisme et Stoicisme," in Mme. L. Prenant and others, La Tradition Philosophique et la pensée française, Paris, 1922.

Schneider, Herbert W. The Puritan Mind. New York, 1930.

Scott, James Brown. Law, the State and the International Community. 2 vols. New York, 1939.

Sée, Henri Eugène. L'Evolution de la pensée politique en France au XVIIIᵉ siècle. Paris, 1925.

Segerstedt, Torgny Torgnysson. The Problem of Knowledge in Scottish Philosophy. Lund, 1935.

Shearer, Edna A. Hume's Place in Ethics. Bryn Mawr, 1915.

Spurlin, Paul Merrill. Montesquieu in America. 1760–1801. University, La., 1940.

Thomas, C. S. "Jefferson and the Judiciary," Constitutional Review, X (1926), 67–76.

Van Duzer, Charles. Contribution of the Ideologues to French Revolutionary Thought. Baltimore, 1935. The Johns Hopkins University Studies in Historical and Political Science. Series LIII, 4.

Wiltse, Charles Maurice. "Jeffersonian Democracy; a Dual Tradition," American Political Science Review, XXVIII (1934), 838–51.

—— The Jeffersonian Tradition in American Democracy. Chapel Hill, N.C., 1935.

Witt, Cornelius Henri. Jefferson and the American Democracy. Trans. by R. S. H. Church. London, 1862.

V. REFERENCE WORKS

Encyclopédie, ou, Dictionnaire raisonnée des sciences, des arts, et des metiers; mis en ordre et publié par M. Diderot. Paris, 1751–65.

Encyclopédie méthodique. Vol. III of Dictionnaire encyclopédique des mathématiques, par d'Alembert, l'abbé Bossut, De la Lande, le marquis de Condorçet. Paris, 1789–97.

Grande Encylopédie, La. Paris, n.d.

New Schaff-Herzog Encyclopedia of Religious Knowledge, The. New York and London, 1908–14.

Index